University of Roehampton
Library and Learning Services

WITHDRAWN

VERGIL'S AENEID
A POEM OF GRIEF AND LOVE

MNEMOSYNE
BIBLIOTHECA CLASSICA BATAVA

COLLEGERUNT

A.D. LEEMAN · H.W. PLEKET · C.J. RUIJGH

BIBLIOTHECAE FASCICULOS EDENDOS CURAVIT

C. J. RUIJGH, KLASSIEK SEMINARIUM, OUDE TURFMARKT 129, AMSTERDAM

SUPPLEMENTUM CENTESIMUM VICESIMUM SECUNDUM

STEVEN FARRON

**VERGIL'S AENEID
A POEM OF GRIEF AND LOVE**

VERGIL'S AENEID
A POEM OF GRIEF AND LOVE

BY

STEVEN FARRON

E.J. BRILL
LEIDEN • NEW YORK • KÖLN
1993

The paper in this book meets the guidelines for permanence and durability of the
Committee on Production Guidelines for Book Longevity of the Council on Library
Resources.

Library of Congress Cataloging-in-Publication Data

Farron, Steven.
    Vergil's Aeneid: a poem of grief and love / by Steven Farron.
      p.   cm.—(Mnemosyne, bibliotheca classica batava.
Supplementum, ISSN 0169-8958; v. 122)
    Includes bibliographical references (p.) and index.
    ISBN 9004096612 (alk. paper)
    1. Virgil. Aeneis. 2. Aeneas (Legendary character) in
literature. 3. Epic poetry, Latin—History and criticism. 4. Grief
in literature. 5. Love in literature. 6. Rome in literature.
I. Title. II. Series.
PA6825.F37   1993
873'.01—dc20   93-6782
                                                                                                        CIP

Die Deutsche Bibliothek – CIP-Einheitsnahme

Farron, Steven:
  Vergil's Aeneid: a poem of grief and love / by Steven Farron. —
Leiden; New York; Köln: Brill, 1993
  (Mnemosyne: Supplementum; 122)
  ISBN 90-04-09661-2
NE: Mnemosyne / Supplementum

ISSN   0169-8958
ISBN   90 04 09661 2

© *Copyright 1993 by E.J. Brill, Leiden, The Netherlands*

*All rights reserved. No part of this publication may be reproduced, translated, stored in
a retrieval system, or transmitted in any form or by any means, electronic,
mechanical, photocopying, recording or otherwise, without prior written
permission of the publisher.*

*Authorization to photocopy items for internal or personal
use is granted by E.J. Brill provided that
the appropriate fees are paid directly to Copyright
Clearance Center, 27 Congress Street, SALEM MA
01970, USA. Fees are subject to change.*

PRINTED IN THE NETHERLANDS

To my Father and Mother
Optimis Parentibus

TABLE OF CONTENTS

Preface		ix
I.	Nisus and Euryalus	1
	A. In books 5 and 9 Nisus and Euryalus are praised for their love for each other despite their immorality and neglect of duty.	2
	B. Vergil's culture greatly admired passionate, self-destructive love	14
	C. Vergil, even more than his contemporaries, admired suffering and dying for love.	19
	D. Modern interpretations of the Nisus-Euryalus episode.	24
	E. Pre-modern interpretations of the Nisus-Euryalus episode.	26
II.	Ancient and modern literary attitudes	31
	A. Ancient and modern interpretations of Greek tragedy.	34
	B. Ancient emotional reactions to literature, history, oratory, painting, sculpture, music, lectures.	39
	C. Modern reactions to ancient literature and literary criticism.	42
	D. Ancient attempts to find meaning in literature and their relation to the *Aeneid*.	48
	E. Ancient and modern attitudes to unity in the Homeric epics.	51
	F. Lack of unity in Apollonius' *Argonautica* and Roman poetry.	56
III.	The poem of grief and love	61
	A. The looseness of the structure of the *Aeneid*.	61
	B. Pathos in the *Aeneid*	63
	C. Pre-modern reactions to the Dido-Aeneas episode.	70
	D. The relation of the Dido-Aeneas (and Nisus-Euryalus) episode to ancient personal love poetry	81
	E. The relation of the Dido-Aeneas episode to ancient mythological love poetry.	92

F. *Benefacta* and betrayal as a source of pathos for
　　　　Dido and other ancient lovers............................ 97
　　G. Guilty conscience as a source of pathos for
　　　　Dido and other characters in the *Aeneid*
　　　　and in ancient literature 100
　　H. The purpose of the Dido episode is not to praise
　　　　or blame Aeneas... 108
　　I. The gods in the Dido-Aeneas episode and in
　　　　ancient amatory literature..................................... 124
　　J. Similarities between the gods in book 2 of the
　　　　Aeneid and in the Dido-Aeneas episode.............. 140
Postscript 146
Appendix: Recent interpretations of the Nisus-Euryalus
　　episode 155
Bibliography... 165
Index.. 172

PREFACE

> To interpret is to impoverish, to deplete the world - in order to set up a shadow world of 'meanings' ... For decades now, literary critics have understood it to be their task to translate the elements of a poem or play or novel or story into something else .... Thus, in the notes that Elia Kazan published on his production of *A Streetcar Named Desire*, it becomes clear that in order to direct the play Kazan had to discover that Stanley Kowalski represented the sensual and vengeful barbarism that was engulfing our culture, while Blanche Du Bois was Western Civilization, ... it was *about* something, about the decline of Western Civilization. Apparently, were it to go on being a play about a handsome brute ... and a mangy belle ... it would not be manageable.
>
> (Susan Sontag, "Against Interpretation", *Evergreen Review*, 1964)

Modern critics of the *Aeneid* assume that all or most of its episodes must serve the purpose of making some comment on Aeneas and his mission to found the Roman people, and through them on Rome and Augustus; whether to explain and propound their positive aspects and achievements, or to show that they are brutal and destructive, or to contrast the public 'voice' of their accomplishments with the private 'voice' of the loss and suffering they cause. In this book I argue that this basic assumption is wrong; the *Aeneid*'s main purpose was to do nothing more than what it obviously does: present a series of emotionally moving episodes, especially pathetic ones. I also show that that is what the ancient Greeks and Romans expected and prized in literature and that that is what the *Aeneid* was appreciated for, from Vergil's time until the late nineteenth century. It was then that scholars began regarding it as their duty to 'correct' this impression. These corrections show that the initial reaction of modern readers to the *Aeneid* is the same as that of earlier readers. If I succeed, I will enable readers to enjoy the *Aeneid* for the reasons it was always enjoyed and for which it is their initial impulse to enjoy it.

I hope to accomplish for the *Aeneid* what C. S. Lewis said, in the 'Dedication' of his *A Preface to Paradise Lost* (1942), Charles Williams had done for that epic:

> the recovery of a true critical tradition after more than a hundred years of laborious misunderstanding. The ease with which the

> thing was done would have seemed inconsistent with the weight that had to be lifted ... the door of the prison was really unlocked all the time, but it was only you who thought of trying the handle.

The gestation of this book is significant. From the time I began studying the *Aeneid*, it seemed obvious to me that Aeneas and his mission are often portrayed unfavourably, especially in the Dido episode, that attempts to interpret that and other episodes as favourable depictions of Aeneas and his mission involved gross and blatant distortions of the text and that the 'two voices' approach was inadequate. Since I shared the premise of all modern critics that the *Aeneid* must have been composed in order to make a statement about Aeneas, his mission, Rome and Augustus, the only possible conclusion was that its purpose was to attack them. I wrote several articles arguing this view and in 1981 signed a contract to write a book which would present these arguments systematically. When I was unable to complete the book by the date stipulated, the contract lapsed. Nevertheless, I continued working on the book. However, the more I did, the further I was from completion. The problem was that my attempts to refute the propagandistic and 'two voices' approaches with arguments from the text, the outlook of Vergil's literary culture and pre-modern interpretations of the *Aeneid* produced interminable chapters, appendices, etc. Finally, when the drawers of my desk and my bookshelves were overflowing with notes, outlines and half-completed chapters, I gave up, consoling myself with the knowledge that my research and thought on the *Aeneid* had deepened my understanding of it, improved my lectures and provided the material for many articles.

However, I then decided to try once again, using the method which Erich Auerbach employed in his *Mimesis*: beginning with a detailed analysis in depth of one passage and then applying the results of that analysis to a broad, general discussion of a topic which has too many ramifications to be expounded systematically. Since the Dido episode has always been regarded as the great glory of the *Aeneid* and much more has been written about it than about any other episode, I decided to approach it through a detailed analysis of the other love story in the *Aeneid*, that of Nisus and Euryalus. Refuting the propagandistic and 'two voices' interpretations of that episode was easy, but to my surprise I discovered that the anti-Aeneas, anti-Roman interpretation also distorted the story. From my perplexity rose the conclusion that the episode's main purpose was not to comment on anything else in the epic, but to depict a very intense, all-absorbing and ultimately tragic love. The first chapter is devoted to demonstrating that this interpretation is the only one that the text can support, that this orientation was natural and to be expected if one considers Vergil's literary predispositions and those of his culture and that ancient Roman readers viewed it in this way.

The second chapter shows that Vergil and his contemporaries regarded the primary function of literature as portraying a series of moving emotional, especially pathetic, episodes; that ancient literary critics, as opposed to modern critics, had little or no interest in the meaning and unity of a work of literature, but concentrated on the emotional, especially pathetic, impact of its parts; and that ancient audiences and readers experienced literature with an amazingly (to us) powerful emotional empathy. The third chapter argues that the main purpose of the entire *Aeneid* was to present emotional episodes, and that by far the most prominent emotion was the pathos caused by the loss of something a character loves: parents bereaved by the death of their children, Aeneas seeing Troy destroyed and having to leave it, Dido losing Aeneas and with him her reputation and the respect of her people. Most of the third chapter is devoted to the Dido episode, which has been regarded as the *Aeneid*'s most important from Vergil's time to ours. As in the first two chapters, I demonstrate that my interpretation is in line with what Vergil and his contemporaries expected in literature and appreciated in it; in particular, the very strong feelings they had about the pathetic losses described in the *Aeneid*: of children, of one's city, of a person with whom one has a sexually based relationship; and I show that pre-modern readers (with very rare exceptions) viewed the Dido episode as I do. This was necessary in order to show that my interpretation seems totally heretical only because modern criticism is heretical. In the future I hope to support this contention further with articles based on the unused material I have amassed on the history of the criticism of the *Aeneid*.

As I explained, the first chapter is a systematic study, but the second and third must be selective and the selection somewhat arbitrary because they cover a vast amount of material. Their 'lumpiness' is increased by the inclusion in them of parenthetical material of a type which is often relegated to footnotes. (Footnotes are used only for long series of references.) I have done this because the use of footnotes for parenthetical discussions seems to me to be a trick used to include such material while superficially avoiding a break in the general analysis. In fact, more of a disruption is involved since the reader must consult the footnotes. By not using footnotes for this purpose I have spared the reader this nuisance and imposed on myself the discipline of not being able to disguise the inclusion of irrelevancies.

Many readers will recognize that the book's title comes from Victor Pöschl's assertion in *Die Dichtkunst Virgils*, on page fifteen of the third edition (1977): *Man hat die Äneis das Epos des Schmerzes genannt. Man konte sie auch den Heldengesang der Liebe nennen. Denn die tiefste Tragik aller Gestalten ist es, dass sie 'zuviel liebten', wie es die der Dichter von Euryalus sagt* (IX 430): *infelicem nimium dilexit amicum*. Pöschl also mentions as examples Juno, Venus, Turnus, Dido, Latinus, Amata, Laokoon, Evander, Aeneas and Mezentius, whose death *ist im Grunde ein Selbstmord aus Liebe* (a theme whose fundamental importance for Vergil and his culture will be explored in this book). To these, G. West added the characters in the title of her article, "Vergil's Helpful Sisters: Anna and Juturna in the *Aeneid*" on pages ten to nineteen of *Vergilius* 25, 1979.

I would like to thank my colleague Professor David Scourfield for reading the first chapter of this book in a rough form and offering suggestions and encouragement; the many students who posed challenging questions to me about the *Aeneid*; the reviewer of the typescript for his corrections; the Centre for Science Development of the Human Sciences Research Council of South Africa for financial assistance in pursuing research in overseas libraries (the opinions and conclusions expressed in this book are my own and do not necessarily represent those of the CSD or HSRC); my darling wife and wonderful children for their emotional support; and last, but certainly not least, my parents. It is to them that I dedicate this book,

Optimis Parentibus

CHAPTER ONE

NISUS AND EURYALUS

> Critics have often puzzled their heads to explain why the immortal episode of Nisus and Euryalus is inserted in this book [9], without any very obvious connexion with the story.

So wrote W. Warde Fowler in 1919 (page 89),[1] and critics have been puzzled ever since. Vergil clearly intended that the activities of Nisus and Euryalus in this episode be regarded as important. They are the first soldiers to engage the enemy after the war is formally declared. On no other character or pair of characters acting together is attention focused continuously for nearly as long, except on Dido in Book 4. The poetic artistry of the episode is universally recognized, even by those critics who attack its content (e.g. Huxley 1974.75). Vergil concludes it with a promise of glory to Nisus and Euryalus (446-9), a promise given in unique manner, a glory granted to no other character (Klingner 1967. 561,563).

In this chapter I will demonstrate that the portrayals of Nisus and Euryalus in Books 5 and 9 are closely parallel and that in both books their conduct to other people is of a nature which was regarded as immoral and contemptible by the ancient Romans, but that is overshadowed by their loving devotion to each other. I will then show that it was natural for Vergil to devote so much space and express such glowing praise for characters of this type since he and his culture were fascinated by and had the highest admiration for romantic love and especially its ultimate manifestation, dying if deprived of one's beloved. So this episode can only be understood if one realizes that the *Aeneid* is basically a poem of grief and love. I will then analyze and point out the defects of previous attempts to explain the episode's meaning. They are all based on the assumption that it must be connected

---

[1] Most secondary works will be referred to by the author's last name, date of publication and pages cited. Full information is provided in the bibliography. I have used the abbreviations of ancient authors' names and works in the *Oxford Classical Dictionary*.

with the rest of the *Aeneid* as a comment on the political, ethical and/or military values, ideals and/or characteristics which are involved in Aeneas' mission to found the Roman people and which make its completion possible. Finally, I will demonstrate that the ancient Romans themselves interpreted this episode in the way I do.

A. *In Books 5 and 9 Nisus and Euryalus are Praised for their Love for Each Other despite their Immorality and Neglect of Duty*

Nisus and Eurayalus first appear in Book 5. Significantly, the contest they enter is a foot race, an *agile studium et tenuissima virtus, pacis opus*, as Statius states (*Theb.* 6.551-2) and Vergil implies (*Aen.* 5.362-3). They are introduced as *Euryalus forma insignis viridique iuventa, Nisus amore pio pueri* (295-6). Vergil usually introduced important characters with a description that mentions the attributes that are basic to their actions and/or tragedies in the entire *Aeneid* (Farron, 1989). *Pietas* for Vergil and his contemporaries often meant loyalty in a love affair (Farron 1992. 274). He concludes their story in Book 9 (446-9) by promising that they will be *insignes* as long as Rome lasts; and in both Books 5 (361) and 9 they are *insignes* for the attributes mentioned when they are introduced.

In Book 5 the crucial action in their episode, which determines the outcome of the race, is described in lines 334-5: Nisus, *non Euryali, non ille oblitus amorum*, trips Salius so Euryalus can win. Donatus pointed out (*ad loc.*), *propter hanc causam superius praemisit amorem magnum inter Nisum et Euryalum fuisse*, and called Nisus' action a *fraus*. Page (1894, *ad loc.*) made similar observations: "The emphatic *non ... non* and pleonastic *ille* call marked attention to the ... devotion of Nisus. To us the action seems ... contemptible." But it seemed contemptible to the Romans also. In line 342 Salius *ereptum ... dolo reddi sibi poscit honorem*, on which Donatus commented, *fraudem sibi dolo quaesitam iustissime querebatur*. Tripping a runner in a race was used as a symbol of immoral conduct in general (Cic. *Off.* 3.42). When Statius' Idas wins a race by *dolus* and *fraus* (*Theb.* 6.614-17), his victory is declared invalid because it was gained by *fraus* not *virtus* (628-30), and Statius described him as *improbus* (644), which means having "lack of regard for others in going beyond ... what is fair and right" (Austin 1955, on 386).

In *Iliad* 23.587-95 Antilochus apologizes to Menelaus because he won by a δόλος (585), gives him the first prize and promises something greater from his possessions so as not to be a 'sinner against the gods'. Antilochus' δόλος (23.419-41) was much less flagrant than Nisus'. But Euryalus is allowed to keep the first prize largely because of his beauty (5.343-4), and Vergil ends the episode by describing Nisus as *egregius* (361) since his *dolus* was motivated by love for the beautiful Euryalus.

That Vergil's sympathy in this episode was directed to Nisus and Euryalus and that he wanted his readers to share that feeling is evident not only from what he says but how he says it. Otis (1963.41-51) used this episode as his first illustration of Vergil's tendency to identify psychologically with the emotions of his characters and to intrude his personal reactions to them into the narrative, qualities which he called 'empathy' and 'sympathy'. His analysis of such devices as the alternation of tenses and dactyls with spondees, sympathetic adjectives, caesurae and diaereses, verbal repetitions and alliteration led to the conclusions (49-50) that the "centre of interest is the friendship of Nisus and Euryalus" and that Vergil "makes it clear that he himself feels most deeply for Nisus and shares Nisus' noble affection for Euryalus".

An analysis of the metrical patterns of the lines in this episode confirms these conclusions. Duckworth (1964.24-5,58-9) pointed out that of the complete, non-spondaic lines in the *Aeneid* which were accepted as genuine by Hirtzel, 14.39% are of the pattern dactyl-spondee-spondee-spondee (dsss) in their first four feet. That makes it the most frequent pattern for those feet in the *Aeneid*, as it is in the *Georgics*, Cicero's *Aratea*, Lucretius, Catullus 64 and Horace's hexameters. He later (1966) discovered that in passages which Otis labelled 'empathetic-sympathetic' the proportion of dsss lines is significantly lower than Vergil's normal frequency, whereas in passages which are unemotional and objective the proportion is significantly higher. In the episode under consideration, of the first five lines (5.286-90), where Aeneas leads the Trojans to the place of the race, two (40%) are dsss. In 291-302, where the contestants are introduced, no line is dsss. In 303-14, where Aeneas announces the prizes, two lines (16.7%) are dsss. Then, in 315-44, the race itself up to and including Euryalus' beauty enabling him to keep the first prize, only one of the 28 complete, non-spondaic lines is dsss (3.6%). That is followed by two straight dsss lines where Diores supports Euryalus' claim for selfish reasons. But when *egregius* Nisus asks for and receives a prize (353-61), none of the lines are dsss. Of the following three lines, which introduces the boxing match, two are dsss.

In Book 9 again Nisus' and Euryalus' actions are very immoral *per se*. They attack the Rutulians at night, and Vergil constantly mentions that the Rutulians are in a drunken sleep (Duckworth 1967.133; Servius on 9.329). The immoral and un-Roman nature of such an attack is made explicit by the words used to describe it. In 236-43 Nisus says that he and Euryalus can get through to Aeneas and return *cum spoliis ingenti caede peracta* because they have seen a place for *insidiae* where the Rutulians have not even kept their fires going because of their drunken sleep (cf. 189-90). In 350 Vergil says Euryalus *furto fervidus instat*. In 428 he has Nisus describe their attack as a *fraus*.

The words *insidiae, furtum, fraus* and *dolus* were commonly used in conjunction with each other, especially in military contexts, and associated with night attacks and consequently thieves (Farron 1992. note 20). But midday could also be *tempus ... fraudis ac doli* for an attack *sine fide*, if those attacked were unready, unarmed and asleep (Caes. *BC iv.* 2.14.1). A victory was *violatus* if a subsequent general defeated the enemy *per fraudem et insidias* because he *hosti gloriam dedit ut videretur aliter vinci non posse* (Florus, *Epit.* 2.17.17). So, *Varro et ceteri invictos dicunt Troianos quia per insidias oppressi sunt* (Serv. Dan. on *Aen.* 11.306; cf. Val. Max. 7.4 *ext.* 2). Indeed, Augustan propaganda used against Antony the accusation that he had gained a victory by *fraus* (Goodyear 1981, on 2.3.1). The Romans of Vergil's time and into the next century constantly attributed such methods to hated or despised enemies and contrasted them with their own *virtus*.[2] So by the following

---

[2] Carthaginians: e.g. *ThLL* 7.1890.63-7; *Ad Her.* 4.66 (*dolis malitiosa Karthago*); Sil. *Pun.* 1.188,219;3.231-4; Florus, *Epit.* 2.6.13; 17.6. Numidians (whom the Romans regarded as similar to the Carthaginians: e.g. Luc. 4.736-42 (*Libycas ... fraudes infectaque semper Punica bella dolis*)): in the *BAfr.* they are an *insidiosa natio* (10), who use *doli* and *insidiae* (7.73;cf. 50,65); Sallust portrays Jugurtha as constantly attacking by night (12.4;21.2;38.4;54.9-10;56.4), which he calls *doli* (14.11;53.6-7) and *insidiae* (55.4); or at day *ex improviso* (58.1) and *ex occulto* (59.2), which he also calls *doli* and *insidiae* (49.5); so, Metellus *videt ... neque Iugurtham nisi ex insidiis ... pugnam facere* (61.1), and Marius ... *hostium ... cognoscere ... insidias* (88.2). Pharnaces II: *BAlex.* 36. (Cf. Plut. *Crass.* 30-33 on

"glorious statement Tiberius tried to put himself on a level with earlier leaders": *non fraude neque occultis ... populum Romanum hostis suos ulcisci* (Tac. *Ann.* 2.88.1). And centuries later Rufus Festus (15-16) recorded that the Parthians *furto ... esse laetatos, vera autem virtute semper Romanos ... extitisse victores* and gave as the primary example, *nocturno adgressus proelio superavit*. For, *das konventionelle Ideal der Römer ist ja der gerade, offenherzige, keiner Tücke fähige Ehrenmann* (Heinze 1915.10).

The ancient Greeks also associated night attacks with theft, deceit, knavery (πανουργία) and sacrilege, regarded victories so gained as unjust and shameful and attributed night attacks to hated or despised nationalities or mercenaries (Pritchett 1974. 162-78). This is well illustrated by what Plutarch (*Alex.* 31.7) calls Alexander the Great's 'well remembered statement' in reply to the advice that he attack the Persians at night: "I will not steal [κλέπτω] the victory." Arrian (*Anab.* 3.10.2) quotes Alexander as saying "it is shameful [αἰσχρός] to steal the victory". Quintus Curtius has Alexander say (4.13.8-9), *Latrunculorum ... et furum ista sollertia est ... Meae vero gloriae ... furtum noctis obstare non patiar ... malo me meae fortunae paeniteat quam victoriae pudeat*.

After Rome became the most powerful state in the Mediterranean, the Greeks tended to think that Romans displayed the military conduct they admired. Thus they granted to the Romans what the Romans prided themselves on. So Polybius (13.3) lamented that in his time the old ideal of fighting battles openly without deceit has been replaced by pervasive κακοπραγμοσύνη. But he added that the Romans still preserve something of the old practices, for "they announce their wars before fighting and rarely use ἐνέδραι [= *insidiae*]". He also recorded (36.9.9-11) some Greeks criticising the Romans' conduct in the Third Punic War because "the Romans' peculiar conduct on which they pride themselves is to fight wars in a simple and noble manner, using neither night attacks nor *enedrai*, rejecting everything done through deceit and fraud (δόλος)"; but against the Carthaginians they had used deceit and fraud, which were "similar to impiety

---

the Parthians.)
 Ovid (*Fasti* 2.214-27) contrasted Etruscan *insidiae* with the *simplex nobilitas* of the Fabii, but *fraude perit virtus*. Val. Max. (7.4. *ext.* 2) contrasted *Punica fortitudo, dolis et insidiis ... instructa* with *nostra virtus*. (Cf. Livy 26.39.11 and *BAfr.* 73.)

and treachery". Those who defended the Romans (36.9.12-17) granted that if the Romans acted that way before the Carthaginians had given themselves into their power, the above accusations would be true.

Among Vergil's contemporaries, the most obvious source for Roman attitudes is Livy. An excellent illustration of his views on this subject is provided by his use of the phrase *artes Romanae*, which appears prominently in the *Aeneid* (6.851-3). In 1.53.4 the worst villain of early Rome, Tarquinius Superbus, *minime arte Romana, fraude ac dolo, adgressus est [Gabios]*. Conversely, one of the greatest heroes of early Rome, Camillus, scorned as criminal an opportunity offered him to defeat Falerii by treachery and said, *ego Romanis artibus, virtute, opere ... vincam* (5.27.8). But the most significant use of this phrase is in 42.47. There Q. Marcius Philippus boasts to the Senate that he fooled Perseus into thinking he could obtain peace, thus gaining time for the Romans to match the Macedonian preparations for war (see 42.43). The older senators, *moris antiqui memores, negabant se ... Romanas agnoscere artes. Non per insidias et nocturna preolia, nec ... improvisos ... ad incautum hostem ... magis quam vera virtute ... bella maiores gessisse* (42.47.4-5; cf. Diod. 30.7.1). Then they elaborated further on proper conduct to enemies, giving historical examples, which include Camillus and Falerii. They call this *religio Romana* and contrast it with Carthaginian and Greek practices (47.6-7). They conclude, *interdum in praesens tempus plus profici dolo quam virtute, sed eius demum animum in perpetuum vinci ... iusto ac pio ... bello superatum* (47.8).

In fact, neither *insidiae* nor *nocturna proelia* are involved in this incident. If the older senators really mentioned them, or if they were in Livy's sources, they illustrate the point made above: the Romans associated these methods with other un-Roman, immoral practices. If Livy added them, they also illustrate that, but have a wider application in addition. Starting with Book 34, Livy narrated several incidents which served as examples of the beginning of Rome's moral collapse (Luce 1977.251ff.). In Book 42 he began to include examples of Rome's dishonorable treatment of non-Romans (Luce. 264-7,270, cf. 262-3), of which Q. Marcius' conduct to Perseus is one. It is significant that the spokesmen for *artes Romanae* assume that such methods make the war unjust and impious despite the facts that the sacrifices and omens were favorable (42.30.8-10) and that Perseus' cause was *deterior* (30.1) because his methods were much worse than the Romans' and incompatible with *iustum bellum* (18.1,40.5-8) and he insulted Roman envoys (25.8-13). (Even if that incident was fictitious (Luce. 123), Livy believed it and he clearly thought the arguments of the older senators valid.)

Vergil fully shared this outlook. *Dolus, fraus furtum* and *insidiae* are nearly always evil in his works when applied to human conduct. For example, in Hades Rhadamanthus *castigat ... dolos subigitque fateri quae quis ... furto laetatus ...* (6.567-8); also horribly punished are *quibus ... fraus innexa clienti* (6.608-9). Allecto, who comes from Hades, is introduced as *cui tristia bella iraeque, insidiaeque et crimina noxia cordi* (7.325-8). In *Eclogue* 4, *fraus* is what the fated child will overcome (31ff.). In the *Aeneid*, the use of *furtum* is an accusation made (e.g. 10.91) and denied (e.g. 4.337), and Vergil contrasts being victorious by *furtum* with being victorious by *fortia arma* (10.735). In 11.702-717 *doli* and *fraus* are the methods of a coward. In 2.390 *dolus* and *virtus* are contrasted, and in 4.93-5 it is assumed that glory cannot be won by a *dolus*.

It is especially Vergil's description of the Greek capture of Troy which manifests contempt for these means. In 1.753-4 Dido asks Aeneas, *dic ... insidias ... Danaum*, where *insidiae* is the first word in its line; as it is also in 2.310, where it again sums up the Greek attack. In 2.65 Aeneas introduces Sinon by stating, *accipe nunc Danaum insidias ... crimine ab uno*. After Sinon's speech (195-6), Aeneas says, *talibus insidiis periurique arte Sinonis credita res*. In 2.36 *insidiae* refers to the wooden horse, in which the Greeks hide *furtim* (2.18,258). The horse is described in 2.44 as having *doli* and in 2.264 as being a *dolus*, as is Sinon's conduct (2.62,152,196) and the Greek attack on the sleeping Trojans (2.252-3). Indeed, the dominant image of Book 2, the snake, emphasizes trickery and concealment (Knox 1950).

Donatus (on 2.152-3), Servius (on 1.754,2.196;cf.2.341) and Servius Danielis (on 2.195, cf. 11.306) pointed out that Vergil constantly mentions Greek *doli* and *insidiae* to show that they did not win by *virtus*. Servius on 2.196 (cf. on 2.341) added that the use of *doli* makes the Greek victory *turpis*.

Nethercut (1971.138-9) observes that Vergil drew the reader's attention to the similarity between the night attack of the Greeks in Book 2 and that of Nisus and Euryalus in Book 9 by the words *somno vinoque*. That phrase occurs four times in the *Aeneid*, all at critical points in the episode in which it appears. In 2.265 it describes Troy when the Greeks begin their attack, restating *doli* in 252-3. Servius Danielis noted (*ad loc.*) that it *ostendere vult nihil magnum a Graecis factum.* Its three other occurrences (9.189,236,316) describe the Rutulians: when Nisus explains his plan to Euryalus, when he tells the Trojan leaders why *insidiae* will work and when he and Euryalus begin slaughtering them. Furthermore, immediately before the Nisus-Euryalus episode begins, Vergil has Turnus pointedly say that he will not undertake an attack on unprepared enemies at night, connecting such an attack with the Greek capture of Troy: *tenebras et inertia furta ... ne [Troes] timeant, nec equi caeca condemur in alvo: luce palam certum est igni circumdare muros. Haud sibi cum Danais rem faxo ... esse ferant* (9.150-5). In Donatus' paraphrase of these lines, he mentions the means by which the Greeks captured Troy, all of which Nisus and Euryalus use: *nulla doli temptamenta perquiram ... nihil insidiarum metuant, superabo hos sola virtute ... per lucem ... non me iuvabunt illorum ebrietates aut tenebrae nec capiam vino sepultos aut somno.*

The Trojan War is also depicted at *Aeneid* 1.456-93. Stanley (1965. 274-7) has shown that the scenes there foreshadow *Aeneid* 7-12 and that "the death of Rhesus (469-73), drawn at least in part from Book X of the *Iliad*, anticipates Vergil's imitation of the *Doloneia* in *Aeneid* IX, 314 ff." (cf. Pavlock 1985.214). The description of the slaughter of sleeping men there is especially brutal. Furthermore, if R. Williams is correct (1960.145-9) that 1.474-8 refers to Troilus being ambushed unarmed by Achilles, then the juxtaposition of "Rhesus slain in his sleep [with] the boy Troilus caught defenceless" prefigures "the *perfidia* and *crudelitas* of the enemy ... described with such force in *Aeneid* 2". In Book 1 and 2 Priam is the ultimately pathetic victim of the Greeks (Farron 1986. 78). The portrayal of his headless corpse ends the depiction of the Greeks' brutality in Book 2 (557-8). Nisus and Euryalus, who use the same methods as the Greeks, also leave a headless corpse, and Vergil's description of it (9.332-4) uses sound and metrical patterns to make it as hideous as possible (Pavlock 1985. 213-14).

Vergil must have assumed that readers of Nisus' and Euryalus' night attack would also keep in mind its model, *Iliad* 10, and notice any differences. R. Schlunk (1974.76-81) points out ways in which Nisus and Euryalus are depicted as being more irrational and brutal than Diomedes and Odysseus. Most significant are the differences in the similes in which Nisus (9.339-41) and Diomedes (10.485-7) are compared to lions as they kill the sleeping enemy. As opposed to Diomedes' lion,

> the Trojan lion is portrayed as having been goaded on by an insane hunger and as roaring out of his bloody jaws ... The phrase, *fremit ore cruento*, is used first in the *Aeneid* to describe ... *Impius Furor* ... (I.296) ... The phrase, *suadet enim vesana fames*, is reminiscent of ... *malesuada Fames* (VI.276).

Schlunk does not point out that in Vergil's simile, but not in Homer's, the helpless terror of the victims is mentioned, nor that it is followed (342-3) by *nec minor Euryali caedes, incensus et ipse perfurit*. That is the only occurrence in any of Vergil's works of the prefix *per* with a form of *furo*. But even if Nisus' lion were not more brutal than Diomedes', it would still be making a criticism while Diomedes' lion does not. For, Vergil, as opposed to Homer, tended to compare characters in similes to things which illustrate their nature and that was especially true of vicious beasts of prey (Pöschl 1977.131-2).

The examples of contemptible military methods discussed above are at least successful. Sometimes the honourable course is explicitly contrasted with what is useful for the state. For instance, in Livy 42.47.9, *vicit ... utilis quam honesti cura*. But Nisus' and Euryalus' sneaky, brutal night attack on men in a drunken sleep is an unnecessary and fatal delay in completing a vitally important objective. Nisus and everyone else know that it is extremely important that a messenger report the Trojans' situation to Aeneas and summon him (192-3, 226-8). He tells the Trojan leaders that that is his purpose (241-3) (see Quinn 1969.202n1). Ascanius emphasises that *sola salus genitore reducto* (257-62, cf. 312). Vergil leaves no doubt that they have not exaggerated the danger of their situation and consequently the importance of this mission. Had Turnus acted sensibly, the next day *ultimus ... dies bello gentique fuisset* (9.759).

Nisus justifies the slaughter of the Rutulians as advancing their mission (*ipsa res*: 320-3, 356). But that clearly is not true. Before they go, Nisus says that the Rutulians in their complacency are in a drunken sleep and have only a few fires burning, among which is a gap (188-90, 236-40). In his notes on 189 and 237-43 Donatus points out the obvious, that the few fires show that they are asleep and can easily be passed through. At the beginning (316-19) and end (351-2) of the slaughter it is again emphasised that they are asleep and totally remiss. Only one of the men who is killed is awake and he is a coward (346) and drunk (350). So he would not have opposed them and probably would not have aroused the others after they had left. Even if the Rutulians had been aroused, in their condition they could not have caught fast runners like Nisus and Euryalus. Finally, they must stop the slaughter because *lux inimica propinquat* (355). It is the light, not the sleeping Rutulians, that is dangerous. Not only is the slaughter unnecessary, but, as Duckworth (1967.133-4) observes, it

> delayed their departure ... had they left earlier, they would have avoided the cavalry ... and they still might have escaped unnoticed, had it not been for the ... helmet; cf. 373f ... Nisus ... did get away, and it was due in part to the *onerosa praeda* (384) that Euryalus ... was captured. Again Nisus *could have done the right thing* and carried out his mission, but his first thoughts were of Euryalus. (second italics added)

Duckworth's conclusion is, "Vergil was ... interested ... in showing that the two young men do the wrong thing and pay the penalty".

Indeed, Duckworth's observations can be strengthened. In lines 386-8 Vergil says, *Nisus abit, iamque ... evaserat hostis atque ... stabula alta*; that is, he "got safely past the farm-buildings where he might have been seen" (R. Williams 1973, *ad loc.*). Furthermore, when Nisus sees that Euryalus is trapped, he forgets his mission completely. The only alternatives he considers are rescuing him or dying (399-401). When the former becomes impossible, he chooses the latter *amens* (424).

There may be validity in Duckworth's argument (1967.146-50) that Nisus' and Euryalus' self-destructive blood-lust prefigures that of other characters, specially Turnus, in Books 9-12. It is also possible that Nethercut (1971.138-9) is correct in asserting that Nisus' and Euryalus' sneaky night attack against the sleeping Rutulians, in conjunction with Turnus' disavowal of such methods, casts a shadow over the Trojans' military activities in the rest of the *Aeneid*. However, Vergil did not intend that Nisus and Euryalus be judged by or remembered for their actions against the Rutulians.

If this episode's purpose was to illustrate immoral conduct, why does it end (446-9) with glowing praise for Nisus and Euryalus?

The answer is that when Nisus got away from the enemy in 386-8, he was not doing 'the right thing', as Duckworth asserts (quoted above). He was, Vergil tells us, *imprudens* (386).³ Conversely, the death which he chooses instead of carrying out his mission is described as *pulcher* (401). Servius (*ad loc.*) explained why: *gloriosum enim est pro amico perire*. That is the glory that Vergil promises in 446-9 will last as long as Rome. It is glorious despite the fact that neglecting their mission for other motives would have been reprehensible. It is so glorious that it completely overshadows their immoral brutality against the Rutulians.

As in Book 5, the low proporation of lines with dactyl-spondee-spondee-spondee in their first four feet confirms the other indications that Vergil's empathy and sympathy are greatest where he dwells on Nisus' and Euryalus' loving devotion, along with Euryalus' beauty, which is a major cause of it, and praises them for it. Duckworth (1966.6-7;cf.1965-6.47) mentions that in the narration of their attempt to escape (9.367-421) 29% of the lines are dsss but none in 422-49, which narrates their deaths, evokes Euryalus' beauty and ends with Vergil's apostrophe. Duckworth states, "the striking contrast [between 367-421 and] ... the *zero* per cent in the description of their deaths ... is perhaps the most amazing fluctuation in the entire *Aeneid*" (Duckworth's italics). But he did not notice that in their attempt to escape there are no dsss lines in 390 through 401, where Nisus realises that *infelix* Euryalus is not with him, sees that he is in danger and considers either rescuing him or suffering a *pulcher* death with him. Sixteen of the remaining 43 lines (37%) in their attempted escape are dsss. That includes the plunder Euryalus took betraying his position and slowing him down, which Duckworth and many others regard as highly significant. There is one more passage in the episode with no dsss lines. That is 207-23, which several editors print as a separate paragraph. These lines also show their devotion to each other: Nisus tries to dissuade Euryalus from accompanying him for fear he will be killed, but Euryalus insists and they leave their position together. In the other passages in the episode, where Nisus and Euryalus formulate their plan, announce it to the Trojan leaders

---

³ Here I accept the obvious meaning of *imprudens*: *scilicet remanentis Euryali* (Serv. *ad loc.*; cf. Asper, *apud* Scholia Veronensia, *ad loc.*). As with nearly every word Vergil wrote, fanciful explanations have been proposed (e.g. Richardson 1938).

and slaughter the Rutulians, the frequency of complete, non-spondaic dsss lines is 13% or higher.

Two other similarities with the Nisus and Euryalus episode in Books 5 are instructive. That also ends (361) with Nisus praised because he did not forget Euryalus and was overcome by love to do what would have been immoral if done for other motives. And both episodes begin by introducing Nisus and Euryalus as being characterized by the factor that will cause the action for which they will be praised at the end: *amor*, along with one of its major inspirations, Euryalus' beauty (9.179-82). Ring composition was very common in the *Aeneid* and in contemporary poetry, especially to frame the beginning and end of an episode (Moskalew 1982.116-22;Ross 1987.40,52; G. Williams 1968.index,*s.v.*;Kenney 1971,on 30). Another example in Book 9 is that, as Servius observed (on 9.176), the introduction of Nisus as being skilled with a javelin prepares for his use of it in attempting to save Euryalus.

There are also two important differences between Books 5 and 9 in the description of Euryalus' beauty, Nisus' and Euryalus' loving devotion and Vergil's praise for it. The first is that they are more emphatic and elaborate in Book 9. There Euryalus is introduced (179-81) as being the most beautiful of the Trojans and as *ora puer prima signans intonsa iuventa*. That was erotically very appealing to Vergil's contemporaries, whether it meant having no hair at all (Murgatroyd 1980, on 8.31-2) or *prima lanugine*, as Servius and Donatus interpreted it (*ad loc.*) (e.g., *Aen.* 10.324-7 (Clytius, whose lover Vergil also apostrophises); Ov. *Her.* 15.85-94, *Met.* 13.753-4). In accordance with ring composition, at the end of the episode, in the passage with no dsss lines, Euryalus' beauty is again mentioned (432-3) and evoked (435-7) by a simile. In it he is compared to two flowers, a "type of imagery [that] was arguably conventional in epithalamia" (Lyne 1987.122). Also, one of the flowers is *purpureus* and is destroyed. That belongs to a literary tradition that "provides ... a set of allusions which implicitly compare Euryalus to a girl at the time of marriage and so stress his effeminate role as the *eromenos* of Nisus" (Griffith. 1985.42-3). The simile clearly conveys Nisus' feelings, as has been observed frequently (e.g., Klingner 1967.564;Otis 1963.388-9;Lyne 1987.229). Vergil often supplied a character's emotions by means of a simile (Lyne 1987.229n30;G. Williams 1983.253-5, cf. 256-8). The parts of the concluding zero-dsss passage before and after the mention of

Euryalus' beauty and the simile (424-30,438-45) describe Nisus' eagerness to die for or with Euryalus. For Vergil and his contemporaries that was the most extreme manifestation of love possible, as will be demonstrated below.

Vergil's overt description of Euryalus' erotic physical attributes and his clear indications of the sexual bond between him and Nisus are especially striking considering the poetic tradition in which he was working and his own normal practices. As Servius observed, *artis poeticae est non omnia dicere* (on *Aen*.1.683, cf. on 1.223). Lessing pointed out in the twenty-first chapter of his *Laokoon* that poets have a strong tendency to avoid descriptions of physical beauty but suggest it by the reactions of other characters. His first example is the reaction of the old Trojan men to Helen's beauty in *Iliad* 3.156-8. For the ancient Greeks and Romans this avoidance of description was particularly true of sex (Henderson 1975.2-6). Among the Greeks, "references to sexual activities by pre-classical and classical poets (apart from satirists and comedians) are generally delicate", and circumlocutions and imagery were usually used (Standford 1983.37-8). The same practice was generally followed even in the *Greek Anthology* (Lier 1914.41-3) and ancient Greek novels (Griffin 1985.111n66). The Roman love poets also normally avoided descriptions of their mistresses' erotic physical attributes and of sex (Lyne 1980.262-4; Lier 1914.41-3; Griffin 1985.104-11 and *passim*; Farron 1983.89,94n42).

The tendency to let readers infer important actions, situations and thoughts without mentioning them was especially characteristic of Vergil. It has been noted by many critics; for instance, Servius in the passages cited above and Dryden: Vergil "says much in little, and often in silence" (quoted by Mackail 1930,on 8.531). More recent examples are, e.g., Henry 1878.833-4; Austin 1955, on 663f.,396,662 and 1971, on 694; and Farron 1985.32n32. Vergil also liked extreme understatements (see, e.g., Quinn 1969.347-8). In particular, he "gives few physical descriptions of his characters" (Highet 1972.40) and he was very reticent about sexual activities. That was true even among animals, as Servius pointed out (on *G*.3.135). His restraint concerning human sex was such that although Pease pointed it out and cited discussions of it (1935.45), he still argued that the reader is supposed to be in doubt as to whether Aeneas and Dido ever had intercourse (ibid.).

The second difference between Books 9 and 5 is that in the

latter only Nisus' love is mentioned when they are introduced (295-6) and operates in the action of the episode. But when they are introduced in Book 9 their love is described as mutual (182: *his amor unus erat*). That is displayed by *pariterque in bella ruebant; tum quoque communi portam statione tenebant* (182-3). It is mentioned again at the end of the episode in the zero-dsss passage, when Nisus says of Euryalus, *tantum infelicem nimium dilexit amicum* (430).[4] As Servius and Donatus saw (*ad loc.*), that explains why Euryalus came on the mission. So he too died because he could not be without his loved one (see Donatus on 446).

These two differences between the Nisus-Euryalus episodes in Books 5 and 9 account for the differences in Vergil's praise at their conclusions. In Book 9 it is much more emphatic and elaborate than in Book 5 and it is for both of them, not just for Nisus.

B. *Vergil's Culture Greatly Admired Passionate, Self-Destructive Love*

That Vergil focused attention continuously on Nisus and Euryalus and Dido for much longer than on any other characters and that he praised the former two in an unparalleled manner, despite their many immoral actions, is natural in view of the outlook of his culture. Vergil's contemporaries were fascinated by passionate, tormenting, self-destructive love, and most of them admired it highly (Farron 1983). Their literary culture was one in which "because of Catullus' writings Lesbia is better known then even Helen" (Prop. 2.34.87-8). In the decade during which the *Aeneid* was being written more first-rate love poetry was published than in any other decade in European, and probably world, history. Propertius' first book was probably published then, his second and third books definitely, as were both books of Tibullus' poems. Ovid was already reading poems in public about Corinna (*Tr.* 4.10.57-60). If we accept what Lygdamus says about himself (Tib. 3.5.17-18 and 3.2.2) he also was composing in that decade (assuming that the year in which both consuls died was 43 B.C., not 69 A.D.). Sulpicia may have been writing then too. Gallus, whose influence

---

[4] For *diligo* see *Aen.* 1.344; 2.784; Catull.72.3-4; 76.23;and Hellegouarc'h 1963.143-6. *Amicus* was closely associated with *amor* (Hellegouarc'h 1963.146-7; Cic. *Fin.* 2.78) and often meant lover (*Thll* 1.1908.3-12; cf.1912.58ff.). It is used as a noun 21 times in Vergil's works, of which five refer to Nisus and Euryalus (5.337;9.198,389,430,444).

as a love poet was constantly mentioned in antiquity, lived into it. The only extant poetry from this decade which was not completely or overwhelmingly about love was Horace's *Epistles I* and *Odes I-III*. But many of the *Odes* are amatory. In 1.6.17-20 Horace characterizes himself as a love poet; and he introduces himself at the beginning of the fourth book of *Odes* as someone whose earlier poetry was about love.

Before 29 B.C. extant Latin poetry which contains descriptions of interpersonal relations consists of the comedies of Plautus and Terence, Catullus, Vergil's *Eclogues* and *Georgics* (i.e. Orpheus and Eurydice, which is its last memorable episode, as will be demonstrated below), Horace's *Satires*, and maybe Propertius *I*. Most of the surviving comedies center around love and its obstacles. Moreover, Horace, the least romantic non-didactic extant poet writing before the *Aeneid*'s publication, assumed that love and its obstructions was *the* subject of Roman Comedy (*Sat.* 1.4.39-53; *Epist.* 2.1.170-2). In the former passage he says that neither his *Satires* nor Comedy are poetry, and the only argument for either being poetry which he considers important enough to be answered is that Comedy revolves around the obstacles to a young man *insanus amica*. Similarly Serivus in his introduction to *Aeneid* 4 says about it, *paene comicus stilus est; nec mirum, ubi de amore tractatur*. (And "tragedy after Euripides was almost as soaked in the passion of love as comedy" (Griffin 1985.208;see also Rohde 1914.107-8)).

Vergil's *Eclogues* are permeated with love (Farron 1983.84-5). When he defines their nature, they are what someone *captus amore leget* (6.10); and love is assumed to be the primary subject of *Maenalii* (i.e. Arcadian) verses (8.21-4, cf. 5.10). For Theocritus, "a constant preoccupation ... is the agony of unfulfilled love" (Bulloch 1985.585), and the identification of the bucolic, Arcadian world with love was common among Roman poets (Nisbet and Hubbard 1975.216;Prop. 1.20.11-12;2.34.76). In the last passage Propertius says that the *Eclogues* are praised by 'the easygoing girls of Rome', to use Camps' paraphrase (1967, *ad loc.*); and everything he mentioned from them (67-76) are either herdsmen who sang about love or incidents of love. Later Romans continued to regard love as the *Eclogues*' subject (Ov. *Tr.* 2.537-8; *Ars Am.* 2.267; Apul. *Apol.* 10; Joly 1978.104,93-4, *passim*).

It is also significant that Catullus' Lesbia poems, his Ariadne and Theseus, the longer erotic subjects of the *Eclogues*, and the love poems of the elegists all develop a story about the vicissitudes of an interpersonal relationship. So they could be used directly as models for an epic poem and were a frame of reference for an epic's readers. But nearly all the extant poetry dealing with non-romantic interpersonal relationships before the *Aeneid*'s publication is either unconnected short poems; or, as in the interaction of the interlocutors in the *Eclogues*, the participants do not act upon each other, they merely fit in with each other (to use T.S. Eliot's distinction between the characters in Shakespeare's and Jonson's plays). So, except for a few comedies and a few of Horace's *Satires*, whose status as poetry was in doubt, *in the extant Latin poetry before the Aeneid's publication all interactions between people traced through a series of vicissitudes are based on love*. That remained true of Ovid's *Amores* and *Heroides* and largely true of Propertius *IV* and Ovid's *Metamorphoses* and *Fasti*. The first extant poetic story about people in which love is not important is Lucan's *Bellum Civile*.

So, all the epic-like Latin poetry before the *Aeneid*'s publication which we can read and evaluate was based on love. The same is true of the extant pre-*Aeneid* epics themselves, at least as the Romans viewed them. The highpoint of Apollonius' *Argonautica* for nearly all readers, and certainly for Vergil, was a love story. Amazingly (to us) the Romans also regarded overpowering, all-consuming love as a basic theme of the *Odyssey* and the basic theme of the *Iliad*. They used Calypso and Circe as examples of passionate lovers and made up incidents to show Calypso's desperation and agony at Odysseus' departure (Ov. *Ars Am.* 2.123–42; *Tr.* 2.379–80; Prop. 1.15.9–16; 2.21.13–14; Heinze 1915. 118n1), as did Vergil's teacher, Parthenius, for Aeolus' daughter whom Odysseus loved and left (*Amat. Narr.* 2). Even as unromantic a character as Scylla was amalgamated by Vergil and many of his contemporaries with Nisus' Scylla, who scarificed everything because of her passionate love (Coleman 1977, on 6.74 ff.; Lyne 1978, on 54). The *Ciris* mentions several other tragic love stories involving Homer's Scylla (70-88), all of which survive in many authors (Lyne 1978, *ad locos*). In lines 68-9 the *Ciris* mentions an interpretation in which the entire *Odyssey* was regarded as an allegory of lust (see Lyne 1978, on 68f.).

The central theme of the *Iliad*, Achilles' anger, was constantly assumed by Vergil's contemporaries to have been caused primarily by his torment at the loss of Briseis, whom he loved passionately (Nisbet and Hubbard 1978, on 4.3; Farron 1983.93n21; Prop. 2.22.29; Ov. *Rem. Am.* 777ff; *Tr.* 2.371-4, cf. 4.1.15-16). The same assumption was also made by other Romans, some of whom were very unromantic (Plaut. *Mil.* 1288-9; Sil. *Pun.* 15.277-9; [Sen.] *Oct.* 807-16; cf. Stat. *Silv.* 4.4.35). The passages from the *Punica* and *Octavia* state that Agamemnon was also passionately in love with Briseis, another common belief (e.g. Sen. *Agam.* 185). References to Briseis' grief at the loss of Achilles, whom she loved intensely, were also frequent (Farron 1983.93n21; Prop. 2.20.1). This was a total distortion of the *Iliad*'s representation of their relationship and of its overall ethos (Farron 1979.27-30). But Homer himself was used as an example of someone overcome by love (Prop. 2.34.45; with Camps 1967, *ad loc.*).

The second cause of Achilles' anger, in the last part of the *Iliad*, was the death of Patroclus. That relationship was also distorted to make it romantic. The distortions in Plato's *Symposium* 179E-180A and Bion 12 (ed. Gow) are especially relevant to the manner of Nisus' death and the reason he and Euryalus are *fortunati* (9.446). In the former the gods sent Achilles to the islands of the Blest (as opposed to *Odyssey* 11.467ff.) because he "chose, having gone to the rescue of his lover Patroclus and avenged him, not only to die for him but also right after him". The last words in this sentence, ἐπαποθανεῖν τετελευτηκότι, describe exactly what Nisus does just before *fortunati*. In the latter are a series of lovers (or friends, the language is ambiguous) who were ὄλβιοι because their affection was reciprocated. Among them are Theseus, who was ὄλβιος because Pirithous went to Hades with him, and Achilles, who "was ὄλβιος dying because he avenged his [Patroclus'] death".

Homer was far from being the only source of stories about Achilles' loves, whether homosexual (Owen 1924, on 411; Servius on 1.474) or heterosexual (Bion 2.21ff.) In the latter passage Achilles, as a typical lover, was desperately in love, but unable to enjoy the relationship. It took place while he was hiding among the girls at Scyros, an incident which was constantly depicted in literature and art (Nisbet and Hubbard 1975, on 8.13). Indeed, it was the most frequently portrayed episode of Achilles' life in Pompeian painting (Schefold 1957.366). So in Ovid's *Heroides* 3.26 Briseis writes angrily to Achilles, *I nunc et cupidi nomen amantis habe*, where *I nunc* is sarcastic and means that Achilles does not deserve his title as *cupidus amans* (Palmer 1898,530.*s.v.*).

This tendency to create romantic incidents and sentiments for Achilles and other Homeric characters began with the Epic Cycle (Griffin 1977.43-5). Also in the fifth century B.C. "the power of Love ... [was a] tragic commonplace" (Heath 1987.158); and the post-classical Greeks and Romans seized on any hint of love in old mythological stories and made them centrally important (Rohde 1914.109), depicting unromantic characters like Heracles, Agamemnon, and even Polyphemus as eager to sacrifice everything for the women and/or boys they loved (Rohde 1914.44, 111ff.; Nisbet and Hubbard 1978,on 4.7; Gow 1952.118). Similarly, the vast majority of mythological paintings in Pompeii and Herculaneum were devoted to the loves of heroes and gods (Farron 1983.87; Schefold 1957.366-73;369 for Heracles, 372 for Polyphemus). And Vergil's contemporaries made into love poets even those post-Classical Greek poets who were not. A good example is Callimachus. Griffin (1985.201n22) expressed scepticism concerning Propertius' and Ovid's familiarity with Callimachus in the form of a rhetorical question: "Could they have gone on referring to Callimachus as a love poet, if they had really read much of his work?" The answer is that if they regarded Homer as a love poet, then why not Callimachus? (cf. note 6 below.)

These facts are crucially important in understanding why Vergil focused attention continuously on Dido and Nisus and Euryalus for much longer than on any other characters. With regard to the 'story of Dido's deeds' (as Donatus called it, on 1.733), modern critics constantly warn us against allowing the romantic orientation of our culture to warp our judgment, since we must judge it by the standards of Vergil's unromantic culture. The same bizarre consideration has probably been an important reason why no modern scholar has argued systematically that love is the basis of the Nisus-Euryalus episode. I point out in the Appendix that many scholars were prevented from following their own insights to their logical conclusions by the belief that this story could not have been about 'merely' love.

Also vital to understanding these two episodes and why Vergil praised Nisus and Euryalus in an unparalleled manner is that he, his contemporaries, and the ancient Greeks and Romans in general thought that the ultimate manifestation of love, and even friendship, was to want to die for one's beloved, with him, or if deprived of him, that this was an aspect of *pietas* (as in *Aeneid*

5.296), and that *laus in amore mori* (Prop. 2.1.47) and conversely *pudor est non ... mori* (3.13.20). So *perit aliqua cum viro, perit aliqua pro viro; illas ... omnis aetas honorabit, omne celebrabit ingenium.*[5] The very words *pereo* and *morior* often meant 'am in love' (Commager 1974.15n35).

C. *Vergil, Even More than his Contemporaries, Admired Suffering and Dying for Love*

Vergil was regarded as a *novus poeta* and *tener* (i.e. love: Pichon 1902.278) poet by his contemporaries (e.g. Suet. *Gram*.16). All his works fully shared the romantic ethos of his culture (Farron 1983. 84-5) and the view that love's ultimate manifestation was dying if

---

[5] Sen. *Controv.* 2.2.11; this and similar statements are introduced (2.2.9) as *loci*, which were *excepta* (i.e. greeted with approval, applauded). Other examples are Parthenius, (Vergil's teacher): 4.7; 5.2; 10.4; 14.4; 16.1; 27.2; 28.2; 31.2; 36.5; Tib. 1.3.65-6; Prop. 2.8.21-4; 20.18; 26.41-4; 28.42; 3.13.15-22 (*pia turba ... certamen habent leti*); 4.3.6,11-16; Ov. *Am.* 2.18.38; *Her* 2.131-48; 3.140-6; 8.121-2; 15.220; 18.195-6; 19.8,117; *Rem. Am.* 591-606; *Met.* 3.469-73,503; 4.107-66; 10.38-9; 11.684-5,704-5; 14.721-38(cf. 14.423-32); *Lydia* 22-4; Lygdamus (Tib. 3.2; 3.3.35-8); Humbert 1972.60-62. This theme in Vergil and his contemporaries was a favorite in the graffiti at Pompeii (Joly 1978.94n11). Griffin (1985. Chapter 7) discusses the close link the Romans, and especially Vergil's contemporaries, felt between love and death and provides examples not mentioned above. On page 208, note 51, he points out how common the combination of love and death was in post-Euripidean tragedy. Commager (1974.13-16 and *passim*) and especially Papanghelis (1987.*passim*) discuss the identification of love with death in Propertius, with examples I have not cited. Very interesting is the latter's demonstration that *laus in amore mori* is central to 2.1 and programmatic of Book 2 (22-6 and *passim*), that Propertius and other Roman poets juxtaposed *amore* with *mori* to show that they are 'very much like each other' (41-2), used *fides* as a metonymy for *mors* (137-8), and that the Romans in general had an *amor mortis* (199ff.).

For dying for or with one's beloved in Greek literature see Norden 1957. 247-8 (cf. 249-51) and Lucian, *Catapl.* 6. For the Hellenistic period in particular see Heinze 1915.133,118 (where he points out that a later writer *in stumpfsinnigem Schematismus* had even the divine Calypso commit suicide for love); Theocritus, *Id.* 1.140-1; 3.9,25-7; 23.21-4 ("is said to be the common cure for lovers' miseries") and L. Purser, *apud* Palmer 1898.419.

Even *vera amicitia* was *qua homines moriuntur, pro qua moriuntur* (Sen. *Ep.* 6.2). Cf. 9.10-11 (*In quid amicum paro? Ut habeam pro quo mori possim*); Cic. *Amic.* 24 (the audience *stantes plaudebant* Orestes and Pylades wanting to die for each other). Valerius Maximus (4.7.4) says it was *laudabilis* and an act of *pietas* that T. Volumnius *in magna fugiendi licentia, examini amico adhaesit ... ut ... causam sibi mortis arcesseret*. And Vergil, in an apostrophe (10.791-3), promises Lausus, *mortis durae casum tuaque optima facta ... non ... iuvenis memorande, silebo*. He then (811-12) has Aeneas call *pietas* Lausus rushing to certain death to save his father (*moriture ruis*: the future participle means 'intending to' (Quinn 1969.12n1; Mackail 1930, on 11.741)).

deprived of one's beloved. Otis (1963.127) gives as examples of the beginnings of Vergil's sympathetic-empathetic style, which culminates with Dido, 'the Damon song, Corydon eclogue and ... Pasiphaë narrative' in the *Eclogues* and 'the Aristaeus-Orpheus narrative' in the *Georgics*. Pasiphae will be discussed later. Damon's song begins by describing the lover as speaking *extrema moriens ... hora* (8.20) and ends with him committing suicide because he cannot live without his loved one (58-60, cf. 41). Corydon introduces his condition as *mori* (2.7) because his loved one has deserted him. For that reason he neglects his duty (58-9,70-2). His resolution to stop his useless self-destruction (68-73) is undercut by the fact that this was the type of thing he said repeatedly (4-5). Vergil ended the *Eclogues* with an account of *Gallus amore peribat* (10.10; cf.Prop.2.34.91-2). When Apollo and Pan give Gallus the very reasonable advice to stop his insane, self-destructive grief since it is useless, Lycoris is gone and will not return (21-30), he acknowledges that they are correct, but says that nevertheless his misery will make him the subject of song and that will console him in death (31-4, with Coleman 1977, on 31). His story concludes with the categorical observation and prescription, *omnia vincit amor; et nos cedamus amori* (69), which is clearly intended as a basic comment on the *Eclogue* book. Vergil follows that by stating that he loves Gallus (73-4), which he says about no one else in his works. The only other place where Vergil follows an account of a character's activities with such glowing praise in his own person is *Aeneid* 9.446-9.

Similarly, the last memorable incident in the *Georgics* is Orpheus dying because his all-consuming love would not let him live after he had lost his loved one. Otis (1963.213) asserts that "Aristaeus stands in some way for the sinful self-destruction, atonement and revival of the Roman people". But his detailed analysis of *Georgics* 4.315ff (pages 190-211) demonstrates that its structure and the way "the diffuse ... unemotional *Aristaeus* sets off ... [the Orpheus section's] concentrated brilliance — its intense, packed drama of human emotions felt and described from within" (208) makes the latter 'the centre of attention' (192), the 'climax' and 'picture proper' for which the Aristaeus story acts as 'the frame' (193), while "Aristaeus remains a shadowy and insubstantial figure" (211). Furthermore, the short part of the Aristaeus story which follows Orpheus' death is 'de-emphasized' because "we cannot quite take his atonement seriously; the sacrifice to the nymphs seems hardly sufficient and there is no real evidence of contrition in Aristacus himself" and "Virgil ... in effect discounted the bougonia by giving a full description of it *before* introducing the Aristaeus story" (210-11, Otis' italics). Again Otis' conclusions are supported by an abnormally low proportion of dactyl-spondee-spondee-spondee lines in the sympathetic-empathetic section: 5.41% in the Orpheus story, as opposed to 14.88% in the Aristaeus story (Duckworth 1966.3). (Similarly, in *Eclogue* 2 the proportion of dsss lines is only 2.74%: ibid.9n12.). Many other scholars, analyzing *Georgics* 4.315ff from other approaches, have also shown that Vergil directs the reader's interest and sympathy totally to Orpheus, even though he represents the self-absorbed, asocial, unproductive mode of existence and Aristaeus resembles the bees in being socially useful and materially productive.[6]

Vergil followed Orpheus' and Aristaus' stories and ended the *Georgics* with an eight line summary of his poetic activities. There he contrasts *Caesar ... magnus ... fulminat ... bello victorque ... dat iura viamque adfectat Olympo* with *me ... dulcis alebat Parthenope studiis florentem ignobilis oti, carmina qui lusi ....* As Griffin (1985.178) observed, "the shape of the period puts the poet, not the ruler, in the climactic position, and Virgil overshadows Octavian". That resembles Vergil's concluding his description of the socially productive, warlike bees with Orpheus' desperate and ultimately fatal agony at the loss of his loved one and making that the center of the reader's attention.

Similarly in the *Aeneid,* just as his contemporaries made Achilles' anger into a love story, so Vergil

---

[6] E.g. Perkell 1978; Segal 1966.310-21; Griffin 1985.165-8,174-8; Bradley 1969.353-7. It is probably because of the Orpheus story that pseudo-Acro, on Hor. *Sat.* 1.10.44-5, understood *molle atque facetum* as referring to the *Georgics,* even though he seems to deny to the *Georgics* the quality of *facetum* (*ioculare*). So he appears to have regarded *molle* as its specific quality. *Mollis* strongly suggested erotic temperament (Pichon 1902.206; Vessey 1969.54,70n8). All modern interpretations of *molle atque facetum* with which I am familiar assume it refers to the *Eclogues* or earlier juvenilia, except Knapp 1917. He argues that Vergil's friends were probably familiar with the *Georgics* before it was published, but his point is that *facetum* refers to it. He does not mention pseudo-Acro. Similarly, modern scholars do not consider it to be a serious possibility that Prop. 2.34.81-2 refers to the *Georgics,* ignoring the tendency discussed above to consider any erotic element in a literary work as its basic attribute.

contulit in Tyrios arma virumque toros,
nec legitur pars ulla magis de corpore toto
quam non legitimo foedere iunctus amor.
(Ov. Tr. 2.534-6)

Dido's intention to die if her loved one leaves her is constantly repeated throughout *Aeneid* 4. Mackail (1930.129-30) points out "the fourfold repetition at intervals of a hundred lines (308,415,519,604) of the single bell-stroke of *moritura*" (which means 'intending to die': Mackail on 11.741;Quinn 1969.12n1). Her resolution to die is also mentioned in lines 323,385,436,451,475,547 and 639; and the last seventy-five lines of Book 4 describe her suicide. Indeed, the wounded deer simile (4.69-73), whose significance for the Dido episode has often been noted (e.g. Pöschl 1977. 104-5), ends with *haeret lateri letalis harundo*. Even before that, in the first two lines of Book 4, Dido is described as wounded and on fire. These two images constantly recur throughout the book and prefigure her death (Newton 1957.37-43; Ferguson 1970-1.57-8,61-3). Ovid, as often, made explicit what Vergil left implicit: *nec mea nunc primum feriuntur pectora telis; ille locus saevi vulnus amoris habet* (*Her.* 7.189-90). We also have evidence outside the text that Vergil regarded Dido's death as central to Book 4. She first mentions it in passing in line 308 and then dwells on it in 323ff. Servius Danielis says of the latter passage (*ad loc*) that Vergil *dicitur ... ingenti adfectu hos versus pronuntiasse ... Augusto*. Given the outlook of his culture, he must have expected that Dido's tragic love story would be the most read and admired part of the *Aeneid*, and I will show in chapter 3 that it was. Just as Vergil made Dido's story the focus of the first third of the *Aeneid*, Aeneas' wanderings, so he began the last third, the war in Italy, with the long, gripping account of Nisus and Euryalus, lovers who die because they cannot bear to be without each other.

For the sake of brevity I will mention only one other example of characters of this type in the *Aeneid*, this one from its middle third. In the center of Book 6 (441-9) are those whom *durus amor crudeli tabe peredit*. They should be added to Pöschl's list of characters who illustrate that the *Aeneid* is the *Heldengesang der Liebe ... Denn die tiefste Tragik aller Gestalten ist es, dass sie 'zuviel liebten'* (Pöschl 1977.15). Vergil's treatment of them is significant since it shows that his fascination and sympathy with people who died for love surpassed even the normal outlook of his own culture in that he totally disregarded monstrous acts they committed, which were usually regarded as their distincive deeds. Thus this passage puts into perspective his ignoring of Nisus' and Euryalus' immorality in Books 5 and 9. Servius (on 6.444) paraphrased *curae* with *crimina*, and Donatus (on 6.445-9) said of them, *iustis diversis causis ... perierunt*. Austin (1977,on 449) sums them up as "an incestuous woman, a notorious traitress, a woman of unnatural lust, a bizarre man-woman; Procris, a jealous and suspicious wife (and ... immoral) ..." and adds, "The common factor is Virgil's pity ... all ... [are] victims of *durus amor*." He points out about Eriphyle in particular (on 445), "She was an arch-traitress of Greek mythology, and Virgil's *maestam* ... is significant of his compassion. Servius records that Virgil was attacked for it". Griffin (1985.153-4) observes,

> The complete absence of moral arrangement leaps to the eye. At line 540 ... the road divides, the wicked being punished in Tartarus, but the killers Phaedra and Eriphyle are not there. Apparently subjection to love overrides everything else, or simply being ... pretty ... (for Eriphyle ... caused her husband's death ... to get a precious necklace) ... Virgil's indifference to the morality of the dead heroines was not emulated by Propertius in his ... use of the motif [4.7.55-68].

The importance of physical beauty here recalls Vergil's emphasis on Euryalus' beauty in Books 5 and 9 and that in 5.343-4 *tutatur favor Euryalum lacrimaeque decorae ... pulchro ... in corpore*.

One of the women in this passage, Pasiphae, also appears in *Eclogue* 6.45-60. That is the only one of Otis' examples of sympathetic-empathetic narrative in the *Eclogues* which I have not yet discussed. Otis (1963.125-6) demonstrates how there "the narrator identifies himself with Pasiphaë" and Coleman (1977,on 46) notes "the singer's more sympathetic involvement in the story [than in the previous stories]" and compares his direct address 'to the suffering heroine' with *Aeneid* 9.446-9. Putnam (1970.214) observes that *Eclogue* 6 contains

> an almost perfectly balanced song of songs ... [which] balance each other and surround ... the strange history of Pasiphaë which, by a six-line margin, receives the most lengthy treatment ... This symmetrical structure ... redoubles the emphasis her story receives.

Griffin (1986.31) puts these facts into perspective: "Both the length and sympathetic tone ... are most remarkable. The passion of Pasiphaë ... was generally regarded as a monstrous aberration, to be explained only as a punishment from the gods". That was true even of Ovid and Propertius, who prided themselves on being champions of love and on flouting accepted moral standards. In the *Metamorphoses* Pasiphae's love is the ultimate *monstrum* (9.735-6), Scylla insults Minos by saying Pasiphae would be a worthy wife for him (8.131-3) and Ovid in his own person speaks of her *foedum adulterium* (8.155-6). In the *Ars Amatoria* her love is called a *crimen* (2.23) and is narrated in 1.289-326 among illustrations that women have a *furiosa libido* which does not *legitimum finem ... habet* (281-2). Many examples of hideously unnatural and/or brutal lust are mentioned (283-340), but by far the greatest length is devoted to Pasiphae's story. For Propertius she is *non proba* (2.28.52); and when he also wanted to illustrate that women's *libido* breaks *frena pudoris*, cannot *habere modum* and is unrestrainable *nequitia* (3.19.1-10), Pasiphae is his first example (11-12), followed by other women who's love drove them to monstrous crimes (13-28). In 4.7.55-8 two examples of evil women are mentioned: *Clytaemestrae stuprum* and *Cressae lignea monstra bovis*.

D. *Modern Interpretations of the Nisus-Euryalus Episode*

I have now argued that passionate love and especially its ultimate manifestation, dying because one cannot live without one's beloved, were sufficiently important and admirable to Vergil and his culture for him to devote a very long, emotionally gripping episode of the *Aeneid* to it and to praise it in an extremely glowing manner despite very serious faults in the lovers involved. That is an extremely heterodox view; so heterodox that it has not been argued by any other modern critic of this episode. All other modern scholars have assumed that the main function of the Nisus-Euryalus episode must be to comment in some way on the political, ethical and/or military values, ideals and/or characteristics which are involved in Aeneas' mission to found the Roman people and which make its completion possible. They have done this whether they think that the *Aeneid*'s purpose is to present Aeneas' mission in a favourable light, or in an unfavourable light, or in a favourable light while undercutting that with disturbing other 'voices', or as involving moral ambiguities, or as completely good but entailing tragic suffering. Since they do not consider the possibility that the main interest of the Nisus-Euryalus episode could be in their loving devotion to each other, there are four approaches to it which they follow. In the Appendix I summarize and criticize examples of each approach. To make that manageable I have excluded everything earlier than Otis' very influential study (1963), except Heinze's monumental book (1915). Below I outline the four approaches.

First, some scholars recognize that Nisus' and Euryalus' conduct in respect to the Rutulians and/or their important mission is seriously flawed, but they take 9.446-9 into consideration and understand it as praise. They argue that it is irrelevant to most of the episode. Some of them interpret it as patriotic, but most of them realize that 9.446-9 refers to Nisus' and Euryalus' personal loyalty, described immediately before it. That is usually obscured by the other approaches.

The analyses of the critics who follow the first approach have two basic defects. First, they underestimate the importance of Nisus' and Euryalus' love and loyalty in the entire episode. Most do not see that those qualities are introduced in the beginning of the episode as their essential characteristics, nor that Vergil explicitly indicates that Nisus should not have gone on without Euryalus and that dying with him is glorious, nor do they see the parallels with Book 5. Similarly, some of them point out the parallels with the Lausus story without seeing that his suicidal *pietas*, for which Vergil apostrophises him, is also constantly kept in the reader's attention. He is introduced (7.649-54) as a *filius* who will suffer because of it, his future death is mentioned during the description of his first actions (10.433-6) and most of the portrayal of him is devoted to his act of suicidal *pietas* (10.789-832). Their second defect is that they minimize the force and significance of the glowing praise in 9.446-9. This is done explicitly in their paraphrases or explanations of it and implicitly by the very fact that they regard it as irrelevant to most of the episode. The first defect is shared by most critics who follow the other approaches. The second characterizes the second approach in a more serious form and reaches its ultimate extreme in the third.

The second approach is to evaluate Nisus' and Euryalus' conduct without considering 9.446-9 and then take it into consideration, regard it as praise and relate it to the episode. Since evaluations of Nisus' and Euryalus' conduct without the apostrophe are nearly always completely negative, this approach produces self-contradictory judgments.

Those critics who want to avoid evaluations which allow contradictions in the episode or in their own judgments of it follow approaches three and four.

The third approach involves the ultimate form of minimizing the significance and/or meaning of 9.446-9. It is evaluating Nisus' and Euryalus' conduct without considering it, which results in a totally negative judgment. These critics either ignore the apostrophe or argue that it should not be taken seriously or that it is ironic in the sense that it means the opposite of what it seems to say and so reinforces the derogatory portrayal of them. The defect of ignoring 9.446-9 is obvious, that of arguing that it should not be taken seriously is discussed in the Appendix. The weakness of interpreting the apostrophe as intending the opposite of its apparent meaning is that if such glowing praise by an author in his own person can be explained like that, then any passage in any text which conflicts with a critic's presuppositions can be neutralized with "the magic wand of irony, by which the commentator converts the sense of a sentence into the exact opposite of what ... it seems to say" (Fraenkel 1962.719).

The fourth approach is the opposite of the third in recognizing that 9.446-9 grants extraordinary praise. It differs from all the other approaches in assuming that such praise must be taken into consideration in evaluating the entire episode. Since critics who follow it think that the episode could not be based 'merely' on love, they argue that Nisus and Euryalus are praised mainly for undertaking and pursuing a patriotic mission and they ignore or explain away their faults in pursuing that mission. In recognizing the meaning and significance of 9.446-9 this approach resembles mine, but not in its attitude to Nisus' and Euryalus' defects. I point out in the Appendix the futility of the attempts to explain them away.

E. *Pre-Modern Interpretations of the Nisus-Euryalus Episode*

The apostrophe in 9.446-9 promises Nisus and Euryalus that if the *Aeneid* has any influence they will be remembered by future

Romans. Several scholars whose views are discussed in the Appendix support their interpretation by asserting that the Romans must have evaluated the episode as they do. For example, Lennox (1977. 333n15), using an argument often employed for many parts of the *Aeneid*, especially the Dido-Aeneas episode, attributes anti-Nisus and Euryalus interpretations to the differences between 'the ideals of Augustan Rome' and those of our culture and assumes that Vergil's contemporaries and all readers of the *Aeneid* 'before our century' regarded this episode and the rest of the epic as a glorification of Augustan and Roman patriotic and military values.

However, there is no reason to rely on assertions and speculations as to how the Romans regarded Nisus and Euryalus. We have many ancient references to them. These show that they certainly were remembered, as Vergil promised they would be. So Seneca, quoting *Aeneid* 9.446-9, wrote, *hoc tibi promitto, Lucili. Habebo apud posteros gratiam, possum mecum diuturna nomina educere. Vergilius noster doubus memoriam aeternam promisit et praestat* (*Ep.* 21.5). And *i [Pompeian] graffiti ... hanno rivelato che episodi come quelli di ... Niso erano ... probabilmente mandati a memoria* (Gigante 1950. 121). The quotations above do not provide the reason for this fame, although Pompeian literary graffiti generally show a fascination with passionate love and the suffering it causes (Farron 1983.86).

All the other ancient references to Nisus and Euryalus with which I am familiar explain why they are remembered. In all of them they are remembered in a totally positive manner, without any hint that they did anything wrong. In this, they agree with the fourth modern approach outlined above. However, as opposed to that approach, Nisus and Euryalus are regarded as admirable and memorable not because of any political, patriotic, or military consideration. Indeed, as opposed to all four modern approaches, only their loving devotion to each other is mentioned, and that is usually described as *pietas*. Thus the ancient references to them confirm my arguments that Vergil regarded their loving devotion as the crucial element in Books 9 and 5, that in 9.446-9 he intended that they be remembered for it and that the introduction of them in 5.295-6 presented the attributes that would be basic for both episodes involving them.

Ovid mentions them three times, all in the *Tristia* and all as a part of addresses to friends who were among the few who remained loyal to him in his difficult and dangerous circumstances. He praises them for their *fides* and compares them to the most famous literary examples of such behaviour. These examples are all centuries old except Nisus and Euryalus, who are always mentioned last, as the climactic illustration. In 5.4.23-6 Ovid refers to himself in the third person and says to the letter's recipient, *te ... (o ... carior illi/omnibus) in toto pectore semper habet;/ teque Menoetiaden, te qui comitatus Oresten,/te vocat Aegiden Euryalumque suum./* Here the climactic position is reinforced by *suum*. In 1.9.23-35 Ovid demonstrates that even enemies praise *quis in adversis ... amat* by using the examples of Pylades; Patroclus, whose *fides* Hector praised; Theseus, who *pius ad Manes ... comes iret amico*; and *Euryali Nisique fide, tibi, Turne, relata/credibile est lacrimis immaduisse gemas./Est etiam miseris pietas*. In 1.5 Ovid uses Nisus and Euryalus to illustrate that his friend's *pietas* (14,38) will not be forgotten. They again follow Theseus and Pylades (19-26). In this passage what is clearly implicit in the other two is explicit: they owe their glory to their *Liebestod: si non Euryalus Rutulos cecidisset in hostes,/Hyrtacidae Nisi gloria nulla foret.* (23-4).

In *Thebaid* 10.347-448 Statius describes the mission of Hopleus and Dymas to recover their leaders' corpses. They are introduced at the episode's beginning (348-50) as *dilecti ... comites* [of Tydeus and Parthenopaeus], *quorum post funera maesti vitam indignantur,* just as Euryalus *infelicem nimium dilexit amicum* (*Aen.* 9.430). Also like Nisus and Euryalus, they do not accomplish their goal (403-4,438). But they are *pii* (384) because of their devotion to their leaders, whom they embrace as they die (402-3,440-1). That is summarized in lines 442-4: *tales optatis regum in complexibus ambo,/par insigne animis .../egregias efflant animas letoque fruuntur* (on which Lactantius Placidus commented, *in facto tali cum voluptate pereunt*; cf. *Fortunati*). This obvious similarity of both to Nisus is followed immediately by the four-line apostrophe,

> vos quoque sacrati, quamvis mea carmina surgant
> inferiore lyra, memores superabitis annos.
> Forsitan et comites non aspernabitur umbras
> Euryalus Phrygiique admittet gloria Nisi.

It is significant that until Hopleus and Dymas are called *pii* in 384, the description of their activities resembles that of Nisus and Euryalus only in that they are two soldiers who leave their camp at night to go on a mission. But in the line after 384 is a verbal echo of *Aeneid* 9.371 and then (386-404) are incidents similar to those in *Aeneid* 9: a cavalry troop sees them, its leader orders them to stop and Hopleus is killed.

Much more space is devoted to Dymas (405-441), and his relation with Parthenopaeus' corpse strongly recalls Nisus' with Euryalus when he was trapped. Dymas does not consider escaping, but is *ad caedem iuxta mortemque paratus* (413) because of his *amor* (418) for Parthenopaeus. Just as Nisus begged to be killed instead of Euryalus and said he was responsible for what they did (*Aen.* 9.427-30), so Dymas begs to be unburied instead of Parthenopaeus because *ego bella audere coegi* (429-30), even though there is no indication elsewhere that he had urged his leader to war. His last act, when dying, is to throw himself on Parthenopaeus' body (439-441). Another significant similarity is that Parthenopaeus is called *puer* in lines 369, 421, 427 and 440 and his tender youth is emphasized in 356-7 and 414-15.

Like Nisus and Euryalus, Dymas and Parthenopaeus participated in a foot race four books before their night expedition. There Parthenopaeus is also called *puer* (6.602), his beauty is emphasized (571-82) and he resembles Euryalus in his *nudae genae* (571-2) and that in his appeal *accessit lacrimarum gratia formae* (623).

Ausonius mentioned *gloria Nisi* among famous pairs of friends (25.23.41-2, ed. Prete), after accusing Paulinus, <u>*inpie*</u>, ... *posses Euryalum ... suo socium secernere Niso* (34-5). His contemporary Donatus in his comment on *fortunati ambo* showed a totally accurate understanding of what the apostrophe was for and its relation to its episode: *Exaequavit amborum fidem, exaequavit laudem; Euryalus enim noluit Nisum relinquere in pericula pergentem, ecce et Nisus, qui evaserat, ne amico examini superstes extisset, properavit ad mortem.* Similarly, the verses in the *Anthologia Latina* on Nisus and Euryalus (77, ed. Riese) showed a totally accurate understanding of Vergil's attitude to friendship and life: *Nomen amicitiae magna <u>pietate</u> colendum est;/maxima pars vitae est nomen amicitiae.*

The poem quoted above was written either in late antiquity or within the sixty years after 476 A.D. One other poem in the *Anthologia Latina*, 653.57-9 (ed. Riese), mentions Nisus and Euryalus. It definitely comes from the early Middle Ages. The passage is, *Caeduntur vigiles et mutua corpora fratrum./Nisus et Euryalus morte et <u>pietate</u> fideles./Dumque petunt laudem, vincunt contraria fata.* As opposed to the references from antiquity, this does not exclude everything except their mutual loyalty. But that is because it is part of an outline of the contents of the *Aeneid*; and Baehrens and Opitz argued that the first line refers to the end of *Aeneid* 9 and should be transposed. Line 58 (*Nisus ... fideles*) obviously presents their important characteristics.

I will conclude with three later treatments of Nisus and Euryalus. These are by very eminent authors and critics who lived at different times and exemplified very different cultural outlooks. But, like ancient authors and critics, they regarded Nisus' and Euryalus' only important characteristic to be their love and loyalty for each other. Boccaccio, in *Amorosa Visione*, Canto 8, lines 62-3, described them as *monstrandosi piagati como foro/ciascun di lor, l'un per l'altro conquiso*. The summary of *Aeneid* 9 which precedes Dryden's translation of it and was written by Addison outlined the episode as, "The Trojans ... send Nisus and Euryalus to recall Aeneas; which furnishes the poet with the admirable episode of their friendship, generosity, and the conclusion of their adventures." (And Dryden himself translated *amicum* in 9.444 as 'lover'.) Lord Byron, in his poetic paraphrase of this episode (in *Hours of Idleness*), added after line 182 of the Latin text, as the last line of the opening description, "Friendship and glory form their joint reward", which indicates why he thinks Vergil praised them at the episode's end. He added to 9.424-6, "Forth, forth he starts, and all his love reveals" (Byron's line 364). He added after 9.443, "Thus Nisus all his fond affection proved –/Dying, revenged the fate of him he loved;" (Byron's lines 397-8). The next two lines, the last before the apostrophe, he paraphrased as, "Then, on his bosom sought his wonted place,/And death was heavenly in his friend's embrace!" That is followed by 'Celestial pair!' for *fortunati ambo*, clearly linked with Nisus' 'heavenly' death.

CHAPTER TWO

ANCIENT AND MODERN LITERARY ATTITUDES

In the course of this century ... there seems to have endured a picture of Virgil as ... shedding warm tears as he contemplates the perennial sorrows of humanity ... there is a certain provincialism ... in the assumption ... that the academic culture of the later twentieth century has achieved an understanding ... denied to the great minds of the past. (Jenkyns 1985.60)

To us Dido is a three-dimensional character ... But we are post-Romantics: our view of Dido is filtered through Purcell, Dryden, Berlioz ... To a Roman of Virgil's day she was probably nothing more than an unbalanced barbarian queen. (Mcleish 1972.127-8)

The Romantics ... admired ... the more intensely written parts of the *Aeneid* (as for instance the portrayal of Dido in Book IV). But they did not respond to the Roman values of the poem. [Many denigrations of Aeneas are then quoted, followed by examples of Victorian emphasis on the *Aeneid*'s pathos.] ... The twentieth-century critic, immersed in this pool of tears ... [should not] substitute for the *Aeneid* an anthology of the most intense parts of the second, fourth, sixth and twelfth books. (R. Williams 1969.132-5)

Les récents travaux consacrés à l'*Énéide* ... dans des voies nouvelles ... sont plus sensibles au pathétique ... tel qu'il ressort de chaque épisode; ils portent un moindre intérêt au sujet même ... *imperium sine fine dedi*. (Perret 1967.342)

The unfavourable view of Aeneas derives, I think, from reading isolated books [2,4,6,8,12]. (Dudley 1961.52)

His speech [Aeneas' in 4.333-61], though we may not like it, was the Roman answer. (Austin 1955, on 331-61)

Les lectures de Virgile aient été moins sensibles que nous à ce qu'il y a d'égoïsme masculin, de brutalité ... dans l'attitude d'Énée [to Dido] ... que peuvent compter, pour un Romain, les peines d'une femme en regard des destinées d'un peuple? ... Le lecteur moderne est très tenté de négliger le point de vue de l'épopée ... C'est là une façon de sentir romantique ... (Constans 1938.147,158)

Aeneas [should be] ... judged by the standards intended by the author rather than by those of some modern sentimentalist ... Heirs of a tradition of romantic and sentimental self-expression, modern readers [must remember, quoting Conway 1914] ... how far less in the ethics of the ancient world the happiness of the

> individual counted as against the welfare of the body politic than it does in our modern sentiment. (Pease 1935.49,42)
>
> The reviving admiration for the *Aeneid* has no word of praise for Aeneas ... [But] if ... we examine Aeneas by the standards of his time he becomes a more interesting ... character, even if he fails to excite that interest which falls always to passionate ... characters ... This was the sort of man that the age of Augustus admired. (Bowra 1933.8,20)
>
> The modern reader may ... criticize Aeneas for ... abandoning Dido ... But ... this modern standpoint ... is justifiable only when the critic admits he is indulging a modern prejudice. The Roman reader ... (Prescott 1927.282)
>
> In Roman social life ... the passion of love was the illegitimate thing. A Roman would understand it all: how Latinus could blame himself ... for abandoning the claim of Aeneas [to Lavinia]: how he had done the wrong thing in preferring the individual passion of a youthful hero not destined to great works of peace and civilization ... it takes an effort to sympathize with Aeneas ... (Fowler 1919.43)
>
> For us moderns ... the scandal of the Dido episode has been quite transferred from Virgil's heroine to his hero ... Our taste has been vitiated by an excess of romanticism ... We are accustomed to think of the love-story as the main part of any story ... In ancient literature the passion of love appears rarely ... (Yeames 1913.139-40)
>
> Virgil is not to be read as if he were a modern writer of romance, but to be interpreted according to the ideas of his time ... Virgil has no intention of exciting such a sympathy with her [Dido's] fate as a modern reader necessarily feels ... (Nettleship 1885.108,129)

Examples of this type of warning can be multiplied indefinitely, and ironically that is not only true of the past century. The scholars quoted above, with the exception of Mcleish, assume that the modern romantic-sentimental-pathetic prejudice is either a phenomenon of our century or goes back to the Romantics. But C. Heyne in his commentaries on Vergil's works, which were published between 1767 and 1775, before the Romantic movement, as it is usually defined, began, conceded in his *Argumentum* of Book 4 that although it is universally admired,

> Aeneas quidem nostris moribus idonei amatoris personam male sustinere videri potest; nec potest negari, vix te ad libri quarti finem legendo pervenire quin Aeneae feritatem et immanitatem exsecreris ... omnino res [Aeneas leaving Dido] nostris moribus ac sensibus non est iucunda.

Indeed, twenty-one years before Mcleish's earliest example,

Purcell's *Dido and Aeneas*, R. de Segrais in the preface to his translation of the *Aeneid* (Paris 1668.35) said,

> Je passe à cette ingratitude ... dont on accuse Enée envers Didon ... il ne faut pas juger d'un siecle par un autre. Comme les jeunes esprits [of today] ... sont plutôt touchez de la passion de l'amour, ils ont tourné en habitude, non seulement de trouver la poësie amoureuse la plus belle, mais aussi d'excuser toutes les fautes que l'amour fait faire. (A fuller version of this passage and a similar argument from de Segrais are quoted in Farron 1983.83)

All these warnings against letting the orientation of our culture cause us to concentrate on the romantic-sentimental-pathetic parts of the *Aeneid* and to ignore its main Roman-patriotic-imperial subject are also ironic in view of the only three references we have concerning the parts that interested and moved Vergil and Augustus and his circle. Donatus' biography of Vergil (32) says that he read only three books to Augustus, one (or two: Murgia 1967.332-5), four and six; and about six, *notabili Octaviae adfectione, quae cum recitationi interesset, ad illos de filio suo versus: 'tu Marcellus eris', deficisse fertur atque aegre focilata*. Servius on 6.861 says, *constat hunc librum tanta pronuntiatione Augusto et Octaviae esse recitatum, ut fletu nimio imperarent silentium, nisi Vergilius finem esse dixisset*. On 4.323, where Dido tells Aeneas that by leaving her he is giving her no choice but suicide, Servius Danielis says, *dicitur ... ingenti adfectu hos versus pronuntiasse ... Augusto*. Servius seems to have proceeded to state that the other books Vergil read to Augustus were one and six (Murgia 1967.332-5). If that is so, then he concentrated on the Dido episode; if it was books two, four and six, Vergil also still did what we are constantly warned against: focusing on the emotional rather than patriotic parts of the epic.

As Fowler observed in the comment quoted at the beginning of my discussion of the Nisus-Euryalus episode, what has puzzled modern critics is it is "without any very obvious connexion with the story", that is Aeneas' mission to found the Roman people. They have devoted their efforts to explaining what the connection is. In chapter one I argued that that episode was not intended primarily to contribute to the *Aeneid*'s 'story' or the meaning and message of that story. Its purpose is to describe the effect of an overpowering emotion. In chapter three I will argue that that is true of the entire *Aeneid*. Now I will demonstrate that my interpretation is in line with the way the ancient Greeks and Romans composed and reacted to literature. This demonstration will of necessity be highly selective and the manner of selection somewhat arbitrary. I will begin with the differences between ancient and modern interpretations of Greek tragedy, a genre whose influence on the *Aeneid* was immense and has often been observed. I will then show how incomparably more emotional ancient reactions to literature, history, oratory, painting, sculpture, music and lectures were than modern reactions. Then I demonstrate the effect of the failure to appreciate this difference on modern evaluations of ancient Greek and Roman literature and literary criticism. After that, I discuss ancient attempts to find meaning in literature and their relation to the *Aeneid*. Then I analyze the disparity between ancient and modern attitudes to unity in the Homeric epics. Finally, I point out the lack of unity in Apollonius' *Argonautica* and Roman poetry.

A. *Ancient and Modern Interpretations of Greek Tragedy*

Typical of the ancients' lack of interest in having the basic plot dominate literary (and historical) works was that their climactic event usually occurred well before the work's end and was followed by various episodes (Farron 1982). (I am using the word 'episode' here as Aristotle often does, to mean an incident which is not part of the plot.) That is fundamentally different from most modern literature. In tragedy this is well illustrated by a statement made by Aristotle, whose insistence on "the overwhelming importance of the plot ... amounts to ... an obsession" (Else 1963. 253) and who constantly argued that the plot must have unity. He used *Iphigeneia in Tauris* as an example of the ideal relationship between plot and episodes (*Poet.* 1455 a34-b15) and said that its plot ends with Orestes' salvation. That cannot refer to his escape by ship, since he mentions that among the episodes. So it must mean his salvation from execution in line 994. The last third of this ideally constructed play is composed of episodes.

There is a "strong thrust in the *Poetics* towards a theoretical separation of poetry from performance, drama from theatre" (Halliwell 1986.337-43). When Tycho von Wilamowitz-Moellendorff (1917) studied Sophocles' plays purely as stage presentations, he, like Aristotle, observed that their plots ended well before the end of the play; in particular, the central character disappears or becomes unimportant before the play is over. Indeed, he demonstrated that the crucial consideration was the impact of single scenes and situations not coherence of plot or character.

Several scholars have followed his insights. Dawe (1963) applied them to Aeschylus. He points out that "much recent criticism ... has been directed at attempts to extract from these contradictions [in Aeschylus' plays] a unified picture of what the poet really intended us to understand" (21) and that "criticism ... has proceeded on the assumption that the function of a literary critic is to assemble everything the poet says on a given topic, and to extract a coherent picture" (60). This has resulted in either attempts to rewrite the plays, of which he gives several examples (24-5), or contradictory interpretations. Among his examples of the latter is the character of Agamemnon in 'the two latest commentaries'. Fraenkel describes him as "a great gentleman possessed of moderation and self-control", Page as unlovable, sanctimonious, cold, hostile and arrogant. "Critics have been fairly evenly divided between these two ... [views] since modern literary criticism of the play began" (46). (The similarity to evaluations of Aeneas' character is obvious.) Dawe concludes that in this and other questions "the bewildering lack of unity among the leading members of our profession" leads to the inference that "they are striving to reconstruct ... a consistent picture that Aeschylus did not want reconstructed" (46, cf. 60). He demonstrates that "Aeschylus was perfectly prepared to allow inconsistencies ... when it suited his purpose" (33) and that that purpose was "to make the utmost out of each successive scene, and to pile different kinds of dramatic thrill one upon the other" (51).

Waldock (1951.49-79) applied Wilamowitz' insights to Sophocles and Euripides. He pointed out that in many of their plays the basic plot, the focus of interest, peters out when the play is half or two-thirds over. He also observed that Sophocles and Euripides made little or no effort to avoid this lack of unity, and he contrasted the unity of the plays of Shakespeare and Racine.

It is indicative of the difference between ancient and modern literary sensitivities that Aristotle did not regard this looseness of structure as a defect but Wilamowitz and Waldock did. The latter introduces his discussion of the 'diptych' plays by describing them as an 'insistent ... problem' at which the modern reader is 'surprised' and 'puzzled' and he attributes them to an unfortunate result of Greek dramatic conventions (e.g. 56-61). The former warns against judging Greek tragedies *nach der modernen Forderung der Einheit der Handlung* (155 and *passim*), but he attributes incongruities to negligence and calls *das Auseinanderfallen der beiden Teile* of the *Trachiniae anstössig* (155).

As Waldock points out (61), "every diptych ... has its defenders". And after him, Kitto (1956.179-98) tried to 'defend' the *Ajax* from Waldock's accusation of lack of unity by arging that it is unified by its illustration of the workings of σωφροσύνη and the conscquences of its absence.

Some critics attack the mistaken search for coherence which dominates modern criticism, but still try to find it. For example, Arrowsmith (1959) points out the damage done to the interpretation of Greek tragedy by the 'itch for conceptual rigor' (36), 'the criteria of orderly reason' (41) and 'our modern preference for the organic' (50). This has led to "the long insistence of critics that Euripidean plays lack unity ... are merely episodes strung together" (51) and to the fact that this incoherence 'has been savagely censured' (44). But Arrowsmith's purpose is still to find 'the dramatist's order' (40), his 'form' (53), "the real coherence of the plays so far as structure is concerned" (51) and "to know again why the plot is the 'soul of the play'" (40). He finds this unity sometimes in a larger-than-life hero, sometimes in "a juxtaposition of antithetical realities — ... the material ... from legend ... and the new reality which the dramatist forces ... from his old material" (52), sometimes in the operation of an intellectual or moral concept or such a concept and its opposite and sometimes in the struggle against necessity (55-7).

The assumptions underlying most modern criticism of Greek tragedy are manifested in the first chapter of Lesky's *Greek Tragedy* (1978.1-26), entitled "What is Tragedy?" His answer is based on the views of eminent philosophers, authors and critics of the past two centuries. He concludes that tragedy must have a conflict (*passim*), *"be relevant to the world we live in"* (10, Lesky's italics), "the protagonist ... [must be] caught in an inescapable conflict ... There will be no tragic effect when a passive victim ... is led to ... execution" (10) and that "we should rate the value of ... moral influence very high ... the 'moral influence' of great and genuine art depends on its being consistent with a strict order of values, so that ... [it] bears witness to these values" (20-21).

The above interpretations of the subjects and functions of Greek tragedy and others with which all Classical scholars are familiar resemble the major interpretations of the *Aeneid*: it demonstrates the operation of moral or intellectual concepts or their opposition to other concepts (e.g. *pietas*); shows the flaws or strengths of its hero; presents conflicts of the hero; comments on the world of the poet, etc. Several common explanations of Greek tragedy are similar to aspects of the now popular 'two voices' interpretation of the *Aeneid*: it juxtaposes legendary material with the author's handling of it, represents the struggle against necessity, the conflict of humans against amoral gods, etc.

Similarly, Heath (1989.6-8) points out that modern criticism of Euripides' *Suppliants* "rejects the interpretation of the play (offered by the ancient hypothesis) as an 'encomium of Athens' on the grounds that it fails to account for the play's pessimistic parts". The "possibility that the play is in part encomium and in part something else" (which is what I will argue the *Aeneid* is) is dismissed because it must have "an evolving and interdependent totality", a 'central idea'. The quest for this central idea leads one eminent modern scholar to assert that the play is "'a coherent and well designed presentation of a single theme', pacifism", which is similar to several current interpretations of the *Aeneid*. But most modern evaluations of the *Suppliants* resemble the 'two voices' interpretation of the *Aeneid*: the actions are 'juxtaposed for contrast' and the "'complex form of the play' ... [is] a 'picture' of the complex forces affecting human decisions"; "the play is 'a tragic satire showing how decent people ... are caught up in a vortex of human folly'"; "the profusion of themes, each treated in an ambivalent or equivocal way, is designed to reflect the ambivalence and uncertainty that is 'a central problem in the life of man'".

What is most relevant for the *Aeneid* is not the validity of modern approaches to Greek tragedy, but the fact that the ancients did not share them. If the delineation of a strong-willed character and his powerful conflicts or of moral and intellectual messages was regarded as important in tragedy, Aristotle would have emphasized them. His argument (*Poet.* 1451b5-6) that poetry is philosophical and serious must be part of his implicit refutation of Plato's condemnation of it (e.g. Heath 1987.34) for showing weak characters and being in general anti-philosophical. But Aristotle frequently asserts that character portrayal is inessential for tragedy (e.g. *Poet.* 1450a16-25), and "in his comments on plots based on the experiences of a single figure, Aristotle shows no sign of anything like the modern sensitivity to personal interest, and does not expect it in his opponents" (Heath 1987.100). As for moral or intellectual messages, Else observes (1963.274), "for Aristotle there is no such thing as *the 'thought' of the poet* ... a 'philosophy of life'" (Else's italics) and (305-7) "There is in fact not a word in the *Poetics* about the ultimate 'secrets of life', about ... man's relation to God, or any such ... matters. These omissions are not accidental".

Instead, "Aristotle thought the *pathos* [is] the basic, indispensable 'part' of the tragic plot" (Else. 229, cf. 356n.38). So he rejects one possible plot as "not tragic because it is ἀπαθές" (*Poet.* 1453b39). He defines πάθος as "an act which is destructive or painful" (*Poet.* 1452b11-12). These παθήματα are pitiful and terrifying events (*Poet.* 1449b27-28), and the purpose of tragedy is to arouse compassion and terror (e.g. *Poet.* 1453b4-6,10-15) through the representation of such events (e.g. 1452a1-3, 1453b15ff; Halliwell 1986.171). That is the 'proper pleasure' that tragedy should produce (Heath 1987.9-10) and epic also (Else 1963.651-3; Halliwell 1986.263, cf. 65). That is what I think the purpose of the *Aeneid* was.

Plato also assumed that the purpose and effect of the Homeric epics and tragedy was to arouse strong emotions, especially compassion, in the reader or audience by depicting emotional, especially pathetic, events and characters. So, for example, he summarizes their subjects as "the πάθη of Niobe, or those of the Pelopidae, or those of Troy or anything else of that kind" (*Resp.* 380A). The discussion which follows shows that Plato thought that these were usually presented with no intellectual or moral meaning or purpose. Instead (*Resp.* 604D-605A) the poet is 'by nature' (πέφυκε) inclined to represent grieving characters and arouse lamentation. Like Aristotle, he also assumed this was the appropriate pleasure of epic and tragedy: "When we hear Homer or another of the tragedians representing one of the heroes being in pain and making a long speech in his suffering ... and beating himself, you know that we feel pleasure" (*Resp.* 605C-606B, cf.*Phlb.*47E-48A); and "we praise as a good poet the one who most shapes our emotions in this way" (*Resp.*605D). So Plato's Ion (535E) rejoiced when his audience cried because of the money that would gain him; and the music which caused the most crying won the prize (*Leg.* 800D). The ancients in general enjoyed pain in art (Macleod 1982.7) and often described crying as a pleasure (Fränkel 1975. 15; Heubeck, West, Hainsworth 1988, on 4.102, their comment reflects modern prejudices); although some, like Plato, attacked this form of enjoyment (e.g. Sen. *Dial.* 6.1.7; *Ep.*99.25; Stat. *Silv.* 2.6.94-6).

B. *Ancient Emotional Reactions to Literature, History, Oratory, Painting, Sculpture, Music, Lectures*

Plato's and Aristotle's assumptions about the nature and goal of literature were typical. To "the ancient critics, the essence of tragedy is in the emotions that it expressed and caused" (Stanford 1983.2). Ancient Greek tragedies concentrated on portraying and arousing extremely powerful emotions by having their characters and choruses "tear their flesh or hair ... tremble and shudder ... fall prostrate ... become dumb or ... utter inarticulate cries — besides weeping, sobbing, groaning and wailing" (*ibid.* 21, cf. 22-48) and by music, noise, gestures, etc. (49-90). Many ancient descriptions of audience reactions show that they succeeded in producing an emotional reaction of an intensity that is totally unparalleled in our culture (*ibid.*3-8, *passim*; Cic. *Fin.* 5.63, *Amic.* 24; Suet. *Iul.* 84.2). For, a successful tragedian is one *meum qui pectus inaniter angit, irritat, mulcet, falsis terroribus implet, ut magus* (Hor. *Epist.* 2.1.211-13, cf. *Ars.P.*99-104). So English cannot translate the full force and empathetic nature of the ancient Greek words for the emotions involved (Stanford 1983.23-4 and *passim*; Kaufmann 1968.44-8; Farron 1983.90).

It was especially the depiction of the pitiful and pathetic that dominated in tragedy (Vickers 1979.59-96; Kaufmann 1968.311-14; Schadewalt 1955.145-6). For, "the supreme tragic emotion ... is *eleos* or *oiktos*" (Stanford 1983.23-4, cf. 10,25-6, *passim*); it was "the common view that suffering ... is the essence of tragedy" (Halliwell 1986.146n14); and for the ancient critics and scholiasts, "*pathos* is the defining quality of the genre" (Heath 1987.10, cf.8-9,13-15,22,172,180). So, for Aristotle, "*pathos* is the ... event ... around which the action ... revolves" (Else 1963.356; cf. Stanford 1983.10) and Aristotle defined *pathos* (*Poet.* 1452b11-13) as painful occurrences.

The ancient Greek and Roman reaction to other literary genres was similar to their reaction to tragedy (Farron 1983). From Homer on, they assumed that the purpose of serious literature was to arouse emotions, especially pity and fear (Schadewalt 1955). 'Poetry as a whole' was defined by Gorgias (*Hel.* 9) as causing "ultra-fearful shuddering and much-weeping compassion and grief-loving longing". (This translation is mostly Taplin's (1978.168), who points out its relevance for Greek tragedy.) Among the Romans, the normal result of a poetry recitation was for the audience to tremble when their innermost beings were 'carved' by the poem (Pers. 1.19-21,81-2). And when someone pretended to like a poem he grew pale, cried, danced and beat the ground with his feet (Hor. *Ars. P.* 429-30).

As for epic in particular, Homer frequently describes the type of poetry he composes as producing an overwhelming, all-engrossing emotional response (Heath 1987.7; Halliwell 1986.188). Especially typical was profuse crying (*Od.* 1.336-42; 8.521-31). Indeed, whenever a Homeric character introduces a story, he always describes its subject as painful afflictions, miserable woes, etc., whose purpose is to arouse compassion. "Hence only what is sorrowful is worth preservation in song" (Fränkel 1975.14-15). And Lucan (7.211-13) looked forward to this type of totally empathetic emotional reaction to his epic. We have ample evidence that audiences and readers did respond in a very emotional way, especially crying and fainting (e.g. Pl. *Ion* 535B,E; Dio Chrys. 53.7; Serv. on *Aen.* 6.861; Donat. *Vita Vergiliana* 32). Ancient critics emphasized the emotional impact of epics, especially in arousing compassion. Servius and Donatus often point out and approve subjects and manners of expression which serve *ad misericordiam/ miserationem eliciendam/commovendam.* Griffin (1976; cf. 1980, chapter 4 and *passim*) demonstrates that the ancient scholia on Homer, which had a profound influence on the *Aeneid* (Schlunk 1974), were incomparably more sensitive to and appreciative of pity and pathos than modern scholars are. The expression 'an *Iliad* of troubles' (Dem. *FL* 148) seems to have been proverbial, as was 'the misfortunes of a Priam' (Arist. *Eth. Nic.* 1.10.14). Indeed, the plight of Hector and "the pitiable sufferings of Andromache, Hecuba and Priam" (Pl. *Ion* 535B; cf. Dio Chrys. 53.7) were among the most popular parts of the *Iliad,* if not the most popular parts, as is attested by the Epic Cycle, Greek art and tragedy and Roman literature (Farron 1986.83n29). So Horace regarded a typical beginning of a poem in the Epic Cycle as *Fortunam Priami cantabo et nobile bellum* (*Ars P.* 137).

Ancient historians also intended to produce pathos; and ancient critics admired the compassion they aroused, even in passages which seem unemotional to us (Walbank 1960.230-2). Indeed, "the [emotion inducing] picture which ancient critics draw of Thucydides, and even of Xenophon, is hardly recognizable" (to modern readers) (*ibid.*) The ancient critics Walbank quotes are Dionysius of Halicarnassus, Vergil's contemporary, and Plutarch. The Romans responded to history in the same way (e.g. Sen. *Dial.* 9.1.12; Cic. *Fin.* 5.62).

Oratory pervaded ancient Greek and Roman life. Anyone familiar with their speeches and discussions of rhetoric knows how effective they were at arousing intense emotions and that that, rather than presenting cogent arguments, was regarded as the heart of oratory (e.g. Cic. *Brut* 89-90, *Orat.* 210; Quint. *Inst.* 6.2.3-7). It was also thought to be necessary for the orator himself to display the emotions he wanted to engender, by his facial features, hitting his face and thighs, stamping his foot, etc. (Cic. *Brut.* 277-8; cf. Val. Max. 8.10.3; Quint. *Inst.* 11.3.123,155). But it was especially the display of misery that was common and drew copious tears from audiences, both in speeches in courts and by characters in literature, of which the *Aeneid* is an excellent example (Farron 1988). However, the ancients reacted ecstatically even when reading speeches of a dead orator (e.g. Dion. Hal. *Dem.* 22). Similarly, erotic poetry and theater productions caused powerful emotional reactions (e.g. Prop. 3.9.45; Ov. *Rem. Am.* 757-65; 751-6; Juv. 6.63-6).

Painting and sculpture also stupefied the ancient Greeks and Romans (Cic. *Parad.* 37: *tabula te stupidum detinet aut signum*; Hor. *Sat.* 2.7.95: *torpes, insane*; Verg. *Aen.* 1.495: *stupet obtutuque haeret defixus*). Men ejaculated on statues of naked goddesses which we admire dispassionately (Pliny, *NH* 36.21), and women were corrupted by erotic art (e.g. Prop. 2.6.27-30). And, as with literature, the ancients wept profusely over paintings and sculpture (Arist. *Poet.* 1455a1-2; Verg. *Aen.* 1.459,465,470, cf. 485). Similarly, music *saepe* had the effect that *pellantur animi vehementius* (Pease 1920, on 80.1; Anderson 1966; Schadewalt 1955.132n2; Plut. *Mor.* 623A; Plato, *Leg.* 800C-D).

Vehement emotional reactions were even common at lectures.

Quintilian (*Inst.* 2.2.9-12) said students should not be allowed 'to leap out of their seats' and 'shout' 'at every *clausula*' of the teacher, 'as usually happens'. Such behaviour is 'appropriate to the theater'. Plutarch (*Mor.* 41B-C) criticized the "screaming, clamour and jumping to their feet of audiences" at philosophy lectures. But he understood this reaction. For, "to a young man who has made real progress in philosophy, these verses of Sappho [31 LP: φαίνεταί μοι] are a constant attribute" (*Mor.* 81D).

C. *Modern Reactions to Ancient Literature and Literary Criticism*

It is very difficult for us to appreciate the intensity and importance of emotions in ancient literature. Some scholars have recognized them in one period, but thought they reflected peculiarities of that period. For example, Havelock (1963) points out that Plato assumes that authors, performers, students and audiences experience literature empathetically (21-4,159-60) and that "in his description of the emotional impact of poetry he seems often to be describing an almost pathological situation ... an intensity of response ... which to us is unfamiliar" (37). Havelock ascribes this to an 'oral state of mind' (38-41), which is characterized by "total personal involvement and ... emotional identification with the ... poetised statement" (44) and "a whole series of motor reflexes throughout the entire body" (157). He asserts that this state of mind ended shortly after Plato's time (e.g. 40-1,44,208-9,216). But once he offers a different explanation, which is, in fact, the correct one: the "curious emotionalism ... of the Greeks which is alien to our experience" (27).

More often, scholars ignore the emotionalism of ancient tragedies and their performance completely. An example of the result of this is the many emendations proposed for *scaenis* in *Aeneid* 4.471 (Geymonat 1973, *ad loc.*), far-fetched interpretations (e.g. Henry 1878.755-6) and criticisms such as, "*scaenis* ... suggests unreality and weakens ... the idea of terror" (Page 1894, *ad loc.*).

Probably the most important specific cause of modern distortions of ancient literature is the failure to appreciate that, as Kaufmann (1968.311-14) points out, "There is ... a very profound difference between the sensibilities of the Greeks and those of ... modern critics ... [who] distinguish sharply between what is merely pathetic and what is truly tragic." Kaufmann demonstrates that this failure has caused a lack of realization that pathos and suffering are the basis of Attic tragedy (*ibid.*). This is also one of the major causes of the modern distortion of the *Aeneid*. That is well illustrated by Norden's comment (1957) on *Aeneid* 6.456 ff.: *der Grundton der Didoszene ist nicht auf sentimentalität, sondern auf heroische Grösse und tragisches Ethos gestimmt (wie überhaupt das ganze Dido-drama ...)*. He quotes the beginning of Donatus' comment on 6.456-7, *dictio mira arte concepta est.* But Donatus emphasizes how Aeneas' crying shows he *miserabilem casum [Didonis] se graviter ferre.*

This difference in outlook between ancient and modern critics is best illustrated for tragedy by responses to Euripides. De Romilly (1961) observes that although Aeschylus and Sophocles often create powerful impressions of suffering and pathos (e.g. 75,85), this was especially Euripides' strong point. Euripides was, after Homer, the most popular poet among the later Greeks (Farron 1983.87), and Quintilian (*Inst.* 10.1.67-8) recommended him because he "is outstanding in all emotions but easily supreme in those based on pity". Aristotle (*Poet* 1453a 29-30) said Euripides "is regarded as the most tragic of the poets". This probably refers to his plays with 'spectacularly unhappy endings' (Lucas 1978.147) and especially his heroes who suffer because they are victims and do not cause their suffering (Else 1963.401-2). To Aristotle this is high praise, despite (γε) Euripides' defects in other matters. For, the ancient Greeks and Romans valued pathos in all the arts very highly and regarded suffering and the pity it arouses as the basis of tragedy. But Schlegel (1809-11.136) said of the *Troades*, which he realizes was the type of play that "gained for him [Euripides], from Aristotle, the title of 'the most tragic of poets'", that it "is a series of situations and events, which have no ... connexion" [cf. Fowler on Nisus and Euryalus] ... [and] 'no ... common aim' and "the accumulation of helpless suffering ... wearies us ... In this way Euripides frequently fails". Jebb (1876.xcix-ci) explained Aristotle's judgement by asserting that the word 'tragic' had suffered a 'degradation' to "come near to 'sensational'", since Euripides is "only ... great in dramatising the accidents of life ... in exciting compassion ... or sympathy", which "mar the symmetry of the larger view".

More recently, Lesky (1978) saw Aristotle's evaluation of Euripides as part of a general ancient Greek defect. They "never developed a theory of the tragic which ... might touch on man's spiritual attitude towards the world" (4). "May we not expect to find in the *Poetics* ... an insight into tragedy?" But in his definition of its goal, to arouse compassion and terror, "Aristotle did not expect any moral effect"; so "it has no connection with a conception of the tragic in the modern, more philosophical sense" (5-6). He proceeds (6), "The same holds good for a passage in the *Poetics* (1453a 29) which at first sight looks promising. Here Euripides is called 'the most tragic' ... of the Attic dramatists." However, "Aristotle only refers to the unhappy endings of Euripides' plays". For Lesky, this judgement on Euripides is typical of a very serious mistake the ancient Greeks made. They regarded "episodes ... [which] involved suffering ... as the core of tragedy".(12) This should be kept in mind when evaluating the constant warnings, some of which are quoted at the beginning of this chapter, not to make the *modern* mistake of regarding the *Aeneid* as a series of emotional episodes. Even scholars who are more favorably disposed to Aristotle than Lesky attack his 'curiously narrow perspective' in ignoring "the poets' views of man and his place in the world" (Kaufmann 1968.2,31; a defect which Plato shared: 20-21), his high regard for 'melodrama' (Else 1963.446) and failure to see what Attic tragedy was really concerned with (*ibid.*). (Other examples are quoted by Heath 1987.38-9.)

Many scholars have tried to save Aristotle from his failure to see the 'real issues' in Greek tragedy by seizing on isolated words in the *Poetics* as keys to providing a 'meaningful', unified interpretation. The two most prominent are *hamartia* and *catharsis*. Aristotle mentions the former in only one passage (*Poet.* 1453a10,16), in an off-hand manner. Yet countless critics have used it as the basis for interpreting not only Attic tragedies but nearly all serious world literature. Lesky (1978.17) points out that although Aristotle leaves no possible doubt that it means error and its purpose is to create pity for someone suffering undeservedly, it was one of the "influences under which tragedy was turned into a demonstration of moral reckoning" and "the contrast between Aristotle's precise statement and the manner in which it was applied ... remains a source of wonder". But Lesky himself finds in *hamartia* something 'anticipating modern views' (6-7), which provides "a genuine theoretical approach to tragedy — ... which is admittedly not developed at all in the surviving text" (18). *Catharsis*, as a goal of tragedy, is also mentioned only once in *Poetics*

(1449b28), as opposed to the frequent mention of compassion, terror and tragic pleasure. However, for centuries it has been regarded as vitally important in showing that tragedy has a moral purpose (Halliwell 1986.300-301). Indeed, "even a full survey of the literature on the subject would require a book" (Else 1963.225). But, although "'Catharsis' has come ... to be one of the biggest of the 'big' ideas in ... aesthetics and criticism ... Aristotle does not *tell* us that catharsis is so important" (*ibid.* 443-4; Else's italics). One need not agree with Else's interpretation of the meaning of *catharsis* to recognize its lack of importance for Aristotle. For example, Lucas says in his review of Else (*CR* 9,1959) that "on most major problems his conclusions do not seem acceptable to me". And in his long discussion of *catharsis* in Appendix II of his commentary on the *Poetics* (1978) he does not mention Else. But he does observe that *catharsis* was of no importance to Aristotle and is not mentioned elsewhere in criticism until the fourth century A.D. (281n3,286-7). Another very big word in criticism, *hubris*, also derives its tremendous importance and incorrect translation, 'pride', from a desire to find a moral meaning and unifying principle in literature. Aristotle never mentions it, a lapse which has been criticized (Fisher 1979.46n13).

The observations I have made so far, especially concerning Greek tragedies, can be supplemented and reinforced by Heath (1987). He points out that recent analyses of works of English literature also differ from earlier analyses because of "one of the most powerful conventions in modern literary reading ... 'Read the poem as expressing a significant attitude to some problem concerning man'" and the "assumption that the constituents of the novel must ultimately be interpreted in terms of a unifying vision of the world" (78). He gives many examples of "the common practice of modern interpreters of tragedy to read the plays as vehicles of ideas", which "embody some vision of the human condition or of the universal order, to explore or perhaps to commend opinions ... in ethics and politics, in philosophy and religion" (37, cf.38,48,90) and of the tendency "to look for a unifying element ... that is something ... to which every other element ... is subordinate" (104). So modern critics either assume that Attic tragedies cannot be 'merely' a series of loosely linked, highly emotional episodes (98-9,133); or, if they recognize the lack of unity, they censure it (92, 108,132-6). (Cf. Heath 1987a, which also points out how totally different pre-seventeenth century attitudes were; and Heath 1986, for the same radical change in critical attitudes to Pindar.)

But the ancient Greeks, from Homer and Hesiod on, regarded the goal of poetry as pleasure, which comes from overwhelming emotional involvement, causing primarily (and to us paradoxically) crying (Heath 1987.5-10,15-16, 180). Moreover, the idea that an entire literary work should display unity, which is fundamental to modern criticism, was not found in ancient criticism. Aristotle did not champion unity in our sense (99-106), and "the scholia on Homer and on tragedy make no use of the concept at all"; "if one wishes to find a Greek critical term for that constancy of theme and focus so admired by modern critics, one might ... choose *homoeideia*: the vice of dull uniformity" (106). The opposite of *homoeideia* was diversity, *poikilia* (106). This was constantly mentioned by Pindar, the scholia, Aristotle, etc. as the principle which should govern the treatment of material. It covers both stylistic variation and embellishment and structural diversity from digressions and contrasting material (105-6, cf. 32,110, 126, 135,137-41,153). Because modern scholars ignore this, they do not see how important conventional forms (e.g. choral tags), characters (e.g. messengers) and subjects (e.g. supplications) are in determining what is said and done in the sections involved, and they try to relate them in a simplistic manner to 'the meaning/message' of the play (e.g. 126-30,145-8,153-7). "Typical situations ... require typical roles: for example, a suppliant-plot implies a victim, a persecutor and a protector ... these 'slots' must be filled"(148).

Modern scholars also do not see that the focus of tragedies is mobile, as one character after another, or two characters linked in some way, are 'the centre ... of sympathetic interest' (96), and the function of other characters is their interaction with them (92-8). For example, in the *Antigone*

> Up to 943, ... Antigone is the focus of emotional engagement ... but after her final exit, remarkably little attention is paid to her ... we are not, for example, invited to dwell sympathetically on her suffering and death; she simply drops out of focus and our attention is switched instead to Creon ... The audience obviously ... is expected to ... lend ... fully sympathetic attention to Creon. Creon, however, has hitherto played a ... unsympathetic role ... the adversary and persecutor of the focal character, marked by tyrannical traits. (92-93)

Heath acknowledges that "tragedy has intellectual (moral, theological, metaphysical) *content*" (71, Heath's italics), and it "moved in the vicinity of large and weighty issues" (72). Sometimes these issues are important to add gravity to a conflict and so help "to excite a strong emotional response" (72). But the issues are not "coherently formulated or purposefully explored" (72). He illustrates this with an analysis of the *Antigone* (73-7, cf. 49-64 on Euripides' representation of the gods). Also, tragedies sometimes appealed to the patriotism of the audience by mentioning national actions or attributes of which they were proud. But "this is not the kind of political significance that has been of most interest to modern interpreters", because the tragedies did not provide "explorations of general political principles, ... allusions to contemporary events, ... interventions in partisan controversy" (65-6, cf. 64-71). Indeed, the ideas expressed in tragedies are commonplaces from folk-wisdom and consequently do not form "a *system* of thought; ideas that are incompatible, or at least in unresolved tension, happily coexist" (160, Heath's italics, cf.157-62).

I have given only a bare outline of parts of Heath's book. He explores and substantiates his observations at length. They are obviously relevant to my view of the *Aeneid*. It contains patriotic statements and general ideas. But its purpose is to arouse emotions, especially pathos, and its focus of interest and sympathy constantly shifts. Sometimes Aeneas is the centre of this sympathetic focus, as when he is the victim of Troy's capture or a wandering exile. Sometimes he is unsympathetic, as when he is in the role of the beloved. For, as I will demonstrate later, in Roman representations of love the focus of interest and sympathy was on the lover (e.g. Dido or Catullus) and the function of the beloved (Aeneas, Lesbia) was to cause him or her suffering. Sometimes Aeneas is absent, as the focus is on Nisus and Euryalus or the pathos of youths of great promise dying, which is an important motif from Marcellus on. Modern critics assume that the *Aeneid* must be 'about' Rome and its embodiment, Aeneas, and the purpose of the other characters and situations must be to comment on them. Either the greatness of Rome and Aeneas is proclaimed, explored and illustrated, and the other characters and situations are contrasts, supports, temptations, dangers, learning experiences, etc.; or the other characters and situations show that Rome and Aeneas are brutal, destructive, deluded, etc.; or the function of the other characters and situations is to form an alternate 'voice' or 'voices'.

D. *Ancient Attempts to find Meaning in Literature and Their Relation to the* Aeneid

There were ancient attempts to derive meanings and messages from literature. But they were totally different from modern attempts, and the cause of this difference is significant. One was allegory (Buffière 1956; Grube 1965.55n3; Heath 1987.39n7). This was clearly a desperate manoeuvre, which, as its name suggests, was based on the premise that a work's meaning was 'other' than what it said. So it need not be considered. But it is worth considering the three examples Lesky gives (1978.18-19) of the ancient view that literature should educate: Plato, Aristophanes' *Frogs*, and Horace's *aut prodesse aut delectare*. These are well known and often cited. Lesky does not regard them as important, that is, similar to modern interpretations, and with good reason. Plato attacks Homer and tragedy for not educating, for causing ignorance and undermining morality, especially σωφροσύνη (e.g. *Resp.* 389Dff.). So Plato saw tragedy as having the opposite effect to that which so many modern attempts to find meaning and message in it argue it has. As Plato observes, his view was already old (*Resp.* 607B; cf. Buffière 1956.13-14). Plato also attacks the idea that poets teach practical skills, such as military strategy and cobbling. But that was accepted by Aristophanes, along with the view that meaning and message are contained in isolated statements, with no regard for the work as a whole. Both these views of the moral and intellectual content of literature remained dominant throughout antiquity (e.g. Buffière 1956.18 and *passim*; Halliwell 1986.15n23,281n46). They resulted in absurdities like Aristophanes' use of Hippolytus' "my tongue swore but my heart did not confirm it" and Plato barring tragedians from his ideal state because they praise tyrants (*Resp.* 568A-B). As opposed to modern critics, the ancients did not look for meaning in the work as a whole. This is in accordance with their indifference to the unity of literary works.

Lesky's third example, Horace's *aut prodesse volunt aut delectare poetae* (*Ars P.* 333), is very important since Horace was a great poet, a friend of Vergil's and a member of the same literary circle.

Actually Horace is recommending neither of the alternatives in this line but a third approach which he mentions in the next line, *aut simul et iucunda et idonea dicere vitae*, and in 343-4, *miscuit utile dulci, lectorem delectando pariterque monendo*. Because of the literary prejudices of our culture this is usually translated as mixing these two elements in the same passage and words (e.g. Fairclough's *Loeb* and Villeneuve's *Budé*). But the ancients regarded the main purpose of the literature as pleasing by arousing powerful emotions. That is the second option in line 333 (*delectare*). If poetry had a use, it was to provide practical advice and/or isolated sententious maxims. So the first option (*prodesse*) must be didactic poetry. The paucity of references to this genre in ancient literary critical discussions seems to indicate that Aristotle's rejection of it as genuine poetry, no matter what is literary merits (Else 1963.50-53), was widely shared. Certainly, what Horace says about his *Satires* is strong evidence that he agreed with Aristotle. He probably included didactic poetry here because he is using a device commonly employed by Aristotle: mentioning extremes so that his own recommendation can be the *aurea mediocritas*, which was commonly regarded as a poetic ideal (Nisbet and Hubbard 1978, on 10.5). Here Horace recommends combining these two components in the same work in the only way the ancients recognized. The emotionally gripping *delectare* element is the story itself, the *ficta* (338), *fabula* (339) (Brink 1971.352-5). 'Everything you will teach' (335) should occur in brief maxims which can be easily remembered (335-7). And their use is practical, a *frux* (341), a word which never before was used metaphorically without a defining genitive (*ibid., ad loc.*). So the emperor Augustus "in reading authors of both languages looked for nothing more than useful ... precepts and examples, these he often copied *verbatim* and sent to household members or rulers of armies and provinces ..." (Suet. *Aug.* 89.2, cf. 40.5).

That is what Horace clearly says, and that is the way later Romans understood him. Pseudo-Acro explicated line 333 with the example, *Delectant Bucolica, prosunt Georgica*. By contrast, Seneca (*Ep.* 86.15) asserted that the *Georgics nec agricolas docere voluit, sed legentes delectare* because their agricultural advice is inaccurate. (It did not occur to pseudo-Acro or Seneca that the *Georgics* could be making a statement about human life, society, the emotions, etc.) Servius in his note on *Aeneid* 6.660 (*hic manus ob patriam pugnando vulnera passi*) says, *animadvertendum illud quod ait Horatius*, quotes *Ars Poetica* 334 and explains,

> Nullam enim maiores nostri artem esse voluerunt quae non aliquid reipublicae commodaret. Unde Vergilius hoc *per transitum* facit. Nam dicendo puniri patriae venditores, contra praemia defensoribus solvi ... fugienda vitia et sectandas docet esse virtutes.

The observations above are reinforced by the reason for Horace's recommendation to mix the useful and pleasing (341-4). The young ignore *austera poemata*, the old reject those *expertia frugis*. So a poem that is generally pleasant (i.e. emotionally gripping) but has some useful parts will be universally popular. In the preceding section (323-32) Horace shows his own preference in this matter. There he contrasts the Greeks, who have outstanding literary ability (Brink 1971, on 323) and are avaricious for nothing but fame, with the Romans, who are avaricious for practical gain. This *cura peculi* militates against the creation of literature of enduring value. Then he advises adding useful sections in poems to please the old, who, as typical Romans, reject anything without *frux*. But he seems to have regarded this as an unfortunate necessity.

Literary criticism and creation are symbiotic; description becomes prescription. Poets put into their compositions what readers expect to find. The pedagogic element which the ancients found in literature was in isolated practical passages and sententious lines, not on-going conflicts of ideas, developments of character or intellectual and moral concepts. Horace is both prescribing and describing what poets who win every vote do (343). However, the sententious lines and passages could easily be distorted by hostile critics. I have mentioned Aristophanes' use of Euripides' 'my tongue swore ...' and Plato's use of his comments on tyrants (*Resp.* 568A-B). But a careful poet could, at least partially, guard himself against that by removing them from dramatic contexts.

I think that that is what Vergil did in the *Aeneid*. He used isolated parts of the poem, such as Jupiter's speech in Book 1, the *Heldenschau* in Book 6, or the description of Aeneas' shield in Book 8, for a practical, pedagogic purpose: to stir admiration for Rome's grandeur and distinctive moral qualities and for Augustus' achievements. But they have no organic connection with the story (or more properly, stories) itself, the *ficta* and *fabula*, as

Horace called it. They were there because the ancients expected poems to have passages which are useful, and among the Romans, as Servius (on 6.660) pointed out, this consisted of *aliquid reipublicae* put in *per transitum.* (This also accounts for Propertius 4.6, Horace's "Roman Odes", Ovid, *Metamorphoses* 15.746-870, etc.) However, the primary goal of the *Aeneid* was to arouse emotional responses. That is what the ancients expected from literature, and that is what readers of the *Aeneid* from Vergil's time to ours have admired and loved in it, as I will show later and as the warnings against it quoted at the beginning of this chapter attest. (It is significant that the passages in the *Aeneid* involving combat, divinities, Rome and Augustus have abnormally high concentrations of the dsss metrical pattern: Duckworth 1965-6.47; 1966.)

Those warnings also attest to the modern prejudice that 'serious' ancient works of literature must be unified around a moral or intellectual 'meaning', which is its main, or sole, purpose. (Although we do not assume this about, for instance, *War and Peace* or Joyce's *Ulysses.*) This must be embodied in the pedagogic statements and the basic plot: Aeneas fulfilling his mission of founding the Roman people by going to Italy and defeating his opponents there. Even those modern critics who recognize the importance of the emotional episodes assume that they must exist to comment on the 'main message' and plot, by showing Rome's brutality, providing a constrasting 'private voice' to the 'public voice', etc. (See the Appendix.)

E. *Ancient and Modern Attitudes to Unity in the Homeric Epics*

As has been pointed out, one of the motives for the search for 'meaning' in Greek tragedies was to find a unifying element since their plots are so structureless. Yet it is a truism of ancient and modern criticism that the epic genre is much more formless and episodic than the tragic. I will now analyze the relationship between the plot and episodes in the *Iliad* and *Odyssey* and ancient and modern attitudes to it. The influence of Homer on ancient literature was overwhelming, as the ancients themselves were fully aware. Indeed, Dawe (1963) conjectures that 'the episodic nature of Homer' (62) was at least partially responsible for the fact that "if consistency of plot and character is ... a criterion of excellence ...Aeschylus, Sophocles and Euripides fall far below ...

script-writers at Warner Brothers" (45). And Homer's influence on the *Aeneid* was especially profound.

Ancient authors and critics, including in particular the scholiasts, constantly observed that "Homer was especially concerned with, and especially skilled in the use of" variation, *poikilia* (Heath 1989.107, cf. 102-118). And the Homeric scholia often pointed out and praised it in reference to episodes which do "not form an indispensable part of the narrative's causal structure" (*ibid.* 112, cf.113-118). This included episodes for emotional effect (e.g. 118). Vergil was very influenced by the Homeric scholia (Schlunk 1974). Indeed, "the Latin commentaries on Vergil take a similar approach" as the Homeric scholia (Heath 1989.159).

Homer had no more ardent admirer or more perceptive critic than Aristotle, nor one who insisted more on the primacy of plot and necessity of unity as a general principle and in relation to Homer in particular. In *Poetics* 1451a16-30 he states that among Homer's superiorities to other epic poets was that he constructed the *Odyssey* and *Iliad* 'around one action'. In 1455b15-23 Aristotle outlines the *Odyssey*'s plot, which he contrasts with its episodes. It consists of the action in Book 5, which is described with genitive absolutes since it forms the plot's prologue, the suitors squandering Odysseus' estate and plotting against his son, Odysseus' arrival in Ithaka, recognizing certain people and killing the suitors. Else points out (1963.512-14) that that amounts to about 4000 lines, the mean length of a tragic trilogy. This explains the statement which precedes the outline of the *Odyssey*'s plot: "In dramas the episodes are brief, but epic is long because of them". The episodes, as opposed to the parts of the plot, do not follow each other by necessity or probability. That is clear from 1451a24-28. There Aristotle says that Homer did not include in the *Odyssey* Odysseus being wounded on Parnassus or pretending to be insane at the gathering of the army, "neither of which became necessary or probable by the other happening". Since the first incident is in the *Odyssey* (19.392-466), Aristotle must have meant that it is not part of the plot (Else 1963.298-9; Lucas 1978, *ad loc.*). Significantly, the *Odyssey*'s 'episodes' were by far its most popular parts among the Greeks and Romans from the seventh century B.C. on, as is attested by their use in art, tragedy and comedy (Touchefeu-Meynier 1968.282-306). Aristotle saw the *Iliad* in the same way (e.g. *Poet* 1457a28-30,1459a30-b7). Its 'plot' was also about 4000 lines in length (Else 1963.603-4). Else points out (582n32) that Aristotle's description of Homer as *thespesios* (1459a30) is extraordinary praise and explains its cause (584-5): Homer "has secured unity-in-diversity ... The main action can be unified ... [it] provides a background against which we can properly ... enjoy the diversity of the episodes".

As Halliwell (1986.289) points out, in the Hellenistic age and among the Romans interest in cohesion and unity of plot declined. So, although the *Ars Poetica* of Vergil's friend Horace begins by insisting on the necessity of unity, it "notably ... refuses to give central value to this principle, and ... mirrors this fact in its own epistolary avoidance of obvious cohesion" (cf. Heath 1989.63-4). So Horace holds up the *Odyssey* as a model to be imitated (140-6), but gives as its basic contents, *speciosa ... miracula ... Antiphaten Scyllamque et cum Cyclope Charybdin*. These are all episodes in Aristotle's terminology. They are not part of the plot and do not follow from each other in accordance with probability or necessity.

Most modern evaluations of the subject and structure of the Homeric epics are totally different. Whereas Aristotle and Horace regarded them as narrating primarily diverse episodes which have no logical connection with each other, and Aristotle regarded Homer's distinctive achievement to be devising a unified plot as a background for them; Lesky (1978.2-3) wrote,

> what characterises epic is the perception of life as a chain of events ... [a] smooth sequence ... what raises the *Iliad* ... beyond the range of typical epic ... is ... a deep connection between events and a single passionate man ... It was a stroke of genius ... to make the motif of anger the crystallisation of the entire poem.

An example of a treatment of the episodes by a modern critic is provided by Camps (1980). He gives an outline of the *Iliad* and *Odyssey*, each of about two pages (9-13). The events of *Iliad* 2-7 are summarized in less than three lines, those of *Odyssey* 6-12 in less than five lines, followed by the observation that they "make up the best known part of the poem". This is the opposite of Horace's emphasis when he gives the *Odyssey*'s basic content. In a section entitled "Unity of Design" (14), Camps asserts, "both the *Iliad* and *Odyssey* are coherent and carefully organized units". Their plots are their 'subjects', which are "of serious and universal human interest": in the *Iliad* "the temporary corruption of a noble nature, with awful consequences before its ultimate self-recovery", in the *Odyssey*, "the reunion ... of man and wife, won by the endurance and wisdom of them both". In the next section, "Imperfections of Detail ..." (15-17), he gives as an example, "the episodes loosely assembled in the account of the first day's fighting are good ... some very good indeed, and have a useful introductory relevance ... Yet ...".

However, modern, like ancient, readers have a very strong impulse to concentrate on the episodes, not the plot. This 'mistake' is deplored by modern Homeric scholars, just as the similar 'mistake' in the *Aeneid* is deplored by modern Vergilian scholars, some of whom are quoted at the beginning of this chapter; for example,

> the stories of Odysseus that everyone seems to know [are] the Cyclopes, Calypso, the Lotus Eaters, and so on ... This gives the reader ... a lopsided version of the *Odyssey* and leaves him with the impression that this great epic is an absorbing adventure story ... hardly worth the attention of serious readers (Clarke 1967.45).

The desire to get rid of these episodic 'imperfections' was a, if not the, cause in the Analytic detour in Homeric criticism. Nearly all the Analysts, although not Wolf himself, based their arguments on the premises that a work of literature is solely a unified plot and that it must be consistent. The former assumption is the basis of by far the most widely accepted Analytic approach, that 'Homer' was the composer of the '*Ur-Ilias*' and '*Ur-Odyssee*'. So Grote, who popularized this hypothesis in Britain (essentially in the form of Nitsch's modifications of Hermann's theory) asserted, in "those portions of the poem which ... constituted the original Achilleis ... the sequence of events ... is ... more unbroken, and more intimately knit together in the way of cause and effect than in the other books" (p.283 of Volume 2 of the *Everyman* edition). This 'continuity' is manifest in Books 1,8 and 11 to 22 (297). The later, episodic, parts could not have been added by the author of the original because they lack "a pervading thread of consensus and organization" (306). But he is glad a later poet added them because of "that splendid poetry ... between the first and eighth books" (300).

Similarly, Leaf, in his edition and commentary on the *Iliad*, which is the best known work of Analytic scholarship in the contemporary English-speaking world, asserts (pages xxi-xxiii of the first volume) that 'the story of the Wrath', contained in parts of Books 1,11,15,16,20-22 and ending in 22.404, is "the main plot to which all else stands in an episodal relation". It "is organically and indissolubly bound together" and has "the real unity of the *Iliad*". So it is 'the oldest kernel', the 'work of a single poet'.

Like Grote and the other Analysts, Leaf was glad that later poets had added episodes to the *Iliad*'s plot. For example, in his introduction to Book 9 he points out its 'glaring' inconsistencies with the *Wrath*, but then states,

> When once we are in Achilles' tent, however, the weakness of the connecting narrative is soon forgotten. Alike in vivid description ... in interplay of character and in glowing rhetoric, the book is unsurpassed in Homer, perhaps in literature ... It is a matter of gratitude that the editor regarded the contradictions with 11 and 16 ... as of small importance — as indeed, from the artistic point of view, they are.

The same approach characterizes modern Analysts. For instance, Mazon (1959.232, cf. 138,236) uses as a proof that most of the *Iliad* is a later addition that the *désordre manifeste dans le poème* is in total contrast with the careful unity of the individual episodes. (The same contrast is also characteristic of the *Aeneid*.) And he also comments on the greatness of the later, added, episodes (e.g. 249).

I pointed out while discussing Aristotle's analysis of Homer that what he called the *Odyssey*'s 'episodes' were by far its most popular parts in antiquity. The same is true of the *Iliad*'s episodes, that is, those parts that the Analysts regarded as later additions. For example, "the *Embassy* [Book 9], the book ... most quoted in antiquity and [which] seems most to have impressed the imagination of Greece, is one of the parts most markedly foreign to its present framework" (Murray 1934. 240). Also, Book 24 was an extrememly popular subject in Greek and Roman art (*RE* 22.186 8ff.; Roscher, *Lex.* 3.2957 ff.; Farron 1986.83n29) and literature (Farron *ibid.*; Stat. *Silv.* 2.7.56; Plut. *Mor.* 105 B-C; Fraenkel, 1957.165; cf. Dio Chrys. 53,7; Plato, *Ion* 535B). Especially, Achilles' compassionate treatment of Priam was often cited a model to be followed (e.g. Cic. *Tusc.* 1.105; Hor. *Epod.* 17.11-14; Ov. *Tr.* 3.5.31-8; 5.1.55; Sen. *Tro.*310-13). It appears prominantly in the climactic scene of the second book of the *Aeneid* (540-3; Farron 1986.78); and in the first, with Hector's death, it is the climactic emotional event (483-7:

tum vero). Before that (461-2), perhaps the most quoted lines in the *Aeneid* are prompted by *en Priamus*.

F. *Lack of Unity in Apollonius'* Argonautica *and Roman Poetry*

The only extant epic composed between Homer's and the *Aeneid* was Apollonius' *Argonautica*. Its pervasive influence on the *Aeneid* is obvious and has constantly been noted since antiquity; as has the fact that it is much more episodic and less unified than the Homeric epics (e.g. Seaton 1912.xi-xiii; Hunter 1989.33). And Seaton is probably correct in attributing that to 'the influence of the age' (*ibid.*; cf. Hunter 1989.35). It is relevant to the *Aeneid* to determine why Apollonius' epic seems more episodic than Homer's. Apollonius emphasized the continuity of his story by frequent cross-references and linkages of various types (Heath 1989.65-7). Certainly a greater proportion of the incidents in the *Argonautica* are relevant to the completion of Jason's mission, whether they delay or advance it, than are incidents in the *Iliad* to Achilles' anger; and, as opposed to Achilles, Jason is nearly always present, even if only as a spectator. However, Achilles and Odysseus are fascinating and compelling characters and the former's anger and the latter's homecoming engage the reader's attention. Apollonius, living in an age in which unity was even less prized than formerly, kept the old procedure of concentrating on episodes interspersed in a plot but saw no reason to make that plot, Jason's mission, interesting and no objection to making *sein Iason ein ganz farbloser Figurant* (W. Schmid, in Schmid-Stählin 2.1.145), "a man of resounding success whom no reader has ever found himself able to admire" (Lawall 1966.168), a character whom "many modern scholars find ... disconcerting as the central figure ... indecisive ... often dismayed, and ... very reliant on the resources of his companions. In what sense, then, is this character heroic?" (Bulloch 1985.590).

Bulloch argues that these unheroic qualities are not significant since they are shared by several characters in Homer (591). But the important point is that they make Jason totally different from Achilles and Odysseus and similar to Aeneas. Bulloch asserts that what "should occupy us [is] ... the almost sinister aspects of his behavior which serve his success as a heroic leader", especially in relation to the woman who loves him and sacrifices everything dear to her for him (591-5): "in his dealings with Medea [he is] ... capable of inflicting great damage" and displays 'treachery' and 'self-interested compliance'. Bulloch also observes that "Jason and his companions remain essentially isolated (one might even say 'alienated') from one another and their environment" (596) and "most critics, disconcerted by the poem's lack of heroic excitement, ... judge that only Book 3 redeems a poem that as a whole is a mediocre failure" (598). All these aspects of the *Argonautica* and its hero also disconcert critics of the *Aeneid*, especially, that its hero seems so cold, uninteresting, unlikable, unheroic and isolated and that in what seems to be the epic's highpoint he behaves to Dido as Jason does to Medea. Some Vergilian scholars argue, as Bulloch does, that these apparent flaws are not real: "the *Argonautica* is a deceptively intricate work, and ... beneath the ... surface are complex allusions and symbols which make the *Argonautica* a very different poem from what it seems to be" (598).

Scholars who are unwilling to dismiss the impression that a literary work gives could argue that the *Argonautica* and *Aeneid* deliberately denigrate their heroes. However, as Lawall points out (1966.168n13), Jason is endowed with strong points (which resemble Aeneas'): "his good deed in carrying Hera across the Anaurus (3.66-73), his diplomatic handling of his men and his democratic spirit ... handsomeness, eloquence, and charm over women". But, as with Aeneas, they are not enough to hold the reader's interest and sympathy. That is especially true since, also like Aeneas, he is "anti-heroic, circumventive, pious, and reliant on the aid of others, both human (Medea) and gods (especially Aphrodite)" (*ibid.* 166), has no enthusiasm for his mission, but "bear[s] his fate with fortitude and piety" (162-3), and when confronted with a woman who loves him passionately and is willing to sacrifice everything for him, he is

> a cautious exploiter of opportunity, he is carefully guarded ... with the infatuated Medea ... He recognizes her overwhelming passion and momentarily wavers with an answering love. Medea desperately tries to lead him into a commitment, but ... before being led into deeper involvement, he breaks off the interview. His sole interest is getting the Fleece and returning home. (*ibid.*)

Lawall argues that these negative, uninspiring, insipid qualities of Jason actually redound to his credit, whereas the engaging qualities of others, such as Herakles' great strength, show that they are not the means for attaining success. This resembles the innumerable attempts to put a positive construction on Aeneas' uninteresting, unengaging qualities and interpret the interesting attributes of characters like Dido as providing a negative contrast. But could not Apollonius and Vergil have been using Jason, Aeneas and their missions as merely a means by which to introduce much more interesting characters? They did not intend to denigrate Jason and Aeneas, but if they were uninteresting, that did not bother them.

There is one other dactylic hexameter narrative involving a famous legendary hero which had an obvious and profound influence on the *Aeneid*: the Ariadne section of Catullus 64. Here the resemblance is especially strong since Theseus, like Aeneas, was the mythical hero of a great nation. Catullus (and Vergil) belonged to a literary culture in which the earlier indifference to unified, continuous narrative had become a conscious antipathy and in which fascination with intense, subjective situations and moving, emotional characters and moods made isolated episodes even more prominent in relation to plot than they had been. The introduction to *Argonautica* 3, "how Jason brought the fleece to Iolcus helped by Medea's love", is an accurate outline of what happens, even though it does not prepare for the focus of the story. Catullus' introduction of Ariadne's story as an example of *heroum virtutes* (50-51) is totally inaccurate, much more inaccurate than I argue *Aeneid* 1.1-11 is for the *Aeneid*; although it is appropriate to a culture which thought 'the anger of Achilles' introduced a love story. Theseus is an even more shadowy, uninteresting character than Jason, and Ariadne's tragedy has been the center of interest for nearly all readers, obviously including Vergil. Modern literary preconceptions about the necessity of unity and meaning have led to ingenious explanations about how the story of Ariadne, and the entire poem, comment on *heroum virtutes*. In most of them the comment is negative, just as many recent critics of the *Aeneid* have interpreted the Dido story and the entire epic as criticizing *arma virumque*. Jenkyns (1982) gives examples of this modern literary preconception concerning Catullus 64 (93-4) and of resulting attempts to assign to it a moral message (90) and shows that its interest was in describing incidents and situations for their own sake. He could have strengthened his arguments by pointing out that the concentration of interest and sympathy on Ariadne's suffering was also characteristic of the many paintings of this story at Pompeii (Schefold 1957.367; Farron 1983.87) and that this fascination with the pathos of love was fundamental to Roman artistic sensitivities (*ibid.*).

Similarly, Papanghelis (1987) has demonstrated that Propertius' interest was in the situations and people he is portraying without regard to unity or 'more important' issues, that he was typical (e.g. 55-6) and that the "fashionable [tendency] to read into Roman love poetry important statements on religious, philosophical and political issues" (4) is misguided.

Even when a contemporary of Vergil's announced that he intended to compose a continuous poem, it is not unified by our standards. The only extant Augustan epic besides the *Aeneid* is the *Metamorphoses*. Ovid introduced it as a *perpetuum carmen*, a description which aligns it with traditional epics like the *Iliad* (Dahlmann 1953.118-127; Brink 1963.61-7). Quintilian (*Inst.* 4.1.76-7) mentions casually, as an obvious fact, that in it Ovid was *res diversissimas in speciem unius corporis colligentem* and that he sought applause by playfully using *sententiae* as transitions, rather than joining one section logically to another. But modern critics try to find its 'principle of unity' (Otis 1970.45). Despite Otis' belief that he has demonstrated its unity, he later concedes (167),

> Ovid's imagination was not primarily on the side of ... the great Romans ... It is in the neoteric episodes far more than in his epic panel or his preparations for an Augustan finale that he is most himself and most successful. There is in fact a decided incongruity between his obvious plan (the designed shape of his *perpetuum carmen*) and his actual execution of it.

My argument is that the same is true of the *Aeneid*, except that I do not think that the epic panel was Ovid's or Vergil's 'obvious plan'.

I will end my analysis of extant ancient literature and modern reactions to it with Vergil's *Eclogues*, which resemble the *Aeneid*, but not the *Georgics*, in that they concentrate on human characters. Towards the beginning of this chapter I summarized Arrowsmith's (1959) attack on previous attempts to find unity in Greek tragedies and his own attempts to find unity of a more complex and sophisticated nature. Recently the same approach has been applied to the *Eclogues*. For instance, in papers presented at the 1990 APA convention and printed in pages 43 to 63 of *Vergilius* 36,

1990, C. Perkell points out and J. Van Sickle agrees that the *Eclogues* are marked by contradictions, illogicalities, incongruities, imprecision and inconclusiveness, and therefore all searches for consistent political, social, moral and emotional meaning have ignored or explained away, and must ignore or explain away, many passages and result in a series of mutually irreconcilable interpretations. However, they still assume that everything in the *Eclogues* must serve a unifying message, but that message must be more complex than has been suspected.

So far I have analyzed only complete literary works since the interpretation of fragments is always questionable. However, very little complete pre-Vergilian Latin poety is extant. Traina (1970, cf. Rostagni 1956) offers a very careful study of how Accius, Livius Andronicus, Naevius, Ennius, Caecilius, Terence and Cicero's verse recast Greek poetic models. He concedes (202) that arguments based on fragments must be hypothetical, but the cumulative weight of his evidence is difficult to question. That evidence demonstrates that the Romans, including Cicero, constantly altered their Greek models to make them even more emotional, subjective, romantic, sentimental, and especially pathetic, frequently substituting pathos for ethos.

CHAPTER THREE

THE POEM OF GRIEF AND LOVE

> The hero [is the] focus of all the poem's [i.e. the *Aeneid*'s] temporalities ... all the other characters ... [are] the facilitators and impediments of his mission, Creusa, Anchises, Dido, Latinus, Evander, Mezentius Camilla, Nisus, Euryalus, Turnus. (Grandsen 1984.3)

In this chapter I will demonstrate that the main purpose of the *Aeneid* is to arouse its readers' emotions, especially compassion. I begin by pointing out briefly its looseness of structure, then the various means Vergil uses to create pathos. After that, I concentrate on the Dido-Aeneas episode, showing that pre-modern readers interpreted it as I do and how closely it resembles other ancient love stories. I then demonstrate that it creates pathos for Dido in the same way and by the same means as other ancient love poetry does for lovers but that this pathos for Dido is not meant to comment on Aeneas. Finally, I show that the main purpose of the gods also is to make Dido's situation more pathetic and that that is similar to Book Two, where they increase the pathos of Aeneas' suffering.

A. *The Looseness of Structure of the* Aeneid

The *Aeneid* is even looser in structure and more episodic than earlier epics. Before the Analytic detour in Homeric scholarship began, many scholars observed that the *Aeneid* shows less of an interest in developing a cohesive story than the *Iliad* or *Odyssey*. An example used by R. Wood on page 20 of his *The Original Genius of Homer* (1769) was that the Trojans do not know where to go in Book 3 despite explicit instructions that their destination is Italy in 2.781-4; and he observes, "inaccuracies of this kind ... are not to be found so frequently in Homer". As for the *Argonautica*, Seaton (1911.xi-xii) criticizes its lack of unity, but, like critics of the same lack in Homer, admits he is glad of it: "it is ... one of ... [its] episodes that gives the poem its permanent value — the ... love of Jason and Medea". Vergil obviously modelled the Dido episode on that, as was observed, with exaggeration, by Servius, in his introduction to Book 4, and by Macrobius (*Sat.*5.17.4). It resembles the Medea story not only in its subject but also in having been the most highly regarded part of the epic since antiquity, as will be shown below, and in that without it "the *Aeneid* would have remained forever within the penumbra of myth" (Austin 1955.ix). However, the Medea story, at least in its outline, is not an episode. It is an integral part of the plot, as Apollonius states (3.2-3). The Dido story is completely an episode. It has no effect on the *Aeneid*'s plot or on Aeneas' moral and intellectual development. It does not even affect the Trojans' geographical location. Immediately before it, the Trojans are *vix e conspectu Siculae telluris* (1.34), which is where they are immediately after it (5.23-4).

I will give just one more example of the *Aeneid* being looser in structure than its models, that is the episode following Book 4, the athletic contests. These were essential ingredients in epics, and such was their appeal to ancient poets, and presumably readers, that poets of much 'gentler' genres also included descriptions of them; for instance, Theocritus. Apollonius justifies his boxing match by making it necessary for the plot, the quest for the fleece, to continue. In the *Odyssey*, Odysseus, the 'man' who is announced as the epic's subject by the its first word, participates himself; and the contests further the portrayal of him by the contrast between him and the Phaeacians, which is an important motif (Farron 1979-80.73-5). In the *Iliad* the contests are at least tangentially connected to the 'anger', its first word, because they show Achilles' devotion to Patroclus, whose death causes Achilles' anger in the last third of the epic. Of course, in all three epics the main interest is in the contests themselves and their participants. In the *Aeneid* the contests show Aeneas' devotion to Anchises, and that helps to motivate his journey to the Underworld; but Vergil does not bother to link that to the games themselves. They also display Aeneas as a generous and concerned leader and as scrupulously religious. But they are much more irrelevant to the epic's plot than the contests in his models. Moreover, the participants, except for Nisus and Euryalus, are without interest or significance in the rest of the poem, as opposed to many of the contestants in *Iliad* 23. Indeed, Vergil did not bother to make Aeneas' friends and companions who survive at the poem's end appealing or interesting, just as he did not bother to do that with Aeneas in most of the epic. It would have been easy to connect the contests with contemporary Rome since many families traced their origins to Trojans (R. Williams 1960a, on 117); but "most of the competitors have no links with known Roman *gentes*, and those who do are not ... linked with the *gentes* most prominent in Vergil's day" (Cairns 1989.225-6). However, a meaning and message could be squeezed even from that fact: "it enhances the status of the Iulii ... and it spreads the effect of heroisation more widely among the Augustan Romans" (*ibid.*). Critics not content, or able, to extract a meaning or message from the description of the contests themselves have seen in it a prefigurement of Aeneas' future trials and conflicts (e.g. Kraggerud 1968.106-232).

B. *Pathos in the* Aeneid

My argument is that Vergil's primary purpose was to provide what his contemporary readers and critics expected to find in a work of literature: a series of emotionally, especially pathetically, moving episodes. One, the Nisus-Euryalus episode, has been analyzed. I will now discuss others in order to demonstrate that the *Aeneid* was mainly a poem of grief and love.

Some of the means Vergil could use to provide pathos would make his readers cry with and for Aeneas, and these he used. The pathos of being driven from one's home into exile was used by Vergil from his first *Eclogue* on. It constantly appears in the *Aeneid* (Bruwer 1974), most prominently in relation to Aeneas. Also, many of the literary and artistic references I cited to illustrate the popularity of *Iliad* 24 dwell on the tearful bereavement of Hector's family. Vergil has Aeneas lose his wife and father. He wrings every tear he can from this situation by having Aeneas weep as he tries unsuccessfully to embrace their spirits (2.790-4,6.697-702, 5.740-2; cf.1.405-9 of his mother). Indeed, the pathos of his loss of his father is brought out in his first words in the epic (1.94-6).

The most pathetic situation that could focus the audience's sympathy on Aeneas was the destruction of a city. "The destruction of cities and the fate of their inhabitants were a favorite theme for poets" (Ogilvie 1965.120-1). Austin (1966, on 746) provides many examples among Vergil's contemporaries of the capture of a city being used as "a stock example of horror". Polybius (2.56.2-12) attacked Phylarchus for his aim of "moving all the Greeks to tears" by his descriptions of the pathos of captured cities, since that is the goal of tragedy, not history. But ancient Greek readers reacted very emotionally even to descriptions of captured cities in Thucydides which seem restrained to us (Walbank 1960.230-1). Certainly, the descriptions of cities being captured in Vergil's contemporary, Livy, were very influenced by tragedies like Euripides' *Troades* and Ennius' *Destruction of Alba* (Ogilvie 1965.120, 320). It was especially the capture of Troy which fascinated poets and painters from the Epic Cycle on (Austin 1966.x-xi) and was a source of proverbial descriptions of misery (e.g. Dem. *FL.* 148; Arist. *Eth. Nic.* 1.10.14). It was probably particularly because of Euripides' plays on this subject that he "is regarded the most tragic of poets" (Arist. Poet. 1453a29-30; see Lucas 1978, *ad loc.*; Schlegel 1809-11.136). These tragedies were highly admired by the Romans (e.g. Gell. *NA* 11.4), as were the many Roman tragedies based on them. For example, Cicero (*Tusc.*3.45-6, cf. 44; 1.85) exclaimed about passages in Ennius' *Andromache*, *O poetam egregium* and *Praeclarum carmen! Est enim et rebus et verbis et modis lugubre.*

Vergil used all his skill to make readers of *Aeneid* 2 cry. When Ogilvie (1965, on 2.33.8) points out how completely Livy's descriptions of captured cities are influenced by conventional representations of the destruction of Troy in epics and tragedies, all the ingredients he mentions play a prominent role in *Aeneid* 2. Indeed, Vergil used the means for arousing crying which Polybius attacked Phylarchus for using (Austin 1966, on 486,490) and which Ennius used in the passage whose pathos Cicero extolled (Austin 1966, on 499). Cicero says that that passage is so pathetic because of the contrast it creates between present misery and past happiness (*Tusc.*3.45). That contrast was also used constantly by Euripides in his plays on Troy's capture (de Romilly 1961.72-3). When Cicero listed ways to arouse pity and tears in speeches (*Inv. Rhet.* 1.106-109), the contrast between present troubles and past good fortune is the first (107). The power of this contrast to cause compassion and crying was recognized in many other passages in the rhetorical manuals of Cicero and other Romans (Schrijvers 1978.489; Quint. *Inst.* 6.1.23), and it was constantly used by Greek and Roman poets, orators and historians (Dover 1974.197; Schrijvers 1978.489-90; Austin 1966, on 554). The ancient commentators were sensitive to Vergil's use of this contrast (Schrijvers 1978. 488-9), especially to arouse *dolor* for Priam, Troy and Hector

(Donat., on 2.486-90; Serv. Dan., on 2.363 and 274), as he did for Dido, Latinus, Evander, etc.

Aeneas himself cries constantly and profusely on seeing depictions of the Trojan War (1.459,465,470) and says that because here *sunt lacrimae rerum* ... there is some hope for salvation (1.461-3; with Serv. and Donat. *ad loc.*). That attitude was typical. The ancient Greeks and Romans thought all life to be extremely pathetic, cried constantly and regarded crying as a very important virtue, especially for heroes; and these feelings are manifested throughout the *Aeneid* (Farron 1988; Brown 1987, on 1177). By contrast, Page (1894) in his note on 1.459 takes into consideration that the ancients had different attitudes to crying from moderns, but still says that three references to Aeneas crying is 'excessive' and 'feeble'.

It is noteworthy that Vergil "could have used [for Book 2] a very different tradition" in which Aeneas is "a resolute, resourceful, and formidable military leader, poles apart from Virgil's hesitant, frustrated, uncertain figure" (Austin 1966.xv-xvi). Austin asks, "Why did Virgil reject what he could have used effectively to the honour of Aeneas?" It does not occur to Austin that the reason is that Vergil tried to make the capture of Troy as pathetic as possible, that that was what the ancients expected and admired in literature and that by doing that he succeeded in making Book 2 one of the most popular books in the *Aeneid* and one of the few places where Aeneas has always gained readers' sympathy. Instead, Austin assumes that Vergil must have intended Book 2 to serve the plot, 'meaning' and 'message' of the *Aeneid*. So its function is to be part of the slow, painful process by which Aeneas learns self-discipline. This explanation is common (e.g. Quinn 1969.123-4). For Lyne (1987) however, although Books 2 is part of Aeneas' development of self-discipline (106-7) and despite its 'further voices' (212-14), at the end Aeneas displays "Roman dutifulness rather than love or compassion" (185), which "the Augustan reader" saw as "a hesitant demonstration of that quality which makes the Augustan hero" (188-9).

However, Vergil would have been totally at odds with the literary feelings and expectations of his culture if he had limited his poem's pathos to only Aeneas' losses. Except for Juno, who also suffers great losses, *all the major characters in the Aeneid die or are the father, husband, wife or son of someone the pathos of whose death is evoked.* That includes Iulus, Latinus, Venus and Jupiter (10.469-71). Of these types of death that of a child was most pathetic. There are many accounts, usually narrated with admiration, of the care Roman parents took in rearing their children (e.g. Lyne 1987.151-2; Hor. *Sat.* 1.4.105-30,6.65-97; Quint. *Inst* 6. prooemium). Also relevant are Lucretius 3.894-9 and 4.1234-9, despite the fact that Epicurus discouraged marrying and having children. Many stories were told about how during the triumvirs' proscription fathers and sons risked their lives to save each other or committed suicide because the other was killed (e.g. App. *BCiv.* 4.20-21 (cf. 22-3); Dio Cass. 51.2.5-6; Suct. *Aug.* 13.2). A father's love for his son was paradigmatic (e.g. Catull. 72.4), as was a father's overlooking his children's defects (e.g. Hor. *Sat.* 1.3.43-50; Ov. *Pont.* 3.9.9-10). So Greek and Roman literature constantly dwelt on the agony of parents whose children died (Farron 1986.80; Pease 1958, on 2.72; Lyne 1978, on 293-4; Nep. *Dion* 6.2; cf. Bates 1930. 42-51). This was true even of animal parents (Farron, *ibid.*). But it was the misery of parents whose children were killed in war that especially attracted the attention and commiseration of Greek and Roman authors (*ibid.*). I have already pointed out that the sufferings of Priam and Hecuba were regarded by the Greeks and Romans as a major aspect of the *Iliad* (*ibid.*; Pl. *Ion* 535 B; Dio Chrys. 53.7; Hor. *Ars P.* 137) and that 'the misfortunes of a Priam' (Arist. *Eth. Nic.* 1.10.14) seems to have been a proverbial expression.

Vergil's feeling that parental affection was natural and all-pervasive and his sensitivity for the agony of parents bereft of their children was unusually acute even for his culture. For example, he attributed parental affection to ravens, in opposition to normal Roman opinion (Serv. on *G.* 1.414); and in similes in the *Aeneid* he inserted prominently parental concern for offspring in distress where it did not exist in the similes' literary models and was irrelevant to their context (Wiltshire 1989.38-43). Indeed, "in every book of the *Aeneid*, whether in simile, allusion, or narrative detail [there are] the persistent laments of mothers" (*ibid.* 38). The misery of parents whose children are killed in war is often referred to briefly (Farron 1986.83n31) and is the subject of some of the most moving and memorable passages in the poem (e.g. 2.531-51; 9.473-502; 10.833-906; 11.148-63). The second and third of these are especially noteworthy. From the beginning of the Nisus-Euryalus episode, Vergil impressed on the reader the terrible misery

Euryalus' death would cause his mother (9.216, 284-94). She is *mater* in 9.216 and 302 and *parens* in 289. When she enters the foreground of the action it is as *matris ... Euryali ... miserae* (474-5). She is *infelix* in 477 and *miserae matri* again in 484. She is never named since her sole function is to feel and express the sorrow of a bereft mother and to arouse pity for it; which she did in characters in the *Aeneid* (9.498-501) and in its readers. Ancient critics commented on the skill with which her misery was represented (e.g. Quint. *Inst.* 6.2.32; Macrob. *Sat.* 4.1.5; Serv. on 9.479).

Mezentius has always been regarded as one of the most interesting and memorable characters in the *Aeneid* (Farron 1979-80a 30; Gotoff 1984.192). Extremely striking to a modern reader is the radical change in the attitude towards him which Vergil directs us to have. Most of the representation of him is as a hideously vicious monster (Farron 1979-80a.30-31,33), but suddenly Vergil uses all his skill to make him the focus of sympathy (Farron 1979-80a.31-2. For his address to his horse see Cic. *Inv. Rhet.* 1.109). This radical change is introduced by *Interea genitor* (10.833), which was prefigured by *genitor nati* (800). After that he is *parens* in 840 and *genitor* in 848, but his name occurs only once, in Aeneas' taunt (897), despite the fact that it is used eighteen times elsewhere. He is now, like Euryalus' mother, primarily a bereaved parent. To concentrate attention on Mezentius and thus gain the maximum pathos from his situation, Vergil was willing to have Aeneas in the background and so deprive him of what could have been one of his most glorious moments. This was not intended to make any sort of comment on Aeneas. Rather, it is an example of the mobile focus of sympathetic interest which Heath observed in Greek tragedies and illustrated with the change of center of attention and compassion in the *Antigone* from Antigone to Creon, who earlier had been unsympathetic (1987.92-8, see "mobile focus" in the index). To this should be added Traina's (1970) demonstration that Latin literature was even more interested in pathos and less in ethos than Greek literature.

It is instructive to consider a recent, detailed analysis, H. Gotoff's "The Transformation of Mezentius" (1984). He points out that Mezentius is at first 'a figure of unmitigated evil' (193), but then he is made the object of great sympathy (200-210). Gotoff constantly uses the words 'pathos' and 'pathetic' to describe Vergil's treatment of Mezentius, observes that he fits into 'a pattern of pathetic family loss' which constantly recurs in the *Aeneid* (198-9) and rejects several attempts by other scholars to interpret the portrayal of Mezentius as serving the depiction of Aeneas, the nature of heroism or a political theory (194-7). However, like so many critics of the Nisus-Euryalus episode, Gotoff is prevented from following his own observations to their logical conclusion by the presupposition that the purpose of a major episode could not be 'merely' to depict and arouse emotions. He begins his analysis by stating that the 'important' point is "what effect does the audience's sympathy ... for Mezentius ... have on its feelings for Aeneas" since "it cannot be doubted that Aeneas ... is Virgil's sole main character" (192). He follows his analysis by stating, "The finale of Book 10 would suffice to make a tragedy, if Virgil were writing a tragedy of Mezentius." However, "this was not Virgil's overriding concern, any more than in the fourth book he was writing the tragedy of Dido", although both Dido and Mezentius are the focus of 'his audience's sympathy' (210). Gotoff then mentions the ends of Books 10, 4 and 12 as examples of scenes whose purpose is to "take the glitter away from Aeneas, although Aeneas is clearly doing what is entirely appropriate" (211). The 'result' of 'the transformation of ... Mezentius' "was to reinforce and enhance a pervasive sense of frustration and personal unfulfilment in Aeneas" (215). However, Gotoff rejects the view that the *Aeneid* is anti-Aeneas or anti-Roman (216-17,213). Instead, he favors the 'two voices' interpretation: the *Aeneid's* purpose is to show the tragic conflict between Aeneas' 'public stance' (212) and the 'frustration, suffering, and personal loss' of 'the private man' (215), which reflected the conflict between the 'unparalleled success' of the Roman Empire and the 'personal sacrifice' it necessitated (218). He ends his article with a warning against being mislead by modern 'Romanticism'.

In passing (198, notes 21 and 22) Gotoff mentions two instances of pathos for a son's death in Book 6: Daedalus and Brutus. For the former he notes that in 6.30-33 "the narrator intrudes to heighten the pathos". In the latter, emphasis is not on Brutus' tremendous importance for Roman political history but on the fact that he was *infelix* (822) because of his actions which are introduced by *natosque pater* (820). Much has been written on the 'meaning' of the former episode. Probably the most popular modern interpretation of the latter is that of the 'two voices' approach (e.g. Commager 1966.11-12), which Gotoff supports (198n21).

These dead sons are part of an even more pervasive means for producing pathos: the death of youths with promising futures, many of whom are also physically beautiful (Moskalew 1982. 100-3). This includes not only those whose parents' bereavement is mentioned, but many others; for instance, Dido, Nisus, Camilla and Turnus. The ancient Greeks and Romans regarded premature death as extremely pathetic (Farron 1988.777), especially that of youths of promise (Schrijvers 1978.487-9). Vergil was even more sensitive to this than most of his contemporaries. Indicative is that for most Romans *puerilis* was a word of disapproval, but Vergil used *puer* with affection and even respect (Curtius 1963. 18-19). He constantly emphasized the youth of those killed, and explicitly and implicitly drew his readers' attention to the pathos of this situation (Farron 1988.777; Duckworth 1965-6.47). The ancient commentators were fully aware that Vergil was using this to arouse pity (e.g. Serv. and Donat. on 7.531). We know that the Marcellus passage had the desired effect on Augustus' family. But modern critics assume that this pervasive pathetic effect must serve the 'message' of the *Aeneid*, to attack Aeneas' mission and Rome, to offer a contrasting 'voice' to them or to show that, although they were thoroughly constructive, they involved great sacrifice. An example of the last approach is Heinze (1915.469-70). He discusses these dead youths as an example of *Pathos: Mitleid* in a chapter in which he uses many examples to show that for the ancients the goal of literature was to arouse powerful emotions. But he cannot leave it at that. So he says that their purpose is to demonstrate that *tantae molis erat Romanam condere gentem* (470). By contrast, Servius (on *Aen.* 3.718) states that Books 2, 3, 4, 5 and 6 all end with the death of a character. His descriptions of the ends of Books 2 and 6 (*mors Creusae, Marcelli citum deflet interitum*) ignore the passages that follow them, which are part of the *Aeneid*'s plot: Aeneas' mission to found the Roman people. That is especially noteworthy in Book 6, where after the Marcellus passage, *Anchises natum per singula duxit incenditque animum famae venientis amore* (888-9), which strikes modern scholars as extremely significant.

Another type of pathos Vergil offered his readers is the destruction or bereavement of nature, which is endowed with feeling. This, again, was a typically Roman interest. Traina (1970.84-9) points out that just as in Roman versions of Greek tragedies and epics pathos overwhelms the original ethos, so in Cicero's version of Aratus' *Prognostica, il pathos della natura* overwhelms the original's scientific accuracy. This is, of course, very prominent in the *Georgics*, where its 'meaning' has been much discussed. Vergil also used it constantly in the *Aeneid*. Many instances are obvious; for example, the portrayal of *maerentem Nilum* in 8.711-13. Not so obvious to the modern reader is that many of the Italians who are killed have names of Italian rivers (Fordyce 1977, on 7.532), including the first two fatalities of the war, Almo and Galaesus. And the latter river had powerful emotional resonances for the Romans (Nisbet and Hubbard 1978, on 6.10). As always, much has been made of the contribution that the pathos of nature makes to the 'meaning' and 'message' of the *Aeneid*, whether that is anti-Roman and anti-Aeneas (e.g. Nethercut 1971.123-6; Farron 1981. 103) or 'two voices' (e.g. Commager 1966.10-11). Indeed, Parry began his seminal "The Two Voices of Virgil's *Aeneid*" (1963) with the pathos of nature.

C. *Pre-Modern Reactions to the Dido-Aeneas Episode*

By far the most intense, powerful and memorable pathos Vergil offered his readers is Dido's. Vergil chose to concentrate interest and sympathy nearly completely on her, as I will demonstrate and others have shown (e.g. De Witt 1907.28-35). The explanations I will present for why the Dido episode is the most memorable episode in the *Aeneid*, why interest and sympathy are focused nearly entirely on Dido and why it is composed in the way it is will, hopefully, prove my contention that it was intended to be nothing but a love story which arouses pity and that it makes no comment on Aeneas or Rome, whether positive, negative or 'two voices'. Before that, I will show that that is the way it was regarded in antiquity. I have already mentioned Servius Danielis on *Aeneid* 4.323 (with Murgia 1967.332-5) as evidence of the importance of the Dido episode for Vergil and Augustus and what interested them in it. The only extant Augustan poet who referred to and used the *Aeneid* in extended passages was Ovid, who was reciting poetry in public while it was being written. His explicit statement in *Tristia* 2.533-6 that the Dido episode is about love and was the most read part of the poem has been discussed. His *Heroides* 7 is the first treatment of Vergil's Dido in extant literature. Its close similarity to Vergil's account is obvious. A long list of the details in which they 'correspond perfectly' is provided by Means (1929. 41-2). He concluded it by observing, "It would be a difficult task to sift from Ovid any fact, other than the most minor detail, not found also in Vergil." It is significant that this first extant representation of Vergil's Dido is in a series of poems about the suffering of women who have been abandoned by the men they love.

Ovid makes explicit two facts which are implicit in *Aeneid* 4. First, the actual wound with which she kills herself is a culmination of the metaphorical 'wound of love' Aeneas earlier inflicted on her (189-90). Second, she constantly emphasizes that she is dying with the sword that was Aeneas' gift; for instance, the inscription on her tomb begins (195), *Praebuit Aeneas et causam mortis et ensem.* In *Aeneid* 4 that was a *Dardanium ... quaesitum munus* (647) and she died with it because it was a *monimentum* of Aeneas (495-8). Her desire for a greater *monimentum*, a *parvulus Aeneas*, was not fulfilled. (*Parvulus Aeneas* became proverbial; e.g. Juv. 5.138-9). That Dido died with Aeneas' sword was also important in other ancient versions, as will be shown. It was as close as she could get to the ideal of dying with the beloved, which Nisus did. When Ovid mentions the *Heroides* in *Amores* 2.18.21ff, his longest description is of number 7, which he sums up as *quodque tenens strictum Dido miserabilis ensem dicat.*

In *Ars Amatoria* 3.31-40 and *Remedia Amoris* 57-8 Dido is again assumed to be a typical victim of love and the man she loved. In the former Ovid, as opposed to modern scholars, shows a true understanding of *pietas* in *Aeneid* 4 (Farron 1992. 272). *Metamorphoses* 13.623-14.608 ostensibly describes Aeneas' activities from the time he left Troy until his deification, but in fact that constitutes a very small part of the narration. The lines which summarize the Dido episode (14.78-81) mention her generous welcome of Aeneas and suicide with his sword after he left. *Fasti* 3.545-50 also dwells on her wretched death by a metaphorical and real fire and wound from Aeneas' gift, just as Vergil had. Ovid follows that (551-4) by stating that immediately after Dido's death the Numidians invaded and Iarbas captured her palace to avenge being rejected as a suitor. That is what Dido said would happen, to increase the pathos of her situation, in the speech which, according to Servius Danielis, Vergil read to Augustus *ingenti adfectu.*

It might be argued that Ovid distorted the Dido episode because he was largely a love poet. But love was basic to Vergil's literary culture, the *Fasti* constantly lavish fulsome praise on Augustus (Farron 1980a.66n22) and that argument certainly cannot be used for the next extant treatment of Vergil's Dido, in the extremely unromantic, patriotic and anti-Carthaginian *Punica* by Silius Italicus. Silius greatly admired Vergil (e.g. 8.593-4), and, indeed, literally worshipped him as a god (Schanz-Hosius II.527). He constantly imitated the *Aeneid*'s episodes, narrative technique and language (Schanz-Hosius II.528). His imitation of Vergil's word order, frequency of elision and location of caesurae caused him to differ in those respects from most Silver Age Latin poets and helps to understand Vergil's practices (Pearce 1968a.346). Similarly, the fact that he, like Ovid, made explicit implicit connections between metaphors and actual occurrences in the *Aeneid* has been used to explain Vergil's intentions (e.g. Knox 1950.139-40).

Silius, like Ovid, constantly dwelt on Dido's death and the fact that her death was caused by Aeneas' sword, the concrete embodiment of the wound of love he inflicted on her (1.90-1; 8.50-3,148-9). Anna's description of Dido's death (8.81-103,116-158), ending with Iarbas preparing to invade (cf. 54), is filled with obvious reminisces from the *Aeneid*. The actions which Silius has Anna add to Vergil's story show Dido's desperate longing for Aeneas after he left (e.g. 84-6,95-7). Silius' main means for showing this is the same as Vergil's: Dido's passionate attachment to objects which remind her of Aeneas. He adds some objects not in the *Aeneid* (e.g. 126-7), including *amens ... sideream fulgentis Iuli effigiem fovet amplexu* (91-2, cf. 106-7). The adjectives and situation recall *Aeneid* 1.710,717-18; 4.83-5 and her desire for a *parvulus Aeneas*. These objects Dido *congessit in atram cuncta tui monumenta pyram et ... dona* (102-3). Silius also retells the Dido episode at length in 2.406-25. There also he follows the *Aeneid* closely, with some additions and conflations, focusing entirely on *infelix* (415) Dido: her city, her generosity to Aeneas when he is shipwrecked and helpless, the *furtiva ... foedera amantum* in the cave, her calling back Aeneas' departing ships in vain and her on the pyre. In addition, Silius adapted the Dido episode to focus attention on the suffering that a later great Roman hero caused the woman who loved him by doing his duty (6.377-520; see Farron 1992. 275 n32).

There are also two poems in the *Anthologia Latina* (255 and 83) which are based on Vergil's Dido's episode. Both are in the form of addresses by Dido to Aeneas. The former is a fifteen line elaboration of Dido's accusations in *Aeneid* 4.365ff. She attacks Aeneas for *perfidia* and *periurium*, as Vergil's Dido does, and also for cowardice in war, which Vergil's Dido does not and which has no basis in the *Aeneid*. The latter is a letter of a hundred and fifty lines, which makes no such departure from the *Aeneid*. It dwells on Dido's *dolor* (11,14,16,89) and reiterates the accusations of *perfidia*, *periurium*, *fraus* (35-6,86,119,123,130-1) and ingratitude for all she did for him (6,31-2,100-1,105-6,111-17). She sums up her criticisms in a series of vocatives (124-5): *Improbe, dure, nocens* [for her death], *crudelis, perfide, fallax, officiis ingrate meis*. In that passage the author shows that, like Ovid and unlike modern scholars, he understood the meaning of *pietas* in *Aeneid* 4 (Farron 1992. 272).

When Saint Augustine recounts the standard Classical education of his time in *Confessions* 1.13, the emphasis was also on Dido's suffering, as it had been from Vergil's reading to Augustus on: *cogebar ... plorare Didonem mortuam, quia se occidit ab amore*, and he describes himself as *flens Didonis mortem, quae fiebat amando Aenean* and *flebam Didonem exstinctam ferro ...* . Here again Aeneas is of interest only as the cause of Dido's love and death. The same is true of the summaries of *Aeneid* 4 in the outlines of the books of the *Aeneid* which were so popular in late antiquity and the early Middle Ages and must have reflected orthodox interpretations. Eight such synopses occur in the *Anthologia Latina*. Number 1 has a one line summary of each book followed by a fuller summary in ten lines. The one line for Book 4 is *Uritur in quarto Dido flammasque fatetur*. Of the ten lines only one and a half are devoted to Aeneas: *Monitus tum numine divum Aeneas classemque fugae sociosque parabat*. Number 594 has five lines on Book 4. Aeneas is mentioned in half a line: *navigat Aeneas iussu Iovis*. Number 634 has one line on each book. That for 4 is *Quartus item miserae duo vulnera narrat Elissae*. Of the six lines devoted to *Aeneid* 4 in 653 and the four in 654 one in each is about Aeneas: *Aeneas altum sociis et classe petivit* and *postquam Anchisiades fatorum est iussa secutus*. Number 672a summarizes each book of the *Aeneid* with one or two nouns. The summary of Book 4 is *amores Elissae*. Number 717 summarizes each of the first six books with one noun. Book 4 is *vulnera*. Number 720a devotes one line to each book. That for 4 is *Ardet amans Dido fatum sortita supremum*. Similarly, the miniature paintings on the Vatican manuscripts from late antiquity and the early Middle Ages concentrate on the pathos of Dido's death; when she is lying dead she has Aeneas' bloody sword in her hand; and when she is with Aeneas at the banquet, all emphasis is on her (McKay 1987. 227-30).

Servius and Donatus saw the Dido episode in the same way. Servius introduces *Aeneid* 4 by describing it as *paene totus in affectione, licet in fine pathos habeat, ubi abscessus Aeneae gignet dolorem ... de amore tractatur.* Donatus comments on Dido's statement in 1.733 (*nostrosque huius meminisse minores*), *sicuti factum est, ut etiam nunc duret de actibus Didonis fabula.* (Note: not *Didonis et Aeneae.*) At the beginning of Book 5 he summarizes the last part of Book 4 as *descriptio actuum Didonis et mortis.*

The versions of the Dido episode discussed so far accurately reflect Vergil's account with two exceptions: the accusation of cowardice in *Anthologia Latina* 255 and the constant description of Aeneas as Dido's husband (Farron 1992. 274 n27). The former adds to the accusations which Vergil's Dido did make. The latter accepts Dido's assessment of the nature of her and Aeneas' relationship, ignoring the fact that Vergil supports Aeneas' argument that he is not married to Dido (*Aen.* 4.172). Similarly, because Dido accuses Aeneas of not crying for her misery (*Aen.* 4. 369-70), the scholia on Juvenal 13.133, assuming that the *lacrimae* in *Aeneid* 4.449 are Aeneas', give them as an example of tears with no feeling behind them (cf. Ov. *Her.* 6.58-63). And Servius (on *Aen.* 3.718) states that the end of *Aeneid* 1 is about *miseratio Didonis*, even though only one of the last thirty-four lines of Book 1 mentions that (749). The rest describe the joyful banquet. These distortions result from the concentration by ancient readers on Dido's love, suffering and death and the belief that Aeneas should have stayed with her and was emotionally cold and unfeeling to Dido's suffering.

The same orientation of interest and sympathy and the same belief are also manifested in the three extant ancient attempts I know of which counter the normal ancient judgement, whether explicit of implicit, that Aeneas was a villain in the Dido episode. As one would expect, they come from Ovid's *Fasti* and Silius' *Punica*, the two Roman propagandistic works which recreate the Dido episode, and from Donatus' commentary on the *Aeneid*, which assumes that Aeneas is *vacuus omni culpa*, that Vergil *inventis occasionibus omnia genera virtutum animi scilicet et corporis adplicare [Aeneae] non cessat* and that *omni occasione Vergilius laudat [Aenean]* (vol.1,page2,line24; p.66,ll.19-21; p.116,l.19ff.; cf.p.10,ll.13-14; p.91, l.27ff. of Georgii's Teubner edition).

In *Fasti* 3.612 Aeneas weeps on being reminded of Dido and swears in an elaborate oath that when he was at Carthage the gods *saepe meas increpuisse moras, nec timui de morte [Didonis] tamen, metus abfuit iste* (616-18). These excuses for Aeneas' conduct were supplied by Vergil. The gods did order him to leave and he did not know his leaving would cause Dido's death (5.3-5; 6.456-8,463-4; 4.72:*nescius*). However, Ovid's *saepe increpuisse* is an exaggeration. Only Mercury's speech in 4.265-76 can be described as *increpuisse*, and Aeneas shows no hesitation in obeying (4.281,571-81).

Silius also has Aeneas swear an elaborate oath that (8.108-11) *respiciens aegerque animi tum regna reliqui vestra* and that he would not have left Dido's bed chamber *ni magna minatus meque sua ratibus dextra imposuisset et alto egisset rapidis classem Cyllenius Euris*. Thus, Silius resorts to much more radical distortions than Ovid had. *Respiciens* is from *Aeneid* 5.3, but earlier in that sentence Aeneas *tenebat certus iter fluctusque ... secabat*. Silius' main means of exculpation is the same as Ovid's: divine compulsion. But he betters Ovid's exaggeration by having Mercury put Aeneas physically on his ship and drive it out to sea, in total contradiction to *Aeneid* 4.576-83.

Donatus also greatly exaggerated the number of divine orders (e.g. on 4.361) and Aeneas' reluctance to obey them and leave Carthage. For example, he comments on 4.281-2 (*ardet abire*), where Vergil gives no hint of such reluctance, *non inanis deliberatio ... fuit ... Occurebant enim Didonis humanitas et ipsa ... coniunctio et terrae iam dulces ... Cumque uno ex latere metus divinae iussionis insisteret, ex altero pudor*.

When discussing the first extant reproduction of Vergil's Dido, *Heroides* 7, I cited Means' (1929.41-2) useful list of details in which they 'correspond perfectly'. Means also states what he regards as a fundamental difference (43): "Ovid is writing rather from Dido's point of view, Vergil from Aeneas's", and (44) Vergil's "Aeneas suffers a fearful agony ... as to where his duty lies". But if this or the other modern interpretations of the Dido episode are correct, then Vergil failed utterly. All extant ancient treatments made the same 'mistake' Ovid did. All assumed that interest and sympathy in the Dido episode is completely with Dido, especially her suffering, and that this was not commenting on anything else. That is true even of the three attempts at exculpating Aeneas, in the patriotic *Fasti*, the patriotic, unromantic and anti-Carthaginian *Punica* and Donatus' fanatically pro-Aeneas commentary. Indeed, Silius, eager as he was to excuse Aeneas' conduct, devoted much less space to that than to Dido's love and suffering. Furthermore, although Ovid, Silius and Donatus resort to blatant distortions of Vergil's text in order to exculpate Aeneas for leaving Dido and although Silius liked to depict public duty and personal desire struggling for a hero's soul, with duty winning in the end (e.g. 15.18-132), none of them used as an excuse for Aeneas that it was his duty to leave Dido. They assumed that it was morally correct for him to stay at Carthage. *Fasti* 3.616-18 suggests that if Aeneas had feared that the god's orders to leave Dido would cause her death, he might have disobeyed them and would have been right to do so. Donatus opposes the divine command to moral considerations (cf. on 4.331-2, 361). This is in accordance with the ancients' interpretation of *pius* in *Aeneid* 4.393 as commenting on Aeneas' actions in lines 393-5 in opposition to 396 and with their belief that the gods frequently commanded what is immoral (Farron 1992. 260-2, 275-6). It is extremely ironic that modern readers have exactly the same reaction to the Dido episode as ancient readers did, but are constantly warned that that is because of the romantic, sentimental orientation of our culture.

Another reaction of modern readers which is constantly corrected by appeal to the Stoic, stoic or at least stoical values of ancient Rome is that the Dido episode is the great glory of the *Aeneid*, the episode which above all else makes it a great poem. According to all modern interpretations, its purpose is to make some sort of comment on the plot and so contribute to the *Aeneid*'s meaning and message. I have already discussed *Tristia* 2.533-6 and Servius Danielis on *Aeneid* 4.323 (with Murgia 1967.332-5) as evidence that Vergil, Augustus and their contemporaries regarded the portrayal of Dido's love and especially her suffering as the *Aeneid*'s highpoint. That is also evident from the way it is intruded into the *Fasti* and *Punica*, to whose subjects and nature it is irrelevant. Ovid's excuse for including the story of Dido's death is the narration of the origins of the goddess Anna Perenna. Ovid seems to have invented the identification of Anna Perenna with

Dido's sister to have a reason for retelling the story of Dido's death (Roscher *Lex.* I. 356-7). After it, he mentions other explanations of her identity (3.657-74), including one which *nec a veri dissidet ... fide* (662). Silius also used the identification of Anna Perenna with Dido's sister to justify his recreation of Dido's love, suffering and death in 8.50-149. Indeed, he, as opposed to Ovid, also needed an excuse for introducing Anna Perenna and her background (8.25-47). He wanted that recreation enough to intrude the irrelevant Anna and then use most of the space supposedly devoted to her for Dido. He obviously found this double irrelevancy embarrassing since he began it by stating it would be short (48-9), which it is not. Silius also retold Dido's story at length in 2.406-25 and mentioned her frequently in passing (Pease 1935.64n492). However, only once did he mention Aeneas without Dido (7.474-5): *Tum pius Aeneas, terris iactatus et undis, Dardanios Italia posuit tellure penates.* That is what Vergil announces in the beginning of the *Aeneid* will be its plot. Modern scholars assume that is what the *Aeneid* is 'about', to praise it, condemn it, or offer contrasting voices to it. But the extremely patriotic Silius, who was extraordinarily unromantic for a Roman poet, had absolutely no interest in it. These lines begin Proteus' assurance to the Nereids that Rome will endure. But that is only an excuse for the long description of the judgement of Paris which precedes it (437-71), most of which is devoted to Venus and her Cupids.

Ausonius, like Silius, was an avid admirer and constant imitator of Vergil. He mentions Aeneas twice. Both are in the book of epitaphs (Book 5 in Prete's edition):13.3-4 and 19.5-6 (the epitaphs of Deiphobus and Polydorus). In both Aeneas is mentioned incidentally as part of the dead man's pathetic situation. But when Ausonius mentions Dido, she is the center of attention. Poem two of Book 14 (Prete) is a long poem based on the *Lugentes Campi*. Dido is there, carrying Aeneas' sword (37-9). In 26.23 a man whose loved ones hate him is advised to seek Dido's advice. The anonymous poems which Peiper prints as Book 22 of his edition of Ausonius have only one about a character in the *Aeneid* (8): *Infelix Dido, nulli bene nupta marito. Hoc pereunte fugis, hoc fugiente peris.*

The way Vergil's works were taught confirms the evidence of poetic imitations. In the Augustan period Vergil was taught as a neoteric poet (Suet. *Gram.*16). As has been pointed out, Saint Augustine, receiving a standard Classical education, was taught primarily to cry for Dido. In chapters 13 and 17 of Book 1 of his *Confessions* he mentions three other parts of the *Aeneid* that he was taught: *verba Iunonis irascentis et dolentis quod non possit Italia Teucrorum avertere regem; equus ligneus plenus armatis, et Troiae incendium, atque ipsius umbra Creusae* and *tenere cogebar Aeneae nescio cuius errores*. Do not most modern readers react to Aeneas in the same way: *Aeneas nescio quis*? If Augustine had been taught about an internal struggle in Aeneas, he certainly would have mentioned it. He attacked his education because it deflected his attention from his own grave problems to those of fictional characters (Aeneas' 'errors' not his own, crying for Dido's death not his own before God, etc.), and the basic theme of the *Confessions* is his internal struggle. (Cf. Lucian, *Salt.* 46.)

On ancient paintings, mosaics and manuscript illuminations representing scenes from the *Aeneid* Dido also predominated (Schanz-Hosius II.102; McKay 1987.228-30). Macrobius summed up the subsequent effect of the Dido episode in *Saturnalia* 5.17.5-6:

> fabula lascivientis Didonis ... per tot ... saecula ... per ora omnium volitet, ut pictores fictoresque et qui figmentis liciorum contextas imitantur effigies, hac materia vel maxime in efficiendis simulacris tamquam unico argumento decoris utantur, nec minus histrionum perpetuis et gestibus et cantibus celebretur.

Macrobius points out that Vergil produced this tremendous subsequent fame for Dido by *pulchritudo narrandi* and *dulcedo fingientis*, despite the fact that the story was not true. The 'true' story was that Dido never met Aeneas, was chaste after Sychaeus' death and killed herself to escape Iarbas' advances. A few ancient authors, mostly African, said that Vergil's version 'slandered' Dido (Pease 1935.65-6). These are sometimes quoted to show that in antiquity the Dido episode was regarded as slandering Dido. Macrobius records the effect of this 'slander'.

Medieval and early modern readers saw the *Aeneid* as the ancients did. Waddell points out (1934.xxvi) that "Dido ... was the romantic heroine of the Middle Ages ... Dido they took to their hearts, wrote lament after lament for her, cried over her". She prefaces these observations by stating that "Virgil ... they read as we do not". What she did not realize is that it is our, modern, interpretation of the Dido episode that is unique. That is obvious in the many modern corrections of medieval and early modern interpretations which resemble Means' correction of Ovid. For example, Nitchie observes (1966) that Chaucer's recreations of Dido in *Hous of Fame* and *Legend of Good Women* were based on a thorough knowledge of the Latin text (41), that "the sympathies of the Middle Ages had been chiefly with the deserted Dido, and Chaucer too treated her as one of the 'saints of Cupid', a true sister of Ariadne" (8) and that "the elaboration of the sentimental part of the story, especially the long account of Dido's 'compleynt', is in full harmony with the medieval romantic tendency" (46-7). But she says that Chaucer greatly distorted "the Vergilian conception of the characters of Aeneas and Dido. The former is no longer the Fate-driven hero, the destined founder of the mighty Roman race ... but the 'fals lover', the 'traitour'" (50). R. Williams (1982.32) illustrates the general observation that Book 4 "has always been the most widely read ... part of the poem and the story of Dido has influenced subsequent literature more than any other from Roman literature" with specific examples. Among them is that Dido is "a favorite character in twelfth- and thirteenth-century French romances ... Shakespeare and Spenser, Marlowe's *Dido, Queen of Carthage* ... Purcell and Berlioz". He adds, "She is generally presented as the innocent victim of fate, or of Aeneas, but Vergil's version is subtler than that." Similarly, Langmuir (1976.165) attributes the importance ascribed to Dido and especially the force of her love and suffering in sixteenth century Italian art and literature to a 'whitewash of Dido'. Dido was also an immensely popular subject in plays, operas, ballets and cantatas from the sixteenth through the nineteenth centuries (Pease 1935.68-9; Newmyer 1990; Henry 1878.544-6; Nitchie 1966.116-17). For most of these Rand's observation (1931.349-50) about "Renaissance playwrights of various nationalities" holds true: they "present her fate as the chief, if not the sole, dramatic motive ... Aeneas is a shadowy figure, and, by implication, a villain". In those cantatas and operas in which he is not a callous villain he wants to disobey Jupiter and stay with Dido, or he actually does that (Newmyer 1990).

Even Dryden made the same 'mistakes' as nearly all readers of the *Aeneid* until recently. He acknowledged that the 'episode of Dido and Aeneas' is the most popular part of the epic (195 in Ker 1926) and thought that "love was the theme of his Fourth Book" (190) and that its great achievement was depicting so well that love and Dido's misery (190,200). I say 'even Dryden' because he is often cited as an antidote to the twentieth century, or nineteenth and twentieth century, sentimental-romantic distortion of the *Aeneid*, which ignores its public, patriotic message by concentrating on Dido's love and suffering (e.g. Martindale 1984.4; R. Williams 1969.135,1967.30). But Feder (1954.203-6), who quotes Dryden's discussion of Book 4 at length, introduces it as an example of the common mistake of regarding Dido "as the heroine ... and Aeneas as the unfeeling deserter. The chief reason ... is that this book is ... treated as a work in itself, whereas it is only an episode in Aeneas' struggle to accomplish his mission". She concludes,

> Dryden's criticism of the fourth book demonstrates that he has little understanding of its intrinsic relationship to the rest of the poem. The fourth book is not merely about a passionate love story; it is concerned with ... the acceptance by Aeneas of a tragic sense of life as the price of his achievement ... Virgil makes it perfectly clear that Aeneas and not Dido is the major figure.

Moreover, medieval and early modern attempts to exculpate Aeneas were based on emphasizing divine compulsion, not a conflict between personal inclinations and public duty, stoic morality, etc. In this they were the same as ancient attempts. They were also identical to ancient exculpations in exaggerating Aeneas' resistance and misery at having to leave and their assumption that the moral course was to stay with Dido.[1] Chaucer recognized that divine compulsion was the excuse Vergil supplied for Aeneas. In *Hous of Fame* 1.293-8 he says, "Eneas ... betrayed hir, allas! And lefte hir ful unkindly". Then (383-426) is a long description of other women in Greek and Roman literature who were similarly lied to and betrayed, especially Ariadne. In 427-32 he states, "but to excusen Eneas fulliche of al his greet trespas, the book seyth Mercurie ... bad him go to Italie, and leve ... Dido". Dryden also recognized this (188-9 in Ker 1926): "an immediate revelation dispenses with all duties of morality", "there was a fault somewhere; and Jupiter is better able to bear the blame than

---

[1] E.g. Marlowe, *Dido, Queen of Carthage* 4.4.56-9;5.1.24-41,80-2,103-4, 125-7,139-40;Purcell, *Dido and Aeneas, passim*;Gavin Douglas, lines 410-44 of the prologue to his translation of Book 1;Philip Sidney, *Defense of Poetry* (pages 98-9 in K. Duncan-Jones and J. van Dorsten, *Miscellaneous Prose of Sir Philip Sidney* (Oxford: 1973): "obeying God's commandment to leave Dido, though not only all passionate kindness, but even ... virtuous gratefulness, would have craved other of him").

either Virgil or Aeneas" and, "Oh how convenient is a machine sometimes in a heroic poem! ... Mercury is plainly one: and Virgil was constrained to use it here, or the honesty of his hero would be ill-defended." (For gods causing characters to do what is immoral in the *Aeneid* and other Latin poems and the recognition of this by ancient, medieval and early modern scholars, see Farron 1992. 260-2, 273, 275-6.)

As Heinze (1915.133) observed, Vergil's artistic skill so surpassed that of his models *dass seine Dido die einzige von einem römischen Dichter geschaffene Figur ist, die in die Weltliteratur übergehen sollte.* By contrast, "at no time has the character of Aeneas excited any strong human interest. No later poet or moralist set it up ... as a subject of ethical contemplation" (Sellar 1908.397). The difference between subsequent lack of interest in Aeneas and the great interest not only in Dido but also in Nisus and Euryalus is very striking.

D. *The Relation of the Dido-Aeneas (and Nisus-Euryalus) Episode to Ancient Personal Love Poetry*

It is natural that the Dido episode is the greatest glory of the *Aeneid* in view of the interests, orientation and aptitudes of Vergil and his literary culture. As was demonstrated in my discussion of the Nisus-Euryalus episode, Vergil and his fellow Romans were fascinated by overwhelming, tormenting, self-destructive love, the ultimate manifestation of which was the lover dying because he could not live without his beloved. Indeed, they assumed that passionate love had been the central theme of nearly all earlier literature, from the *Iliad* on. Consequently, the two love stories in the *Aeneid* involve the longest concentration of attention on a character or pair of characters in the epic; and, since they were to be the most gripping parts, Vergil placed them in Books Four and Nine. That made as short as possible the space between them and between each and the poem's beginning and end.

The two love stories in the *Aeneid* also share another common practice of its literary culture. Catullus, whose influence on Vergil and his contemporaries was immense, wrote both heretosexual love poems and poems in which the beloved was an adolescent boy. The former were more important, memorable and cumulatively longer. Tibullus followed this procedure, as did Vergil in the *Eclogues* and *Aeneid*.

The ancients were not obsessed, as we are, with literary unity and cohesion. But Vergil tried to integrate episodes into the *Aeneid*'s plot when it was possible. This could be done with his homosexual lovers by making them soldiers. Vergil could then adapt the night expedition in *Iliad* 10 for their main episode. He may have also used it to show how important Aeneas was to the Trojans and especially to Ascanius and to show the destruction caused by lust for plunder and slaughter. But even if he intended to do that, they were of peripheral interest. The integration of the heterosexual love story into the plot had to be more tenuous. I will explain below how it was done.

To understand the nature and orientation of the heterosexual love story, and the entire *Aeneid*, it is necessary always to keep in mind two factors. First, Hellenistic and Roman poetry, especially epic, was characterized by a mingling of genres (lyric, history, romance, drama, etc.) in the same work, and this was extremely prominent in the *Aeneid* (Grant 1952.194 and *passim*). So Vergil's teacher, Parthenius, says in the Preface of his *Erotic Sufferings* that it is for use in 'epic or elegiac'. Second, although these genres were combined in the same work, each had a canonical, accepted form and pattern (for, e.g., speeches of eulogy see Marrou 1956. 272-3); and these were learned largely by studying and imitating earlier treatments of them. The conventions for types of characters and subjects had a great influence in determining what is done or said in different parts of ancient literary works. In my discussion of Attic tragedy I summarized Heath's (1987) demonstration that modern scholars tend to ignore the formal elements of recurrent ingredients, like messenger speeches and supplications, and try to relate them to the 'meaning' and 'message' of the plays.

The powerful influence of a canonical pattern of passionate love on various poetic genres and on Vergil's culture is obvious and has been noted frequently (e.g. Griffin 1985). This pattern forms the basis of Catullus' Lesbia poems. Vergil probably never considered the possibility that his heterosexual love story, the highpoint of his epic, would follow any other pattern than the one which made Lesbia better known than Helen while he was composing the *Aeneid* (Prop. 2.34.87-8). The similarities have often been observed (e.g. DeWitt 1907.18-25; Saylor 1986; Cairns 1989. 135-49). However, because of the preoccupation with unity and meaning, I do not think anyone has noticed how completely the Dido episode is controlled by the pattern found in the Lesbia poems. An important general similarity is that, excluding Ovid's *Metamorphoses*, the Dido episode is the only description of a love affair from its beginning to its end in any extant ancient epic; and the narration of the development of a love affair from its beginning to end with all its vicissitudes seems to have been Catullus' invention (Lyne 1978a.176-7).

For specific similarities, let us look at the Lesbia poems, beginning with poem 51. The sight of the beloved produces an overwhelming passion (cf. *Aen.* 1.613), like a fire or powerful blow (cf. *Aen.* 4.1-2 and *passim*), which makes him *miser* even before the affair beings (cf. *infelix* Dido, who is *miser* or *miserrima* six times because of her affair with Aeneas). This leads to *otium*, which *beatas perdidit urbes* (cf. *Aen.* 4.86-9). This *otium* stanza was part of Poem 51 as Catullus wrote it and influenced other poets contemporary with Vergil; *otium* was regarded as a basic component of love; it refers to neglect of political and military duties and in Catullus' case was caused by him not satisfying his desires (Fredricksmeyer 1965: Fraenkel 1957.211-13; Frank 1968; Saylor 1986.74-5). When the lover and beloved first meet as lovers it is in a hidden, isolated place (68.67). For a short time the lover is happy with the affair despite carping rumours, but he realizes that the beloved does not reciprocate his total commitment, a commitment which obliterates all other considerations. He becomes bitter and indignant, claiming that the beloved has deceived him because she offered marriage and, indeed, recognized their relationship as a marriage. (For this theme in Catullus and other Roman love poets scc Lyne 1980.34-8,56-60,79-80,185; G.Williams 1958.25,27.) This claim of marriage is extremely improbable and shows that the lover had deluded himself into thinking that the love was mutual. But despite his resentment and scorn, the lover cannot stop loving. (For Dido see Highet 1972.133-4; Servius Danielis on 4.496 and Servius on 4.659.) He alternates between hatred and desperate thoughts of continuing the love, even on very compromising terms. He expresses this agonizing *odi et amo* condition with strikingly compact brevity (cf. *Aen.* 4.532 ('saevit amor ... irarum...') with Austin 1955, *ad. loc.*). (Aelius Donatus in his note on Terence, *Andria* 718 cites Dido and Catulus as the two quintessential examples of the ambivalence between *amare* and *bene velle minus*.)

Finally, the lover viciously attacks his rivals and the beloved, wishing that they be miserable and the beloved not enjoy the rivals and be without love (cf. Nisbet and Hubbard 1975. 289-90; Murgatroyd 1980, on 6.77-84; Ov. *Ars Am.* 3.59-80). (I will point out the parallels in the Dido episode. Monti 1981.59-60 observes that these maledictions with which lovers ended affairs were also common in Hellenistic literature and that Dido's follow the normal pattern of wishing on the beloved that he suffer other torments he made her suffer, besides being without love.)

Very striking is Catullus' use of political terminology to describe Lesbia's disloyalty. Roman "politics operated by the exchange of services (*officia*) and favors (*benefacta*) ... From this exchange resulted *gratia* ... The indispensable quality ... was *fides* ... The sacredness of ... *fides* was underscored by ... the term *pietas*". This explanation is from pages 9-10 of R. Monti's *The Dido Episode and the Aeneid* (1981), which is largely devoted to demonstrating how basic these and related terms are to the Dido story. Their importance in the Lesbia poems has been much discussed (although this has not prevented *officium* in 75.2 from being translated as 'devotion', contrary to its meaning elsewhere, including in Catullus). The longest poem in which this series of ideas is developed is 76. It begins, *siqua recordanti benefacta priora voluptas est*, where *si* with the indicative does not suggest doubt (Page 1894, on 3.433; Nisbet and Hubbard 1975, on 32.1). Then Catullus calls himself *pius* and mentions his *fides* and Lesbia's *ingratia*, talks about himself as being *ipsa in morte* and says that the gods do not want him to be miserable and will end his agony because they pity wretched people and reward *pietas*. But this poem and the others concerning Lesbia show that the gods do not help him. Similarly, in poem 109 Catullus calls on the gods to bring it about that Lesbia's promise of a *iucundus perpetuus amor* is sincere and will be fulfilled (cf. 30.4,11-12).

Vergil, writing a narrative of a love affair, could make these assertions and this situation objectively real. His lover really is *ipsa in morte* and the reader sees the *benefacta* she recalls and the manifestations of her trust in the gods' benevolence, pity and morality (as will be demonstrated), along with their indifference to fulfilling that trust. The reader even hears the beloved acknowledging her *benefacta* in glowing terms and assuring her that the gods will reward her *pietas* (1.597-605). In showing these phenomena as actual events, the Dido episode was in the tradition of Roman mythological love stories, which will be discussed.

The descriptions of disillusionment, anguish and desperation have always been regarded as the most memorable and greatest of Catullus' poems. When "he describes in [Poem] 64 Lesbia's desertion of him in epic terms" (Putnam 1961.170), it is devoted to Ariadne's agony. And Propertius 1.1, which is the first extant programmatic exposition of love after Catullus' poems, is also concerned completely with its pains. Similarly, 'the very heart of the *Metamorphoses*' is Ovid's "preferred theme, amatory *pathos* ... the anguish of human passion" (Otis 1970.166). That is natural for a culture which was extremely melancholy and lachrymose (Farron 1988) and so regarded even those involved in a mutually satisfying love as miserable (*ibid.*) and pathos as the core of literature.

Vergil integrated the Dido episode as well as he could into the *Aeneid*'s plot. In this, its greatest episode, Aeneas had to be involved. But he could not be the lover. It is he who must leave and, in accordance with the ideal which Vergil admired even more than his contemporaries, the lover must die. So Aeneas is the beloved and could not be the focus of interest and sympathy, as he is in Books 2 and 3. This must have seemed perfectly natural because, as I will demonstrate, in narratives of mythical love affairs the lover was nearly always a woman deserted by her beloved, and he was usually the leader of her country's enemies. Vergil used this pattern to integrate the Dido episode into the *Aeneid*'s plot. The lover is the founder of Rome's historical arch-enemy, and her rival, for which the beloved leaves her, is Italy and the future Rome. Thus, along with her wishes that Aeneas be miserable and without love, she wishes that he not enjoy Italy and that it be made miserable by the Punic Wars, the most traumatic experience in Rome's history. This desire to integrate a love story into the political plot partially explains Aeneas saying of Italy *hic amor* (4.347; cf. *pulchrum Latium* in 4.432). He certainly gives not the slightest indication of loving Italy anywhere else in the first five books.

The basic elements in Catullus' Lesbia poems are important ingredients in all the amatory literature of Vergil's time. So Propertius says (2.32.45-6) that Cynthia cannot be blamed for doing what Lesbia did. Of course, emphasis sometimes falls more on one element, sometimes more on another; for instance, self-delusion in Tibullus. Also, some are more specified; for instance, the hidden, isolated place for the lovers' meeting is often a cave, as in *Aeneid* 4 (e.g. Hor. *Carm.* 1.5.3; Prop. 3.13.33ff.; Ov. *Her.* 15.137ff., *Ars Am.* 2.623; cf. Verg. *Ecl.* 9.41-2). Moreover, reactions differ; for example, it was normal to be concerned about one's reputation and, therefore, bothered by gossip about the affair, as Dido is but not Catullus (Saylor 1986.76; Prop. 3.25.1-2; Tib. 1.4.83-4; Ov. *Am.* 3.1.17-22; cf. Prop. 1.5.25-6). Furthermore, the Lesbia poems are few and short; they omit several basic amatory elements. These will now be mentioned.

At approximately the time that Vergil began the *Aeneid* Propertius published his first book of poems. It was read in *toto foro* (2.24.1-2, cf. 26.22; 4.7.78). Graffiti from Pompeii show that Propertius was just as popular there as he had been at Rome, as were the other Roman love poets (Farron 1983.93 notes 25,26,28; Gigante 1979.185-221). The first poem is programmatic, setting forth the essence of his love. Many of its elements are also found in the Lesbia poems. The poet introduces himself in the first line as *miser* and in the second as *contactum*, which "combines the associations of two meanings ... 'hit' by a missile, and 'infected' by a disease" (Camps 1961, *ad loc.*; cf. *Aen.* 4.1-2 and *passim*). He goes on to compare himself to Milanion, who was wounded by a club (13-14) and *amens errabat* (11, cf. *Aen.* 4.68-73), thus manifesting "the typical *inertia* of the elegiac lover" (Cairns 1974. 98). However, Milanion's *preces et benefacta* (16, which involved rescuing his beloved in distress) helped him in love, whereas Propertius', like Catullus' and Dido's, do not (17-18).

Propertius 1.1 also emphasizes some common basic aspects of love which are mentioned only in passing in the Lesbia poems. Catullus describes himself as *vesanus*, which is obviously an appropriate description (cf. *sana* in 83.4). Propertius says he is *non sanus* (26), just as Dido is *male sana* (4.8), lives *nullo consilio* (6) and describes his love as *furor* (7). *Furor* and its related nouns, adjectives and verbs are applied sixteen times to Dido, more than twice as much as to any other character in the *Aeneid* (Farron 1985.621; cf. Saylor 1986.73-4; Pease 1935.92-3). Also, Propertius elaborates on and makes specific Catullus' suggestion of hostile gods in the same way Vergil does. He summarizes his condition as *adversos cogor habere deos* (8); mentions Venus and *Amor* as the agents of his torture, in contrast with those *quibus facili deus annuit aure* (31-4);

and in lines 3-6, *improbus Amor* is parallel with Cynthia (1-2) as the cause of his condition, the first of whose attributes is his broken pride (cf. *Aen.* 4.412-14).

Propertius 1.1 also contains elements of love which were very common but not mentioned in the Lesbia poems. One is the lover showing his desperation by resorting to a magician, who claims to have miraculous power over nature, to win the beloved back, even though the lover does not believe this will work (Camps 1961, on 1.19). This "preoccupation with magic in connexion with love ... becomes something of a parable bringing home the deadliness of love" (Papanghelis 1987.202). It was very common in the erotic poetry of Vergil's time, as it had been in Hellenistic erotic poetry (Papanghelis 1987.39-41), whence Vergil adapted *Eclogue* 8.64-108, which also ends by casting doubt on the magic's efficacy. Another attribute of love is that *in me nostra Venus noctes exercet amaras* (33). *Amarae noctes* often described the sleepless nights of lovers (e.g. Prop. 2.17.3-4; 4.3.29; Ov. *Her.* 12.169), and sleeplessness is the first characteristic of love Ovid describes (*Am.* 1.2.1-4). It plagues Dido from the beginning of Book 4(5) on (e.g. 80-5) and is the setting of an extremely powerful speech (529-32). There her *insomnia* is emphatically contrasted with the normal sleep of others. Propertius does the same with his sleeplessness (31-3). However, although Propertius depicts himself as different and isolated, he appeals in desperation to his friends for help (25-6), as Dido does to Anna.

That love of this nature was not merely a literary convention but was common in life as clear from the attacks on it by contemporaries like Cicero and Lucretius. The latter's constant practice, rooted in Epicurean epistemology, was to describe what he sees and to appeal to his readers to confirm it from their own perceptions. Indicative of this is that he uses forms of *video* two hundred and eighteen times. So he introduces the main section of his description of romantic love with *Haec Venus est nobis* (4.1058), which Smith (1942, *ad loc.*) aptly translates as "this is sexual love as we know it". Lucretius then (1061) addressed the reader as a lover (*ames*). He says that even in a stable and successful love (1141-2) the lover is wounded (1048-55,1068-70,1120) by Venus (1052), sees the loved one and hears her name when she is absent (1061-2), is insane with frenzy (*furor*: 1069,1117; *rabies*:1083,1117; cf. 1075), burns with love (1077, 1086-7,1090,1116; cf. 1098-1100,

1199), gives his loved one luxurious, exotic, gifts (1123-30), loses his property and good name (1123-4, 1129), ignores his obligations (1124), idly wastes his time (1136), suffers from a guilty conscience (1135) and is constantly suspicious for no reason (1137-40, which might be abbreviated as *omnia tuta timens (Aen.* 4.298; cf. Ov. *Her.* 19.109; Prop. 2.34.19-20)). So lovers are *miseri*, as opposed to the *sani* (1075-6, cf. 1067,1096). Those involved in an unsuccessful love are also *miseri* (1159,1179) because they deceive themselves about their loved ones (1151-70) and "often cry as an excluded lover [*exclusus amator*]" before their loved one's door (1177-9). Interestingly, even when Lucretius gives the alternative, of which he approves (1278-87), a love that is not caused by 'Venus' arrows' but by long association and habit, one falls in love by 'light but frequent blows' and so 'dissolves [*labascit*]'. Every aspect of love which Lucretius attacks as an important experience occurs in the erotic poetry of Vergil's time, including the Dido episode. The only one which Vergil does not represent exactly is that Dido is never a weeping *exclusa amatrix*. That would have been literarily gauche. Instead, *miserrima fletus fert refertque soror* (4.437-8). The reason that the representation and analysis of this type of love were done so well and were so popular was that it was a vital experience of the poets, and they wrote for 'similar' lovers (Farron 1983.86; Wheeler 1910; Prop. 3.3.19-20; cf. Ov. *Am.* 1.15.27-8). Similarly, Sappo's φαίνεταί μοι (31 LP) seems to us to be wildly exaggerated. But when 'Longinus' quotes it, he says (*Subl.* 10.1-3), "Sappho always takes the emotions that accompany the madness of love from those which occur in real life [ἐκ τῆς ἀληθείας αὐτῆς]" and "all such things occur to lovers" (cf. Plut. *Demetr.* 38.4; Apul. *Met.* 10.2; cf. Plut. *Mor.* 763A).

It is because the Dido episode was formed by the pattern of love which the ancient Greeks and Romans experienced and wrote about that interest and sympathy are focused completely on Dido, a fact which modern critics either try to deny or explain as contributing to the *Aeneid*'s meaning and message. The ancients distinguished sharply between the ἐραστής and ἐρώμενος. Sometimes the love was mutual. Even then, as Lucretius observed, it was a cause of misery; and for it to have the intense pathos the ancients craved in serious literature further suffering was usually added by occurrences extraneous to the love, as in Vergil's Orpheus and Eurydice and Nisus and Euryalus. But the major love story of the *Aeneid* had to be in the pattern of the great loves of literature, in which the pathos and tragedy was inherent in the one-sidedness of the passion. This one-sidedness was reflected in the concentration of interest and sympathy completely on the lover. In personal poetry that was the author. So in Sappho's tremendously admired and universally experienced φαίνεταί μοι

> We do not know who the girl is, who the man is, or where or when the incident took place. All Sappho's energy and all our attention are focused on her own violent sensations ... The poem begins, 'He *seems* to me', and the long recital of the poet's agonised sensations ends, 'I *seem* to myself.' ...we are not to know what really happened but how she felt. (Jenkyns 1982.17; his italics)

Similarly, in Catullus 64 "not one word is said of the feelings of Theseus and in the Argonautica we are only told that Jason felt love enter his heart from the love of Medea. His emotions are nowhere described or further mentioned" (De Witt 1907.27).

The same focus of interest is obvious in Latin personal amatory poetry. The only attributes and actions of the beloved which are mentioned are those that are causes or indications of the lover's feelings: his love, pleasure (which is rare), jealousy, hatred and suffering. That is very obvious in Vergil's *Eclogues* 2, 8 and 10, the shorter descriptions of love in the other *Eclogues* and Tibullus' poems to and about Delia and Nemesis. In the case of the Lesbia poems the lack of interest in the beloved is sometimes obscured by the reader unconsciously filling out Catullus' poems with what he knows about the historical Clodia. Catullus himself says remarkably little about Lesbia. Indicative is poem 86, where, to provide his reason for loving her, he says she is very beautiful and has *omnis Veneres*. But he gives no specific description of her, in contrast with Quintia, who is described in the same poem. Catullus' lack of interest in portraying Lesbia is in sharp contrast with his penchant for depicting the mannerisms and character traits of people in his *vers de société*.

Excluding Ovid's *Amores*, which partially play with the pattern of love, the only exception to this principle of total concentration on the lover seems to be Propertius' poems to and about Cynthia. But the reason is that Propertius gives a much fuller description of an affair than his contemporaries, so the loved one's actions and attributes which cause or indicate the lover's feelings are more numerous. Thus, Cynthia made Propertius love him not only by her beauty but also by her talents and accomplishments. Her imperious jealousy was also intended primarily to characterise him. On some occasions it indicates his hope that his love is reciprocated. As Griffin observes (1985.122) (his citation of Catullus 82 should be 83), "the elegists hope for the marks of passion", which consist mainly of the mistress displaying "jealousy, anger, loss of color". For, *in amore haec omnia insunt vitia: iniuriae, suspiciones, inimicitiae, indutiae, bellum* (Ter. *Eun.* 59-61). On many occasions the Roman elegists advised lovers to cause quarrels because anger increased love (Lier 1914.36-7), "but usually lovers ... had no need for these instructions, for they attacked each other on their own impulse"; and often hatred was interpreted as a sign of love (Lier. 37-8). This is explicit in Propertius 3.8 and Tibullus 1.6.69-72 (see Murgatroyd 1980, *ad loc.*). On other occasions Cynthia's rage causes misery (e.g. 2.29.31-42); or her anger provides Propertius with the masochistic pleasure of being a *servus amoris*, a role which he and the other elegists relished. So in 1.7.6-12 he says that all the reputation and the fame he wants is *servire dolori cogor et aetatis tempora dura queri* and *iniustas saepe tulisse minas* (cf., e.g., 1.4.3-4,1.5). This often made him a *supplex*, which he and his contemporaries regarded as a typical situation of a lover (Pichon 1902.271). (Cf. *Aen.* 4.412-14.)

The longest description of Cynthia's jealousy is in 4.7. There she seems to be the lover, swearing that she was faithful and accusing Propertius of *perfidia* and *ingratia*. However, in the next poem her jealousy is again typical of a loved one. She is being unfaithful, as she often is (4.8.16,27). Propertius in revenge tries to be unfaithful but cannot. Her savage, brutal jealousy makes her beautiful to Propertius and he accepts his servility. These two poems must be put in context. The end of the affair had been proclaimed in 3.25 in the typical manner, with prayers for the loved one's future misery and lack of love. But "he who says too often 'I do not love' is in love" and "he who finished an affair with hatred either still is in love or will end his misery painfully" (Ov. *Rem. Am.* 648,657-8). So in lines 135-47 of the introductory poem to book 4 Propertius summarizes his adult life and work as writing *elegos, fallax opus* and being totally, inescapably dominated by his beloved, who makes him miserable by being unfaithful and, as Aeneas with Dido, *eludit palmas*. Poem 4.7 shows that her domination does not end with her death.

Very different from Cynthia's jealousy is that of the woman in 2.20. It is truly pathetic. In 1.1 Cynthia is emphatically named as the object of Propertius' all-consuming, agonizing love, and in 4.1.140 *una puella* has the effect described in lines 135-47. In 2.20 the woman is the lover and Propertius the beloved. She is the *supplex* (33), just as Propertius often is to Cynthia. He did not *temere* begin to be her lover (35-6). That makes him like Lucretius' ideal unromantic lover (4.1278-87), as opposed to the invariable manner in which romantic love begins, *ut vidi, ut perii* (see Fordyce 1961, on 64.86). The woman, like Dido, cries and cries and *insana* calls on the gods about the loved one's *fraus* and *fides* (1-5). Propertius, like Aeneas, swears he will not forget her (28). Her qualities are the opposite of Cynthia's and other loved ones' (20-25): *servitium mite, ianua mollis, nec mihi muneribus nox ulla est empta beatis* (as opposed to 2.8.11,16.17-18,23.8, etc.)

This focus of interest and sympathy on the lover, as opposed to the beloved, also characterizes descriptions of love affairs in which the poet is not involved. A typical example is Horace's *Ode* 1.5. Quinn points out (1984.130) that this is "the first love poem in the collection" and cites examples to show that "the theme is a frequent one in Horace's love poetry: the battle of the sexes as waged between unequal partners". In the first line *gracilis* evokes "the fragility of the boy and the risk he runs of being crushed by an experience beyond the strength of his emotions or understanding" (Quinn 1963.67); and *multa ... in rosa* was "a traditional symbol of luxurious living; the boy, i.e., has spared no expense" (Quinn 1984, *ad loc.*); just as Dido and other lovers give luxurious gifts. *Perfusus* in line two shows the extreme care the lover has taken with his appearance (Nisbet and Hubbard 1975, *ad loc.*; cf. *Aen.* 4.137-9). Lines five to twelve begin with *heu*, "introducing a reaction of pity" (Quinn 1984, *ad loc.*). They contain the typical actions, situation and feelings of lovers: *quotiens fidem mutatosque deos flebit ... qui nunc te credulus ... semper vacuam, semper amabilem sperat, nescius aurae fallacis. Miseri quibus ... nites.* (*Nescius* is a basic characteristic of Dido too: Farron 1989.108-9.) Also significant is *insolens* in line eight. Quinn (1963.71-2) points out that it can indicate the boy's shocked surprise at his first troubled affair, but "the commonest meaning of the word" is 'presumptuous': "The boy is presumptuous in supposing he has any claim on Pyrrha or the gods".

E. *The Relation of the Dido-Aeneas Episode to Ancient Mythological Love Poetry*

By far the most common type of love affair narrated by Vergil's contemporaries in which they were not involved was of mythical characters. In these "the names famous ... are almost exclusively those of women" (De Witt 1907.27). So Purser (*apud* Palmer 1898. xi,xv-xvi) observes that Ovid's making "the heroines the centrepoint of interest" in his *Heroides* was part of a long tradition, going back through Catullus to the Alexandrians, Greek tragedy and Homer (as the Romans interpreted him). ("In [Greek] tragedy *eros* affects women most strongly": Stanford 1983.37.) And Heinze (1915.133,118) points out that Vergil's depiction of Dido's words, feelings, suicide, etc. had many antecedents among women lovers in Hellenistic poetry. Lyne (1978.33-4) observes that the author of the *Ciris*' "preference ... to put the spotlight upon his heroine, in particular upon her emotions and emotional crises ... and ... actively to involve our feelings with the girl and her crises ... probably reflects the general preference of neoteric epyllion". He also ascribes to that source "the space he devotes (e.g.) to Scylla *furens* (163-90), to the long 'nurse scene' (206-385), and to Scylla's lament (404-58) — to direct speech generally". Lyne later observes basic parallels, which are 'widely accepted', not only with epyllia but with Apollonius' *Argonautica*, whose influence on the Dido episode was profound, and the Dido episode itself (36,39, on lines 404-58). The parallels with *Aeneid* 4 are indeed obvious, with Anna as the 'nurse' (although there is also a real nurse), and the fact that it has a higher proportion of direct speech than any other book in the *Aeneid* except six (Pease 1935, on 9). (And much of the direct speech in Book 6 has nothing to do with the characters' interactions.) Lyne ascribes these parallels to copying and adaption, but much of it stems from the overall orientation of Roman and Hellenistic literary sensitivities.

Griffin (1985.137-41) explains this literary orientation by the fact that "the myths offered an inexhuastible supply of passionate and suffering heroines". For, "mythology provided an alternative to the prosaic world of Rome ... The beautiful ladies of myth ... really could be passionate ... living for love and dying for it, carried by it into ecstatic joy or utter despair". A good example, which is not among those Griffin cites, is Propertius 1.15, where he mentions passionate mythological women who suffered for love (9-22) in contrast with Cynthia's indifference, displayed, like Horace's Pyrrha's, by her concern with her hair.

Another reason for the passionate mythological lover nearly always being a woman is suggested by the poem Tibullus chose for the beginning of his first book. "Throughout the poem there is a contrast with the soldier" (Murgatroyd 1980.48). The contrast between the lover and soldier was, of course, very common in Roman love poetry. Tibullus characterizes the soldier as someone who goes on long journeys, leaving his mistress to cry for him (1-6,51-56). This was an obviously rich source for pathos, and was often used (Murgatroyd 1980, on 1.2.65-6). It was so appealing to Vergil that he tried to use it for a male lover left by a woman going off on military service, but the result was unintelligibility (*Ecl.* 10.44-9, cf. 22–3). Similarly, the first three stanzas of Catullus 11 are ineptly related with the rest of the poem, as has been recognized by the unconvincing attempts to make poetic sense of them. Their ineptitude can be explained by the point I am making. The full force of the contrast they create would be achieved by the beloved going off to these places, leaving the flower, in the last stanza, whose existence and destruction were unnoticed by him. But in that case the beloved would have to be a man. In poem 45 Catullus expresses the male lover's devotion by *Acmen mavolt quam Syrias Britanniasque* (21-2) and has him say, *ni te perdite amo atque amare porro/omnes sum adsidue paratus annos/quantum qui pote plurimum perire,/solus in Libya Indiaque ...veniam obvius leoni* (3-7). Here the very common expression 'die for love' is made more real: May I really die if I do not die for love. The implied opposition is between dying for love, that is being totally absorbed in it and completely committed to it, and leaving for distant, exotic places. Acme is never associated with distant places because Catullus did not consider that to be an option possible for a woman.

In the *Erotic Sufferings* by Vergil's teacher, Parthenius, the predominance of women as the lovers is not as overwhelming as in Latin poetry. By my analysis, in the heterosexual stories a woman is the lover, which usually means the sufferer, on thirteen occasions, a man on seven and nine of the loves are mutual. Especially relevant for the Dido story are number two, in which the man sails off, leaving the women tearfully clutching his possessions, and numbers 21 and 22, where a woman helps the leader of her country's enemies in return for a promise of marriage, but is treated cruelly by him afterwards. In number 5 a woman also helps the enemies' leader because she loves him.

Catullus depicts two mythological lovers. Both are women. In 68.73-86,105-118, in a lover's typical self-delusion (as Tibullus is when he says Delia will cry if he leaves), he compares Lesbia to Laodamia *flagrans amore* and her suffering because Protesilaus (like Aeneas) had to leave to fulfil his patriotic-military duty, *quo tibi tum casu, pulcherrima Laodamia, ereptum est vita dulcius atque anima coniugium* (105-7). The verbal influence of the Ariadne story on the Dido episode has been frequently observed. Probably no work of literature had as thorough and direct an impact on it. Some of the more significant parallels are that she is introduced as *indomitos in corde gerens Ariadna furores* (54, cf. 94); which makes her like a Bacchante (61, cf. *Aen.* 4. 301-3) because she *deserta in sola miseram se cernat harena* (57, cf. *Aen.* 4.330,466-8, etc.). (She is also *misera* in 119, 140 and 196.) At first sight of the beloved she *cuncto concepit corpore flammam* (86,91-3), at which time she was secure and happy in her home (87-90). But her destructive love was also caused by Venus and Cupid (71-2,94-8). Then Catullus, like Vergil, narrates the lover's rescue of the beloved when he is in peril (105-15; *nam* in 105 shows that Theseus' achievement resulted from Ariadne's prayers in 103-4: Konstan 1977.41). Ariadne begins her speech by calling Theseus *perfide* twice (132-3, cf. 174) and accusing him of *periuria* (135) and lack of pity (136-8). The *promissa* he violated were of marriage, which is a constant complaint of hers, although a formal marriage was impossible (Konstan 1977.75,77). She brings up against him that *te in medio versantem turbine leti eripui* (149-50). Then she says, also like Dido, *utinam ne ... Cnosia Cecropiae tetigissent litora puppes* (171-2) and that now, in contrast to her happiness and security when he came, she has nowhere to turn since, because of her love, her own people hate her (177-83). She ends by talking about herself as being on the verge of death (187-91, cf. 130) and praying for his future misery by being bereft of his loved ones, as he had deserted her (192-201). As in the depiction of all genuine love stories, interest and sympathy are focused completely on the lover's passion and especially the suffering it causes her. The beloved's only function is to produce these.

Vergil was far from alone in his fascination with Catullus' Ariadne. Just as Catullus used her to represent his experience with

Lesbia, so Lygdamus (Tib. 3.6.39-52) cites *Catullus'* Ariadne's weeping at her beloved's *periuria* and *ingratia* as an analogue to his experience.

Propertius' longest treatments of passionate, suffering women are poems three and four of Book 4. The similarities between Arethusa in the former and Dido are numerous and striking. She writes while 'dying' (6). The cause of her death was her marriage (13-14, cf. *Aen.* 4.169-72), because her beloved left her for distant lands (7-10) in fulfilment of his patriotic-military duty (63-9). She asks indignantly, *haecne marita fides?* (11). She weaves Tyrian clothing for him (18,33-4), cannot sleep (31-2), kisses his *relicta arma* (30), performs religious rites (57-62) and invokes the *foedera lecti* (69). In 4.4 Tarpeia, like Dido, *obstipuit* at first sight of the beloved (19-21), hopes to have children by him (55), assumes he will marry her (82, cf. 90), talks about her marriage bed (62), is the victim of the gods, who *condit in ossa faces* (68-70,85-6) and dies because she helps her country's arch-enemy.

In Propertius 4.4.39-42 Tarpeia compares herself to Scylla and Ariadne, who suffered because they helped their country's enemy. That is also the situation of several of Parthenius' lovers, Medea and Dido. Indeed, Parthenius wrote about Scylla in his *Metamorphoses* (in pages 23-4 of Martini's Teubner text of *Mythographi Graeci*, II.1, *Supplem.*); and Ovid mentions Dido and Scylla among women who suffered for love (*Rem. Am.* 57-68) and has Medea say that Scylla should have killed her and Jason because *debuit ingratis Scylla nocere viris* (*Her.* 12.124). In his *Metamorphoses* 8.101-142 Scylla's lament has many similarities to Dido's speeches in Book 4. For example, she says that she is *deserta* and must remain so since, because of her love, her own people now hate her (113-16) and that his mother was distant, cruel places (120-2) because of his *ingratia* (135). And Scylla's story was told by many other Roman authors (Coleman 1977, on 6.74ff.; Lyne 1978, on 54).

The longest extant version is the *Ciris*. Its overall similarities with the Dido episode and other mythological love stories have been mentioned. Among the specific similarities are that Scylla was seized by *furor* at the first sight of the beloved (130-2); drank fire into her veins and *furor* into her bones (163-4); was like a Bacchante (165-7); constantly tried, day and night, to catch sight of him (171-6); had no more concern for her normal activities

(177-9); thought of herself and talked of herself as dying (182, 267,277,406); mentioned many former suitors (411-13); claimed that her beloved promised marriage, although she may have deluded herself (Lyne 1978, on 187). Also "there is nothing *at all* on the confrontation of Minos and Scylla after the event" (*ibid.*, on 386-458, Lyne's italics). Interest and sympathy are focused on the lover's agony. The beloved's function is to motivate it. And Scylla is constantly described as *infelix* (71,155,167,190,318, 402,517) and *miser* (187,234,254,482,508,530). Scylla also resembles Dido in that she is a victim of the gods (Lyne 1978, on 156-7) and of her devoted and loving confidante, who convinces her that her moral scruples are misguided (335-9).

The *Ciris* also illustrates the basic feeling of Vergil's culture that if an act is motivated by love, that is more important than any immorality involved. As was demonstrated, in the Nisus-Euryalus episode and elsewhere in Vergil's works erotic motivation completely obliterates any immoralities and makes the lover unqualifiedly admirable or at least sympathetic. That is not true in the *Ciris*. Scylla is introduced as *impia* (48, cf. 219) and *scelerata* (52). However, although "at 48-50 ... the metamorphosis is explicitly announced as Scylla's punishment ... Amphitrite ... clearly sees it as a kindness ... [and] in 204-5 the metamorphoses ... are described ... as an *honour.* cf. too 522" (Lyne 1978.9-10, Lyne's italics). Furthermore, as Lyne observes (on 188-9, cf. on 190), "The poet throws his emotional weight behind the sympathetic interpretation of Scylla's action (*sive illa ignorans*) — and sympathetically leaves the plausible interpretation ... unspoken." And most importantly, he "put the spotlight on ... her [Scylla's] emotions and emotional crises ... [and tried] to involve our feelings with the girl and her crises" (Lyne 1978.33).

Ovid's *Metamorphoses* is full of love stories in the basic, canonical pattern being discussed. When Lyne points out the similarities between the *Ciris* and neoteic epyllia, Vergil's Dido and the *Argonautica*, he also mentions "the technique of many episodes in Ovid's *Metamorphoses*" (1978. 34n1, cf. on 404-58). And when Griffin observes that "the myths offered an inexhaustible supply of passionate and suffering heroines"; he says, "It is not without deliberate intention that such extensive use has been made here of the *Metamorphoses*" (1985.137). Very many of its stories have specific resemblances to the Dido episode; for instance, the lover kissing and crying on the *nota vestis* of the beloved before suicide (4.117); or,

> The Scylla/Claucus/Circe episode bears a remarkable similarity to the story of Aeneas and Dido: in both, strangers come by sea asking the ruler of the place, a woman, for help; they are offered love by the woman; they ultimately reject the woman and leave because of their dedication to another purpose; and the woman ... turns her hostility, in one case, against another woman, in another, against herself. (Ellsworth 1986.30)

The most concentrated compendium of the stories of passionate mythological women is, of course, Ovid's *Heroides* 1-15. All are letters by women to men who have left them. I pointed out while discussing ancient treatments of Vergil's Dido episode how accurately *Heroides* 7 reflected it. It is, therefore, significant how typical *Heroides* 7 is of the *Heroides* in general, with their constant emphasis on the lover dying without the beloved and accusations of *perfidia* and *periuria*. Of special relevance are Phyllis' claim of *iura, fides ... commissaque dextera dextrae ... promissus ... Hymnenaeus* (2.31-4) and her reminder that she refitted her beloved's smashed ships (45-6), welcomed him, gave him many gifts and her kingdom (107-14); Hypsipyle's claim of *cunubialia iura* (6.41) and her reminder that she received her beloved in her city (55); Ariadne's recollection of her *officia* (10.124); and Medea's accusation of *ingratia* (12.124).

F. Benefacta *and Betrayal as a Source of Pathos for Dido and Other Ancient Lovers*

This pervasive pattern in Roman mythological love stories of the woman, who is the lover, helping her beloved in distress, being deserted by him and complaining about it was also popular in Greek literature, beginning with *Odyssey* 5.130-36. It was basic in Euripides' *Medea* (e.g. 476-89) and Apollonius' *Argonautica* (e.g. 4.360-68,1031-41), whose influence on the Dido episode was profound. Furthermore, these stories were very popular in Pompeian wall paintings. (For the desertion of Ariadne see Schefold 1957. 367 and Farron 1983.87.) The question imposes itself: why? Sullivan (1976.92,100) shows that Propertius' love for Cynthia, and the literary love affairs of his contemporaries, follows a pattern of love observed by Sigmund Freud, among whose basic attributes is "a desire to 'rescue' the beloved". Sullivan thinks that "the most striking manifestation ... is ... poem 2.26 (*Vidi te in somnis fracta, mea vita, carina*)". That is one possible explanation. But I think more important is the ancient craving for pathos in literature. Cicero in *De Inventione* 1.106-109 lists sixteen *loci communes* to arouse pity (106) and tears (109). As he says later (2.4), he drew his precepts from a wide range of sources; and anyone familiar with ancient rhetorical theory and practice has frequently seen these sixteen *loci*. All are used in the *Aeneid*, most of them prominently and often. Several are used for Dido; for instance, one and two: *quibus in bonis fuerint et nunc in malis ostenditur* and *in tempora tribuitur per quem quibus in malis fuerint et sint et futuri sint demonstratur*. (For the ninth see Servius on 4.659.) For the question under consideration, numbers four, six and thirteen are especially relevant: *res turpes et humiles et illiberales proferuntur, et indigna esse ... fortuna pristina, honore, <u>beneficiis</u> quae passi perpessurive sunt; praeter spem in miseriis demonstratur esse, et, cum aliquid exspectaret, non modo id non adeptus esse, sed in summas miserias incidisse* and *cum indignatione conquerimur quod ab eis a quibus minime conveniat male tractemur ... amicis quibus benigne fecerimus, quos adiutores fore putarimus*.

While I was trying to explain why mythological lovers are overwhelmingly women, I cited Tibullus' imagining a woman crying because her beloved left her as a rich source of pathos. Her situation is much more pathetic if he leaves her after she saved him and gave him valuable help. Even in the rare case of the beloved taking her with him after being helped, as Jason does with Medea, a woman was in constant danger of being deserted. By far the most common type of help was given to the leader of the woman's country's arch-enemy because that shows the full depth of her love, which *omnia vincit*, and greatly increases her *benefacta* and so her agony and indignation at his *ingratia*. When discussing the parallels between Catullus' Lesbia poems and the Dido episode, I pointed out that Catullus and Dido use political terms (*benefacta, officia, fides, gratia,* etc.) to express what their loved ones owed but did not give them. The prevalence of this pattern of mythological lovers helping their loved ones to a political goal and then being rejected by them could be a cause. To the mythological heroines, as to Catullus in 76.1-2, *recordanti benefacta priora voluptas est*. That certainly includes Ariadne, whose relationship with Theseus clearly mirrors in many ways how Catullus saw his relationship with Lesbia (Wiseman 1985. 175-8; Putnam 1961).

The lover's betrayal of her country and with it her family was used for another source of intense pathos. It could cause Cicero's tenth *locus communis* for arousing pity: *inopia, infirmitas, solitudo demonstratur*. So Dido says to Aeneas, who is the founder of the country which will be her country's arch-enemy and destroyer, that because of her love for him she now has nowhere to turn since her own Tyrians hate her (4.320-3). Here again Vergil was using a very common motif in mythological love stories. Euripides (*Medea* 502-8), Apollonius (*Argon.* 4.378-80,1031-41), Ennius (*Scaenica* 276-7, Vahlen²), Ovid (*Her.* 12.109-13) and Seneca (*Medea* 451-60) have Medea say to Jason that by rescuing and helping him because of love she betrayed her family and country and so has nowhere to go if he deserts her. And in *Heroides* 17. 226-32 Helen uses this situation of Medea as a reason for rejecting Paris' offer to run off with him. Catullus (64.180-1, cf. 150-3,117-23) and Ovid (*Her.* 10.63-72) have Ariadne say the same to Theseus.

The test of the validity of a hypothesis is that it explains the phenomena in question more plausibly than other hypotheses. Konstan (1977.41) points out that Catullus introduces Theseus' victory over the Minotaur with *nam* (64.105), which indicates it is not a result of his virtues and courage but of Ariadne's prayers, which were motivated by her love. He explains that as contributing to the 'message' of poem 64: an indictment of Theseus and through him of Rome. Vergil also greatly emphasized Dido's *benefacta* to Aeneas. Those scholars who have tried to explain this also relate it to the portrayal of Aeneas and of Rome. For example, Horsfall (1986.14-15) ascribes the fact that in *Aeneid* 1.599 Aeneas and his men are *omnium egenos*, whereas in most stories he was permitted to take treasure from Troy, to Vergil's desire that he not incur 'the suspicion of treason'. Austin in the introduction to his edition of Book 1 (1971.xvii-xviii) points out that in that book "Vergil draws all our sympathy to her" (i.e. Dido) and in Book 4 "the sympathy ... deepens continually, until grief for her dominates all else". He asks about Vergil, "Why did he take such pains to draw her so? Why did he invent that strartling offer of common citizenship between Carthage and Rome?" He offers two tentative answers: "Dido is a woman whose highmindedness and honour match the most exacting Roman ideal ... a woman worthy of Aeneas" and "to show the intensity of Aeneas' personal sacrifice in obeying the will of the gods". I ask the reader to judge between the plausibility of these explanations and mine.

G. *Guilty Conscience as a Source of Pathos for Dido and Other Characters in the* Aeneid *and in Ancient Literature*

My approach can also explain another basic ingredient of the Dido episode more plausibly than any other. Of the utmost importance to Dido is the obligation she feels to Sychaeus never to remarry. As Servius Danielis and Donatus pointed out (on 4.9), Dido begins her first speech to Anna *suspense et pedetemptim* and *per longos verborum circulos* because of her *pudor*. When she does mention her *pudor* with regard to Sychaeus (24-9) it is to pray that she die before violating it. Austin (1955) observes in his notes on these lines that *optem* in line 24 is 'much stronger' than *velim* because it 'marks an ambition', that *pudor* means 'virtually "conscience"' and that the use of the indicative mood in line 27 "made the pledge more vivid". Donatus and Servius pointed out that she cries in line 30 because she thinks of Sychaeus and *quod urgebatur efficere quod animo respuente damnaverat*. When she tells Aeneas she will die, one of her reasons is *exstinctus pudor* (322). We then learn (457-9) that she *templum coniugis antiqui miro ... honore colebat, velleribus niveis et festa fronde revinctum*. As Page observes (1894, *ad loc.*), citing 3.64, what made this *mirus* was that altars of the Manes were usually *caeruleis maestae vittis atraque cupresso*. So Dido "honoured him, not with signs of gloom and death, but with signs of joy and life as being, though dead, her heart's still living lord". In 547 she says to herself, *quin morere ut merita es* because *non servata fides cineri promissa Sychaeo* (552).

The importance of this feeling of Dido's has been recognized; for example, "the ideal ... of her one marriage to Sychaeus is the key factor in her tragedy" (G. Williams 1958.23). Typical explanations of her failure to fulfil it are that it shows that her death is 'poetically justified' (Heinze 1915.125), that she has faults (Austin 1955.xiii) and that this fault "foreshadows the perfidy of her people ... [and] places in sharp relief the irresistibility of Aeneas' noble nature" (Phinney 1964-5.359, cf. 357). So it proves that Vergil did not intend for his readers to side with her against Aeneas (e.g. Pease 1935.38-9). These critics (cf. Austin 1971, on 344) assume that the Romans felt strongly that widows should not remarry and that this ideal was especially important for Augustus' moral reforms (e.g. Heinze, 126). That is the view of most critics. However, it is an example of the documentary fallacy, a fallacy which is probably so common because of the empathy great literature produces. Although Dido says of herself, *morere ut merita es*, Vergil says in his own person that she *merita nec morte peribat* (696). Moreover, as Monti (1981.55) observes, "only Dido condemns remarriage. It offends ... no one else". Indeed, the last line of her last appearance (6.474) confirms Anna's argument in 4.34.

Moreover, as has been frequently observed, remarriage of both men and women was extrememly common and routine at Rome, and that included Augustus and his family (e.g. Conway 1921.155-7; Bailey 1965.265; Luck 1959.14). Indeed, in the passage that is probably most frequently cited to prove that not remarrying was regarded as a virtue (Livy 10.23), Livy says that the practice that only a woman *uni viro nupta* could sacrifice in the temples of Pudicitia *in oblivionem venit*. This subject has been studied exhaustively by M. Humbert in *Le Remariage à Rome* (1972). He demonstrates that there was no *prescription générale ... excluant des dévotions matronales les femmes remariées* (32), that the few cultic privileges for *univirae* did not imply *réprobation quelconque à l'égard des femmes remarieés* (57), that epitaphs praising widows for not remarrying were very rare and there it was *estimé ... sous la forme indirecte d'un désir* (73, cf. 75,109), that many epitaphs show an easier acceptance of remarriage than we have (104-8) and remarried women are often described as endowed with *pudicitia* and *castitas* (102-3), that this attitude prevailed throughout *l'époque historique* (111ff.), that Augustus, following Republican precedents, tried to make remarriage a patriotic obligation enforced by legal rewards and punishments (138-60) and *les conceptions romaines du mariage ne sont pas heurtées ... par le devoir imposé aux veufs de se remarier* (171). So, *les secondes unions ne sont pas des unions de second rang; le remariage est un phénomène très fréquent*, which *n'exclut pas la* fides *à l'égard du premier conjoint* (179). Indeed, *les secondes noces ... garantir la prospérité de l'Etat* and *la législation d'Auguste développa cette conception* (180).

So why did Vergil make Dido's horror of remarriage so important? My answer, of course, is primarily to increase pathos. For, *nihil est miserius quam animus hominis conscius* (Plaut. *Mostell.* 544). Vergil was frequently not satisfied with the objectively extremely pathetic situations he contrived for his characters and heightened their pathos with an intense feeling of guilt, even when there was no reason for it. This guilt was often, as Dido's, felt for violating an obligation to those dear to them. I will illustrate this briefly with Aeneas' major adversaries in the second half of the *Aeneid*: Turnus, Mezentius, Amata and Latinus. The first three, like Dido, feel so guilty that they think they deserve death. In 10.673-86, after having been tricked into following an image of Aeneas away from the battle, Turnus calls his desertion of his men a *nefas*, prays for death and tries to commit suicide three times. In 12.638-49 and 666 7, after having been removed again from the heart of the battle by a supernatural intervention, Turnus feels *ingens pudor*, blames himself for the death of his men, including Murranus, *quo non superat mihi carior alter* and resolves to die. As for Mezentius, although he had been rendered *inutilis* (10.794) by a wound, he blames his son's death on his cowardice (10.846-9), suddenly and unexpectedly feels guilt for his *crimen* against his people, to whom *debueram poenas* and *omnis per mortis animam sontem ipse dedissem* (851-4), and resolves to die (855-6). In 870-1 he feels *ingens pudor* for his son's death. He tells Aeneas he comes *moriturus* (881) for it and *iugulo ... haud inscius accipit ensem* (907). Amata *subito mentem turbata dolore,/se causam clamat* [of Turnus' death] *crimenque caputque malorum, multaque per maestum demens effata furorem* (12.599-601) and hangs herself (602-3). As R. Williams observes (1973, on 600), "the violence of Amata's outburst is emphasized by the fierce alliteration of *c* and *q* ... the unusual trochaic break in both fourth and fifth feet ... and the vivid use of *crimen* ('the guilty one') and *caput* ('source')". Vergil calls hanging an *informe letum* (603). It was a very rare form of suicide because it meant the corpse could not be buried (Voisin 1979.259-60). It had not been the method of her suicide in earlier versions (*ibid.* 263). Latinus also feels tremendous guilt for violating an obligation to those dear to him even though objectively he is innocent. When his city is attacked, he *multa ... se incusat, qui non acceperit ultro ... Aenean* (11.471-2). In 12.30-36 he blames the many deaths his people have suffered on the fact that *vincla omnia rupi; promissam eripui genero, arma impia sumpsi*. Yet, he had immediately and gladly acknowledged Aeneas as his fated son-in-law and been very generous to him (7.255-85), and he had stood fast against his wife's ravings (7.373-4) and the ravings of all his people as long as was possible (7.586-600).

No critic I know of has recognized this constant occurrence of causeless guilt. For instance, just as most scholars think Dido's agonizing guilt at violating her loyalty to Sychaeus was motivated by an actually existing moral code, so the two critics whose observations on Amata I cite (Williams 1973, on 600 and 603; Voisin 1979.262) assume that her guilt was justified, even though its cause, Turnus' death, had not occured. They also attribute the method of her death to Vergil's dislike for her. (*L'humanité de Virgile, sa pitié ... n'existent pas pour Amata.*) They ignore the tremendous pathos of his description of her guilty feelings, which her means of suicide reinforces. Similarly, G. Williams (1983.176-7) desperately tries to find an objective cause for Arruns' feeling of guilt.

Vergil was far from unique in his use of causeless guilt. For instance, in the *Phoenissae* Seneca has Oedipus wish he had the courage to kill himself, because *totus nocens sum* and his heart is *tot scelerum capax* (155-81). Antigone tells him that no *culpa* touched his heart, he is *innocens* (203-5), which is manifestly true. But that does not deter him from raving about his hideous crimes, hoping for the death he deserves and even blaming his sons' crimes on himself (216-53,305-6,328-47). Jocasta also expresses a powerful feeling of guilt for her and her sons' crimes (363-9), although she realizes that *error invitos adhuc fecit nocentes, omne Fortunae fuit peccantis in nos crimen* (451-3). Concerning Oedipus, she says, that *scelere ... nullo nocens* he blinded himself for an *error* (538-40), yet in his judgement *erroris quoque poenae petuntur* (554-5).

As Brown demonstrates (1987, on 1135), "the theme of conscience is widespread in ancient literature". In the form of guilt to loved ones it was used to increase pathos from the *Iliad* on. Helen's guilty conscience is basic to Homer's portrayal of her character (Farron 1979.16-22). In 3.240-44 she says that Castor and Polydeuces may not be among the Greeks because they fear the shame and reproach that attach to her. As scholia b and T observe on line 242, "by accusing herself she wins pity". In 18.82 Achilles says that he killed Patroclus (translating ἀπόλλυμι by its primary meaning in Homer and elsewhere). Scholia b and T characterize this as περιπαθῶς πάνυ.

Feelings of guilt were especially common among lovers. When Lucretius describes 'love as we know it' (4.1058), one of its components is *conscius ... animus se ... remordet* (1135). Often this guilt is felt towards the beloved. So Tibullus regards as a typical activity of lovers weeping because they have cursed or beaten their women (2.5.101-4; 1.10.53-6; cf. Ov. *Am.* 1.7). Frequently, as in the *Aeneid*, the guilt is causeless. For example, in poem 1.5.5-6 Tibullus asks that he be deservedly burned and tortured, although the rest of the poem shows that he was the victim. Similarly, Propertius usually shows that he is Cynthia's victim, but he often says he is suffering deservedly for what he did to her (e.g. 1.17.1-2). In 4.8.64-6 he says Cynthia viciously beat and bit him, *praecipueque oculos, qui meruere, ferit*. But in fact he had neither heard Phyllis and Teia singing to him nor seen their bared breasts because he was thinking about Cynthia (47-8), and he resorted to them only because of her infidelity (27). Ovid's Deianira says four times to herself, *inpia, quid dubitas, Deianira, mori?* (*Her* 9.145-64), although she was tricked by Nessus (159-63). Seneca's Deianira realizes that what she did was an *error*, but says, *scelera quae quisquam ausus est hic error vincet*, so she prays for torture in Hades (*Her. Oet.* 938-82); and in answer to Hyllus' argument that she is innocent (982-3), she tells him to kill her for her *nefas* (984-91).

However, in mythological love stories by far the most common cause of guilt is, like Dido's, the lover's feeling that she betrayed members of her family by her affair. While discussing lovers' *benefacta* I mentioned that this type of betrayal increased her pathos by showing her total devotion to the beloved and leaving her alone when the lover deserts her. I provided as examples several versions of the Scylla, Ariadne and Medea stories. Even more intense pathos was provided by her guilt for betraying her family. Often, as Dido, the lover says she deserves to die because of it. When Propertius' Tarpeia weeps for her wound of love (4.4.29-30) and expresses her excruciating guilt for betraying her obligations (36,43-6), she mentions as parallel cases *patrios Scyllam saevisse capillos* (39) and *prodita ... fraterni cornua monstri* (41). Ovid has Scylla say, *exige poenas, Nise pater! ... nam, fateor, merui et sum digna perire* (*Met.* 8.125-7), and in *Ciris* 277 she says *merui ... mortem*. Catullus' Ariadne talks about her brutality to her 'brother' (180-1) and says she chose Theseus over her 'brother', *pro quo* she will be torn apart by animals and not buried (150-3; cf. Ov. *Her.* 10.69-70).

Ovid's Medea (*Her.* 12.109-126) says she should be killed because of her betrayal of her father, mother, sister and brother (cf. Eur. *Med.* 483, 502-8). But it was Apollonius' Medea who, along with Catullus' Ariadne, had the greatest influence on Vergil's

Dido. Her dream (3.627-32) crystallizes her conflict between her father and lover and her 'measureless pain' at her parents' anger because she chose the latter. Again in 3.742-3 αἰδώς seized her for helping Jason in opposition to her father. She talks and thinks constantly about her terrible crime (3.891,1161-2; 4.412-13) because "with ἀναίδητος will I left my country ... home and even my parents, which are the most important things to me" (4.360-2). Like Dido (4.321-5), she exclaims that when her αἰδώς and glory are gone she wants to die (3.785-800). Her disgrace there consists in choosing love over her home and parents, and the death she wants is by hanging. We saw in reference to Amata that this shows the depth of her feelings of guilt. Again in 4.373-81 Medea says she deserves to die for what she did to her family. Indeed, she nearly commits suicide twice (3.806-9; 4.20-21).

This type of conflict was a basic ingredient of most Roman and Greek amatory literature. Konstan (1977.79) observed that the "conflict between filial piety and the demands of love [was] the central theme of new comedy, especially as Terence handled the genre". And Monti (1981) provides many examples to show that Dido's guilt towards Sychaeus was part of a pervasive pattern. Among them is that Parthenius' collection is (51)

> for the most part a series of accounts in which the indulgence of a passion has to be balanced against the infringement of some positive moral prescription ... from the sphere of family relations - to name just some, incest (*narr.* 5,11,13,17,31,33), marriage (*narr.* 4, 23, 25, 27, 37), the bond of guest-friendship (*narr.* 1, 2, 3, 4, 18) and the obligations to father and fatherland (*narr.* 5, 9, 21, 22).

(Indeed, Parthenius' Alcinoe (27) feels such guilt because she left her husband and children for her lover that she commits suicide.) Monti also notes that in "love stories told by Hellensitic poets whose tradition is represented in Parthenius' collection ... the choice of indulging a passion ... must be invested with an air of immorality and even criminality" (52).

As in the case of Dido, many literary lovers exaggerate the extent of their immorality to family members caused by their love or feel guilty to family members for no objective reason at all. For example, when Helen speculates that her affair with Paris has brought such shame on Castor and Polydeucus that they avoid the other Greeks, she calls them "full brothers, whom the same mother bore" (3.238), which they were not in most versions.

Similarly, Ariadne speaks of her brutality to her 'brother', even though the Minotaur was only her half-brother. When discussing the portrayal of Scylla in the *Ciris*, I quoted Lyne's observation (1978, on 188-9, cf. on 190), "The poet throws his emotional weight behind the sympathetic interpretation of Scylla's action (*sive illa ignorans*) — and sympathetically leaves the plausible explanation ... unspoken." So she is not a villain but *heu tamen infelix* (190). Yet, though she betrayed her country *ignara*, she still considers herself worthy of her punishment (416-20) and says she deserves to die (277). Another example of this phenomenon is Europa in lines 25 to 76 of Horace's *Ode* 3.27. Typically, nearly all of it is devoted to her expression of misery because of the affair. The main cause of her misery is her guilt towards her father. Her lament begins, *pater, o relictum filiae nomen pietasque ... levis una mors est virginum culpae ... ploro turpe commissum*' (34-9). Then she prays for death (49-56) and imagines her father urging her, *vilis Europe ... quid mori cessas?* (57-8). The first form of suicide she imagines her father urging is by hanging (58-60). Yet Horace's introduction established her innocence: *sic et Europe niveum doloso credidit tauro latus* (25-6).

The use of causeless guilt to increase the misery of love was also prominent in Attic tragedies. For instance, in Euripides' *Hippolytus*, lines 239-49 Phaedra keeps talking about how miserable she is and wishes she would die because of her αἰδώς, which comes close to meaning a guilty conscience (Barrett 1966, on 244). In 401 she says she has resolved to die (cf. 407-9). After Hippolytus' frenzied denunciation of women and Phaedra for plotting evil (649-50), which she did not do, she says, "I have found justice" (672). Phaedra's innocence, indeed her nobility, is explicitly stated by Artemis in lines 1300-5, and the "judgement here is certainly the poet's own" (Barrett 1966, on 1305).

As the scholium on *Hippolytus* 386 observes, Phaedra is tortured by the conflict between love and αἰδώς, which "she regards ... as her own great failing" (Barrett 1966, on 385-6). We have seen that the same conflict tortures Apollonius' Medea. Pichon (1902.243) supplies very many examples in the love poetry of Vergil's time of *pudor amori contrarius*. For, *non veniunt in idem pudor atque amor* (Ov. *Her.* 15.121; cf. *Am.* 1.2.32). In the *Hippolytus*, Euripides used Phaedra's interaction with the nurse to bring out the full force of this agonizing conflict with powerful dramatic effect. Such interactions were also very common in Hellenistic love stories (Pease 1935.496-7; Heinze 1915.127n2). Vergil probably could not have imagined his love story without such a conflict and such an interaction. Dido was too mature and independent to have tormentingly powerful feelings of loyalty to her parents, and her brother had done her great harm. So the source of this conflict and cause of the interaction was her feeling of loyalty to Sychaeus never to remarry. Vergil probably got the idea of her confidante being her sister rather than a nurse from Apollonius. Phinney (1964-5.358) observed that "the struggle in Medea's soul between love and honour ... forms the basis of the third book of the *Argonautica*", that "this struggle is most graphically portrayed" by her interaction with her sister and that there are many parallels between that and the Dido-Anna scene. I have pointed out how moving Dido's conversation with Anna about *pudor* and love is and that that was appreciated by the ancient commentators. It was also appreciated by Seneca, who borrowed extensively from Dido and Anna's interaction for his nurse and Phaedra (Fantham 1975.2), whose feelings of guilt are also extremely prominent.

So far I have explained the pathos Vergil derived from Dido's feeling that she was obliged never to remarry by the struggles and guilty conscience it caused. It also heightened her pathos in three other ways. First, it added to what she sacrificed in order to have an affair with Aeneas, along with her reputation, affection of her people and security of her city. So his leaving was all the more painful. She gave up everything that was important to her and was left with nothing, not even a clear conscience. (For many lovers in ancient literature, like Medea, Ariadne and Scylla, the struggle and guilty conscience concerned performing their *benefacta* for their loved ones, thus increasing their significance.) Second, the ancient Greeks and Romans constantly defined pity as being felt for those who suffer undeservedly (Schrijvers 1978.485-6; cf. 487-90; Isoc. 16.48). (Cf. *immerita* of Troy in *Aen.* 3.1–2.) Third, they knew that *is probus est quem paenitet quam probus sit et frugi bonae; quis ipsus sibi satis placet, nec probus est nec frugi bonae* (Plaut. *Trin.* 320-1).

These must be the main reasons for the constant emphasis in the *Aeneid* and throughout ancient Greek and Latin literature on characters tormented by a guilty conscience, while the author informs the reader that they have done nothing wrong, indeed, that their actions are often praiseworthy. They explain why Vergil said that Dido died *non merita*, while she says she *merita* to die for violating an obligation which no other character in the *Aeneid*, nor any of Vergil's contemporaries, thought existed.

There may be two other reasons, besides pathos, why Vergil invented Dido's feeling of obligation to Sychaeus never to remarry and made it so important. The first is that it really was a characteristic of certain types of love, which Freud analyzed and which constantly recur in modern as well as ancient literature, that "there must be an injured third party, whether a husband or a fiancé ... who has right of possession' (Sullivan 1976.91-2). The second is,

> The upper class of Roman society ... notoriously played fast and loose with marriage ... Amid their [the love poets'] praise of free love they sometimes praise true Roman conjugal union ... the magnetic pull of the idea of true marriage can be detected in many other places too: in the loving depiction of the power of women's love, and of heroines who, on being abandoned, did not just turn easily to a new union with another man but preferred to languish and even to die ... they were not cool creatures who could marry and divorce at will, but emotional and passionate. (Griffin 1985.140-1)

Vergil's Dido displays this passionate loyalty and the misery it causes her not only in relation to Aeneas but to Sychaeus also.

H. *The Purpose of the Dido Episode is Not to Praise or Blame Aeneas*

The concentration of interest and sympathy on Dido in her relationship with Aeneas is ignored by most critics who argue that her purpose is to create a contrast which highlights Aeneas' (and Rome's) character, attitudes and ideals, and/or to be a test he must overcome, and/or to show how much he must sacrifice and suffer to fulfil his mission. (The last interpretaton is also popular among proponents of the 'two voices' approach.) It is not surprising that so many sensitive critics ignore the manifest orientation of the Dido episode. As I have pointed out, many scholars ignore 9.446-9 in interpreting the Nisus-Euryalus episode and so argue that its purpose is to show their completely negative character traits. If Vergil had not included 9.446-9 that would nearly certainly be the most popular, and maybe the only, explanation of that episode's function. The other indications of Vergil's admiration for them, which are now usually ignored, would be nearly universally ignored, as is the description of Dido's death as *nec merita* (4.696). There would be no need to devise easily refutable justifications for their gratuitous brutality towards the Rutulians and their neglect of their vitally important mission, or find patriotic virtues or moral ambiguities. Most of the critics who recognize the importance of their love would probably assert that it was an aspect of their reprehensible characters to put that before their socially important mission, that death was a fitting punishment and that that shows that Aeneas was right to leave Dido.

I will consider three arguments against interpreting the Dido episode from her point of view. The first two are used by many scholars and appear prominently in Pease's edition of Book 4 (1935), which is a monumental compendium of orthodox opinions as well as of facts and parallel passages. He says (36-7), "Dido exhibits not a few characteristics of the typical Epicurean, and as such stands in sharp contrast to the commonly observed Stoicism of Aeneas" (cf.8-9,47). He later qualifies that by stating that Aeneas is the "obvious representative of Stoicism ... as ... one progressing toward ... perfection" (43). He cites (43-4n322) many scholars who have interpreted Aeneas as a Stoic. The only one he quotes at length is Arnold, whose *Roman Stoicism* (1911) was often used as the major authority for Aeneas' Stoicism into the 1930's. Arnold asserts (389-91), "Much modern criticism revolts against the character of Aeneas [in Book 4, because] it is without sympathy for Stoic ethics". But Arnold concedes that "after the death of Brutus Stoicism ceases for a while to play a prominent part in Roman history" and that Vergil "like so many of his contemporaries ... holds aloof from formal adherence to the sect".

The last advocate of the Stoic Aeneas whom Pease cites is Bowra, calling his article, "Aeneas and the Stoic Ideal" (*G & R* 3, 1933), 'a very full treatment'. He cites it several times later and quotes it at length in note 365 (49). It was to supersede Arnold's book as the most frequently cited Stoic defense of Aeneas (e.g. R. Williams 1967.34-5). Bowra, like Arnold, insists that only by realising that 'Aeneas is a Stoic' can he be understood (11). This takes the bizarre form of his being the opposite of a Stoic in the first five books of the *Aeneid*. Bowra demonstrates that very ably (11-14), *especially for Book 4* ('the climax of his lack of wisdom': 12). Bowra's explanation is that in *Aeneid* 1-5 Aeneas is being tested.

"The moment he arrives on Italian soil ... he is by Stoic notions both wise and brave" (16). However, Bowra then shows (16-19), again very ably, that even there Aeneas often acts in a totally un-Stoic manner. He admits (18) that "this involved indeed an inconsitency with his earlier treatment of Aeneas as a Stoic type" (which consisted in being the opposite of a Stoic).

Furthermore, Bowra's specific proofs for his thesis are extremely meagre. One (10-11) is the *City of God* 9.4, where Augustine says that in 4.449 Aeneas is like a Stoic. But Bowra shows that in Book 4 Aeneas is totally un-Stoic. The other proof is two occurrences of Stoicism's 'technical terminology' (14-15): *exercite* (3.182, 5.725) and *praecepi* (6.105), both of which were common, ordinary Latin words.

However, it is clear from the first two pages of Bowra's article (8-9) that he resorts to a Stoic explanation out of desperation. He begins by stating that current opinion, like that of the nineteenth century, "has no word of praise of Aeneas". He agrees that Aeneas is 'lifeless', as opposed to the other characters in the *Aeneid*. So "with Aeneas ... [Vergil] was more deeply concerned with some end outside the delineation of character". Bowra rejects the normal interpretation that "this end was ... 'Morality! Aeneas was the ideal Roman'" since Aeneas "is a coward, a muddler, and a seducer". Because of his refusal to distort the evidence of Vergil's text Bowra was forced to resort to his Stoic thesis to salvage Aeneas as a hero and then concede the bizarre contortions that this thesis involves in practice. Bowra's honesty is especially striking in his last paragraph:

> Or perhaps the poet in Virgil knew what he was doing, and by making us feel qualms about Aeneas he gave us his own inmost feelings about the heroic type ... it is always the enemies of Rome with whom he makes us sympathize ... Dido ... Turnus.

Such amazing contortions are very common in the arguments of those scholars who insist that the *Aeneid* must be judged by the Stoic standards of Vergil's time. For example, Fowler (1919.43-5) explains that 'a Roman would understand' why Aeneas was a better husband for Lavinia than Turnus because "in Virgil's contrast of his two heroes we may assuredly see the influence of Roman Stoicism" (for which he quotes Arnold as support) and because "in Roman social life ... the passion of love was the illegitimate thing". But he concedes, "In the parallel case of Dido we may be sure that his [Vergil's] heart was with the queen, and there are signs in this book [12] that it was with Turnus too." So Vergil's heart was like ours, and unlike the hearts of his unromantic Stoic contemporaries.

The Stoic interpretation of the *Aeneid* is no longer as pervasive as it once was, although it still has many adherents. Much more popular is the view that Aeneas is interesting and sympathetic in Book 4 because he loves Dido intensely and suffers greatly at leaving her. This is argued by Pease on pages 45 to 47. His argument has been cited frequently (e.g. Otis 1963.266n1). Pease asserts, "to suppose ... that the pleasure of the Trojan sailors at leaving Carthage represented the feelings of their commander is to expunge from the *Aeneid* and from the character of the ancestor of the Roman state ... much of its deepest significance". But when Mercury first tells Aeneas to leave Carthage, he *ardet abire* (281). After Mercury's second admonition, Aeneas says, *iterum paremus ovantes* (576-7). Then (581) his *ardor* is communicated to his men (*idem omnis simul ardor habet*).

Pease argues that in addition to one 'clear declaration' Aeneas makes of his feelings for Dido in Book 4 (which is discussed below), there are "hints [of them] which Virgil, with characteristic parsimony, has thrown out". But Vergil is hardly parsimonious when describing Dido's feelings for Aeneas, or Aeneas' for Troy. His first words in the epic are a wish that he had died at Troy, and when he sees depictions of the Trojan War at Carthage he cries constantly and profusely. In Book 2 his reaction to the instructions of Hector's spirit to flee Troy and pursue his divinely ordained mission across the sea is very different from his reaction to similar instructions by Mercury in Book 4. He immediately and completely forgets them, and he constantly mentions his intention to die in Troy (314-17,353,359,431-4). In the beginning of book 3 (10) he leaves Troy weeping, in contrast to the way he leaves Carthage in the beginning of Book 5 (cf. 3.492-505). Again, in the only speech Aeneas makes to Dido in Book 4, he says that he has no choice, he must go to Italy; but if the Fates allowed him to lead his life as he wanted (and one naturally expects him to tell Dido he would stay with her; but he says) *urbem Troianam ... colerem* (341-2). It is this speech which Pease cites as Aeneas' 'clear declaration' of his feelings for Dido (cf. Austin 1955.xv).

Vergil emphasized Aeneas' love and devotion to Troy because

that was crucial in arousing pathos for its destruction and Aeneas' exile. But it would have detracted from the pathos of the Dido episode for Aeneas to show emotions for her, as will be explained.

These considerations are ignored also by those critics who recognize that Aeneas is much less prominent and interesting than Dido and argue that Vergil used that to highlight his virtues in contrast with Dido and show how much he must sacrifice for his mission. For example, Feeney, in an influential article (1983), states that the coldness of Aeneas' only speech to Dido in Book 4 (333-61), which infuriates Dido and innumerable readers, is to be explained by the fact that "the lassitude which so many readers sense in Aeneas' speeches is ... a restrained disavowal of the fervour which animates the language of the other characters when they seek to influence their listeners" (217). This is admirable since there is in the *Aeneid* a "mistrust of powerful language" (216) and Aeneas' speech in Book 4 implicitly criticizes Dido's speech by showing that in the latter "powerful language distorts reality ... and it exploits ungovernably the emotions of speaker and audience" (216). His speech also displays his "special burden. He must ... repress emotions he does feel, and generally behave not as a free individual, but as the incorporation of a society's needs" (218).

As for his 'burden', the refutation of Pease which I used above is applicable. In most of Book 4 Vergil does not hint at any reluctance in Aeneas to leave Dido and has him manifest extreme insensitivity by telling her that if he were a 'free individual' he would now be at Troy (not with her). Moreover, his earliest actions, chronologically, in the epic are to forget his social duties because of his passionate love for Troy; and the *Aeneid* ends with him acting and speaking *furiis accensus* (12.946) and *fervidus* (951) and doing something which Vergil shows (936-7) serves no social purpose. Furthermore, what infuriates Dido (4.365-70) and most readers is not that Aeneas displays no emotions in presenting arguments, but that he shows no compassion for her suffering.

Most of the above observations are also made by Lyne (1987.161, 165,173). He also demonstrates that there are strong indications in the text that "if Dido had not thought that she was being left by someone callous and unfeeling" her grief would have been much less, might even have been bearable (173-4). He cites and summarizes the many arguments that "Aeneas' comportment and speech are those of a man who has responded to a moral dilemma (love versus duty) [and] exercised moral strength ... Aeneas shows himself ... pretty much the Stoic" (166). Lyne points out some weaknesses in these arguments. Even if Stoic inexpressiveness is demanded here, "earlier in the Dido story, why are we not told that Aeneas uttered feelings ...?" (167). In Book 6 he does show he pities her, tries to console her and "stresses in moving and eloquent terms ... that he wanted to stay" (172); as opposed to his speech in Book 4, where he said he would have preferred to be at Troy. Also, the context of his statement, *nec credere quivi hunc tantum tibi me discessu ferre dolorem*, seems to indicate that had he known, he would have handled his departure differently (174).

Austin (1955), although he argues that "Dido never finds it difficult to let her desires overcome her conscience, but Aeneas' desires are as strong ... [his] conflict was harder than anything that Dido had known ... His hurt is ... as terrible as hers" (xv); nevertheless, begins his discussion by stating about Aeneas, "it is never possible to think of him as any other but the man whom Dido had loved, and who ... had loved Dido" (ix). However, in fact, he was remembered as the man who brutally destroyed her. That is obvious from the many recreations of the Dido episode in which she says that her punishment on him will be his reputation as her destroyer (e.g. Ov. *Her.* 7.63-4; Marlowe, *Dido, Queen of Carthage* 5.1.292-301).

Was the concentration of interest and sympathy on Dido intended to create that reputation and thereby discredit Aeneas and Rome, as many critics, including me, have argued? Or was its purpose to present 'another voice' in contrast to the 'epic voice', as many critics, including Lyne, have argued? Lyne does accept that Aeneas' lack of display of compassion is caused by "his attempt to be the Stoical Roman hero" (176 and *passim*). His argument is that Vergil did not regard this Stoic approach as admirable. He assumes that "the absence [of emotional reaction by Aeneas] must be significant" (167). It, with its consequences, is part of a 'voice' which shows that "we should ... approach the ... imperial attitude of life ... warily and critically" (183). Vergil "is saying something about ... the cost of the Trojan/Roman progress and how it may be repeated", an example of which is the destruction of Dido (200).

I will now advance my own explanantion of Aeneas' conduct to Dido and try to show that Vergil did not intend to make any negative comment about Aeneas. I think that Lyne is very perceptive to see how instrumental in increasing Dido's agony was Aeneas' failure to show, with words, facial expressions or crying and groaning, any compassion, indeed, any understanding of the depth of her suffering (e.g. 4.365-70). But I think that that is its sole purpose. It greatly heightened the pathos of the episode. As we have seen, the Romans were fascinated by the terrible pathos involved in the contrast between the lover, who cares about nothing but his all-consuming passion, sacrifices everything for it and often cannot live when it ends, and the beloved, who regards the affair as a pleasant interlude or a means to an end and leaves it with indifference. So in Horace's *Ode* 1.5 the only action of Pyrrha's is tying back her hair. That is her concern, in horrible contrast to the lover; or Scylla laments that Minos does not pay attention to her lament (*Ciris* 415). This type of pathos was, of course, not restricted to descriptions of love affairs. In the *Georgics* Vergil uses it frequently with regard to the terrible damage farmers cause to living things while they are intent on 'more important' matters and do not notice it. Indeed, he uses this theme to symbolize Orpheus' grief at losing Eurydice (4.511-15).

Catullus also used it to sum up Lesbia's *culpa* (11.22-4), which caused him such unbearable torment. His love was like a flower at the edge of a meadow cut by a plow going past. The agent is a plow not a farmer to emphasize that the farmer did not notice it, presumably because he was intent on considerations that were more important and interesting to him. The cut flower follows Catullus' wish, which is typical of those ending love affairs, that the beloved be miserable and loveless; that is, that she feel the way she made him feel. Partly this is a desire for revenge, but it is more a desire that she feel the type of need he felt for her (cf. *Aen.* 4.383-4) and that at least in retrospect she take their affair seriously (11.21; cf. Prop. 3.25.4; Nisbet and Hubbard 1975. 289-90; Murgatroyd 1980, on 6.77-84; Tib. 1.8.41-48; Ov. *Ars Am.* 3.59-80), in contrast to her bland indifference during it. While discussing Propertius' programmatic first elegy, I observed that among the similarities between him and Dido is that he depicts himself as being isolated, yet he appeals in desperation to his friends for help. In Catullus 11 the flower is at the edge of the field and the rest of the poem is an appeal for help from his friends. But the main purpose of the flower's location is to stress its inconspicuousness to the beloved. That is emphasized by the contrast with the glamorous, exotic and politically-militarily important places in the first three stanzas.

When I was explaining why mythological lovers were nearly all women, I pointed out that that makes it possible for their loved ones to leave them for distant places. That gives concrete embodiment to the psychological distance between them. The loved ones have more interesting, important concerns, completely distinct from their love. I also pointed out that the first three stanzas of Catullus 11 are ineptly related to the rest of the poem because Catullus tried to adapt that theme to a situation in which the lover was a man (himself).

In mythological narratives a female lover and her broken (or *pollutus*: *Aen.* 5.6) love really could be left unnoticed by the beloved departing for constrastingly important places, just as the lover really could make tremendous sacrifices, give great *benefacta*, be the victim of the gods and die for love. Vergil used this contrast for his female lover in the *Aeneid*, as did Catullus when he recast his love in a mythological form. The first adjective used of Theseus is *immemor* (64.58). It is emphatically placed at the beginning of its line and is linked with his neglecting his promises (59). In line 123 it is contrasted with his promise to be her husband. Ariadne begins her accusation of him by accusing him of *perfidia* (132-4) because he left her *immemor* (135), where it again is the first word in its line. As Fordyce observes (1961, on 64.58), "*immemor* regularly implies ... indifference to one's obligations". However, its primary meaning is 'forgetful', especially not keeping actively present in one's mind what one should. So Ariadne prays that *quali solam Theseus me mente reliquit,/tali mente, deae, funestet seque suosque* (200-201: i.e. he will not enjoy the love of the rival for whom he left her (cf. *Aen* 4.612-19). Aegeus had told him to keep his instructions *memori ... corde* (231), but *qualem Minoidi luctum/ obtulerat mente immemori, talem ipse recepit* (247-8). His great crime is that her love and agony meant nothing to him. He promised marriage, but was so *immemor* that *nulla ... res potuit crudelis flectere mentis/consilium ... nulla fuit clementia praesto, immite ut nostri vellet miserescere pectus* (135-8).

That is compounded by the fact that he left her *sola* (200). The first adjective used of Ariadne is *deserta*, which begins its line (57). It is followed by *in sola miseram se cernat harena* and in the next line by a contrast with *immemor at iuvenis fugiens*. Her first accusation is that *immemor ... deserto liquisti in litore* (135,133). Not only is he unconcerned with her torment (cf. *Ciris* 415), but no-one else is aware of it either. She laments *nequiquam* to *ignaris ... auris ... quae nullis sensibus auctae* ... (164-6). Similarly in the Dido episode, it is not only Aeneas who is unaware of the intensity of her agony and therefore amazed at her suicide. The same is true of Anna (4.500-2,675 6).

As has been demonstrated, mythological narratives provided a concrete embodiment for clusters of thoughts and feelings which constantly recur in short personal poems. The only occurrence of *immemor* in Catullus' poems besides 64 is in 30, which begins, *Alfene immemor*. There also this accusation involves *perfidia* and *periuria*, but mainly, *iam te nil miseret, dure, tui dulcis amiculi* (2) and *me miserum deseris in malis* (5). It is because *tu oblitus es* that the gods will punish him (11-12).

Catullus had no interest in exculpating Theseus. In his own person he calls Theseus *coniunx* (123) and says he disregarded his promises (59), thus substantiating Ariadne's accusations of *perfidia* and *periurium*. Vergil's primary purpose in narrating the Dido episode was the same as Catullus' and other love poets', to arouse pathos. So the beloved's torment had to be unmitigated. But he tried to exculpate Aeneas as much as possible without lessening Dido's agony. He gave her good reason to think that she and Aeneas are legally married. The very impressive natural and supernatural phenomena in 4.166-8 are those of a wedding raised to a cosmic scale (Serv. Donat., Pease 1935, Austin 1955, *ad loc.*). "Vergil thus makes the wedding ritually correct" (Austin, on 166ff.); and "in everything that he makes Dido say, Virgil shows her, in public and in private, convinced that she is married to Aeneas" (G. Williams 1968.380). Every other character in book 4, human and divine, except Aeneas, also regards them as married (*ibid.* 379-83; Monti 1981.30-31,45-8). But Vergil says in his own person that they were not married (172). Also, although Aeneas shows no hesitation to obey the command to leave Dido (4.281), he does consider how to tell her in a manner and at a time that will cause her as little pain as possible (283-94). That consideration is not shared by other loved ones in mythological narratives or personal love poetry. However, Vergil used Aeneas' delay to increase Dido's misery, by giving her reason to think that he is trying to sneak away without her knowing (305-6), as Theseus did from Ariadne (Catull. 64.55-9). Vergil also gave Aeneas something else which other loved ones do not have, a speech in which he defends himself against the standard accusations made against loved ones: he did not marry, so he is not guilty of *periurium* and *perfidia*; he will always be grateful for her *benefacta*, so he is not guilty of *ingratia*; he did not try to sneak away. However, this speech has been perhaps the most criticized passage in the *Aeneid* because of Aeneas' cold formality, understatements (e.g. *nec me meminisse pigebit Elissae*), bizarrely unnecessary and very cruel statement that if he could do what he wanted he would choose to be at Troy, and especially his lack of display of compassion, or even understanding of the cause of her misery. He attributes it to *invidia* that he will have in Italy what she has in Carthage. This poetic clumsiness was caused by Vergil's desire to exculpate Aeneas without in any way diminishing Dido's torment.

The climax of Aeneas' defense, his strongest argument (R. Williams 1972, on 4.356f.), is that he is being forced to leave by divine compulsion. Here again Vergil had been careful to inform the reader that Aeneas' argument is accurate. As Moskalew (1982. 110) observes, the verbal repetitions in a short interval of Jupiter's commands and Mercury's relay of them is very unusual for Vergil, and then Aeneas echoes Mercury. Also,

> Divinities *per se* appear directly to mortals just four times in the Aeneid — Venus to Aeneas in *Aeneid* 2, Venus to Aeneas in *Aeneid* 8, Iris to Turnus in *Aeneid* 9, and Mercury to Aeneas in *Aeneid* 4 ... the theophany of Mercury is exceptional. In the other cases, Vergil seems much less concerned with detailed descriptions or instructions of the divinities. In Book 4 Mercury dresses before (or for) our eyes ... Vergil also provides a full account of Mercury's journey ... presents to us a series of powerful visual pictures ... The impression of reality is strengthened later by the words of Aeneas ... to Dido (356-359) ... Aeneas is defending himself ... and ... we ... accept his statement as essentially true. (Jones 1987.29-30)

To further impress this divine compulsion on the reader, Vergil has Mercury come again to drive Aeneas from Carthage.

The ancient commentators realized that Vergil was using the gods to exculpate Aeneas (e.g. Donat. on 4.331–2, 361; Serv. on 331,

393; cf. Serv., on 1.2; Donat. in Georgii's Teubner edition, Vol.1, page 2, line 29 - p.3 *l*.6,p.8 *ll*.4-8,p.155 *ll*.26-9).

Divine compulsion was often used to excuse leaving a lover (e.g. Parth. 4). In particular, it had been much used for another national hero who left a lover. As has been observed, Catullus had no interest in exculpating Theseus. But the Athenians did. Plutarch in chapter 20 of his biography of Theseus says that there were many stories about Theseus and Ariadne. "Some say that she hung herself because she was abandoned by Theseus. Others say ... she was abandoned by Theseus because he loved another woman". Plutarch then quotes a line from this version, "Terrible passion distressed him for Aigle ...", and says, "This verse Peisistratus deleted from Hesiod's poems, just as, on the other hand, he inserted into [*Odyssey* 11] ... 'Theseus and Perithous, glorious sons of the gods' in order to please the Athenians." Plutarch also summarizes a version by Paeon in which Theseus put Ariadne ashore at Cyprus, was driven out to sea by a storm and when he returned and learned that she was dead he was very sad. But the most commonly used excuse for his leaving her was divine compulsion, most often in the form of a god driving him away, but sometimes Dionysus seizing her by force. These divine interventions were constantly represented on vase paintings, especially those from Athens in the fifth century B.C. (Webster 1966.26-8); and we have many summaries of literary versions of them (e.g. Apollod. *Epit.* 1.9-10; Diod. 4.4-7; Paus. 9.40.4; cf. the scholium on Theoc. *Id.* 2.45-6). In the former two versions Theseus was so sad at having to leave Ariadne that he forgot to put up the white sail when approaching Athens, thus causing his father's death.

Vergil used divine compulsion not only to excuse Aeneas for leaving Dido but also for not displaying compassion for her, a fact which was appreciated by the ancient commentators (e.g. Serv. Dan. on 4.393,439; Serv. on 4.331; Donat. on 4.331-2). As has been pointed out, the most glaring aspect of Aeneas' speech to Dido is that it shows no compassion and this lack greatly increases Dido's agony. She begins her reply by asserting that Aeneas is the product of "places in the mysterous North to express coldness and cruelty, just as in *G* IV 517f." (Austin 1955, on 366f.) because *num fletu ingemuit nostro? num lumina flexit?/num lacrimas victus dedit ...?* (369-70). But, just as Vergil was careful to defend Aeneas against the accusations of deserting a marriage and trying to sneak away, so he had explained before Aeneas began speaking (331-2), *Ille Iovis monitis immota tenebat lumina et obnixu curam sub corde premebat.* It is noteworthy that these divine orders serve no purpose as far as the plot is concerned. Aeneas could have gone to Italy just as well after expressing and showing pity. But Dido's torment had to be unrelieved, and Vergil wanted an excuse for Aeneas.

Similarly, in lines 425-8 Dido expresses agonized perplexity as to *cur mea dicta negat duras demittere in auris;* where *duras* is emphatic as the first word in its clause, after the caesura. But twelve lines later Vergil informs us, *fata obstant placidasque viri deus obstruit auris;* where *placidas,* which is the first word in its clause, means 'kindly' (Pearce 1968), and *viri* and *deus* are pointedly juxtaposed. That is why Aeneas *nullis ille movetur fletibus aut voces ullas tractabilis audit* (438-9).[2]

The *lacrimae* in line 449 may be Aeneas', or at least include his tears. If they do, that does not relieve Dido's misery since she is unaware of them. In the same way, Dido's accusation of lack of pity began, *num ... ingemuit? Gemitus* was the sound which usually accompanied crying (e.g. 11.150; 10.465). Vergil was careful to have one place in Book 4 where Aeneas *multa gemens magnoque animum labefactus amore* (395; where *amore* is Dido's, as are *curas* and *dolentem,* which end the previous lines). But Vergil was

---

[2] That Aeneas was not moved nor heard anything although *tractabilis* is an example of a verbal phenomenon which Vergil often employed: juxtaposing with a word or clause an attribute (or attributes) of its subject or object which make it incongruous in some way, so 'although' is suggested. Examples in Book 4, where it is especially frequent, are *fraterna caede* (line 21), *germanique minas* (44), *absens absentem auditque videtque* (83), *ardet abire fuga dulcisque relinquere terras* (281), *omnia tuta timens* (298; *tuta* could be object or subject), *frater destruat* (325-26), *aversa tuetur* (362), *nec ... oculis pater aspicit aequis* (372), *sequar atris ignibus absens* (384), *omnibus umbra locis adero* (386), *altae consternunt terram* (433-44), *his, germana, malis oneras* (549), *inluserat advena* (591), *celerabat/ celebrabat anilem* (641), and *sororem sprevisti* (677-78). Similar are *mene fugis* (314, as Dido presents the characteristics of *me* in lines 314-18), *me fraude petebas* (675; the significance of *me* is derived from *germana* earlier in the line); and *inimico a fratre* (656).

Vergil used this phenomenon consciously. A good indication is that *altae consternunt terram* is modelled on *abies consternitur alta* in a famous passage of Ennius' *Annals* (187-91 Vahlen[2]) Vergil added *terram* to bring out the incongruity. But when he imitated that whole passage in 6.179-82 no verbal incongruity was used. And none was used by the other Roman authors who imitated it (Lucan 3.440-41;Silius 10.529-34). All these incongruities contribute to the pathos of someone's situation. (Several will be discussed.)

equally careful to have Dido faint just before this so she cannot witness Aeneas' *gemitus*.

I have pointed out that ancient, medieval and early modern apologists for Aeneas' conduct to Dido used the divine order to leave her, which Vergil provided in Book 4, greatly exaggerated it and contrasted it with his moral obligation to stay at Carthage. However, it was only after Aeneas left, that Vergil could supply most of the material that Aeneas' apologists used, again with great exaggeration (that is, before the recent tendency to use justifications which Vergil did not supply at all, such as Stoic ethics). Basically, he does this by showing that Aeneas, unlike Theseus, was not *immemor*, that Dido's love and suffering did matter to him. A minor example is his looking back at Carthage (5.3; used by Sil. *Pun.* 8.108-11). The most important are in Book 6, lines 455 to 476. There Dido's tragedy has run its course, she is dead and no longer cares what Aeneas thinks or feels. So Vergil could have him cry for her in her presence and speak to her in the way she (and the reader) wanted in Book 4. As Highet (1972.139) observes, "his refutation in Book Four ... sounded legalistic. Here ... Aeneas' opening words mingle surprise and sorrow. The heart of his speech is a passionately sincere declaration ... Then comes a touching ... conclusion: *siste gradum ... quem fugis?*" Lyne points out (1987.165) that Aeneas' speech to Dido in Book 4 is remarkable in that it does not "respond to the despair of a beloved person ... it betrays no compassion" and in that he tells her that "had he been a free agent, he would have stayed at Troy ... surely the natural thing to say here is, even if it is a white lie: 'were I a free agent, I would stay with you'". In Book 6 Aeneas displays compassion and does tell a white lie for her. He swears that *invitus, regina, tuo de litore cessi, sed me iussa deum ... egere*. This, with major exaggerations, has been the primary excuse used by his apologists (e.g. Sil *Pun.* 8.109-111). Defenders of Theseus also depicted him as being driven away from Ariadne unwillingly. They also said he was sad to leave her, as Aeneas here implies he was to leave Dido. Indeed, in one pro-Theseus version his sadness, like Aeneas', occurs when he learns that she is dead.

That is not the way Aeneas' departure is described in Book 4 (281,571-81), nor is it what he said to her. In addition to saying that his first choice would be to be at Troy, he called Italy his *amor* and suggested he felt for it the way Dido felt for Carthage (347-50). He never speaks that way of his Italian future anywhere else. He generally forgets about it, as in Book 2, or regards it as an unfortunate chore (e.g. 3.493-7). Even when in Italy, in Book 6, he constantly becomes emotionally absorbed in personal interests and must be driven forward by the Sibyl (e.g. 37,539; cf. 719-21). In 6.889 Vergil says Anchises *incendit ... animum famae venientis amore.* But in the second half of the epic Aeneas does not call Italy his love either. I have explained Aeneas calling Italy his love in 4.347 by Vergil's desire to fit the Dido episode into the standard pattern of a love affair. He leaves Dido for a rival and her curse is that he not enjoy that rival. More obviously, it increases Dido's misery.

Other important excuses Vergil provided in Book 6 for Aeneas' conduct, which were used by later apologists, were that he did not know his leaving would cause her death and that Aeneas spoke to her with *dulcis amor* (455; cf. Sil. *Pun.* 8.104). That did not suggest the all-consuming passion which the ancients regarded as the essence of true love. That was constantly described as 'bitter-sweet' from Sappho on, with the emphasis on 'bitter'; for instance: (Parth. 23) "Cleonymus was violently stretched on the rack for her, it was not a gentle love he had"; in other words, he was really in love.

I have pointed out that Dryden, like Chaucer, explicitly stated that Vergil supplied divine compulsion as an excuse for Aeneas leaving Dido since otherwise it was inexcusable. He also thought that the main purpose of Aeneas meeting Dido in Book 6 was to excuse his conduct: "there was a fault ... [and] blame ... The poet ... therefore brings the deserting hero and the forsaken lady to meet together in the lower regions, where he excuses himself when 'tis too late; and accordingly she takes no satisfaction" (189 in Ker 1926). That has not been seen by more recent critics. A typical example is Skinner (1983). She rejects two popular interpretations of *Aeneid* 6.455-76: "one fastens upon Dido's culpability, the other stresses the guilt of Aeneas" (12). These oversimplify because there is "a deeper dimension of moral uncertainty and an exquisite but ultimately futile balancing of rights and wrongs" (12). In Book 4, "When he struggles to ... leave ... Dido, he ignores her pain and his own, and conceals his feelings behind a mask of Stoic detachment." But, "Two books later, he is made to calculate the price of his heroically inhuman austerity in terms of its impact upon the life of another" (14). This "draw[s] attention to the ethical dilemma now perceived in what formerly had been thought of as a right and proper, albeit painful, course of action". So in this passage in Book 6, "Vergil deliberately calls into question that general view of events he was at pains to establish earlier ... Aeneas' stern Stoic deportment loses its heroic quality" (16).

An original and, I think, fruitful observation is made by Lyne (1987.167,172-7,180-3). He points out that Vergil has a strong tendency to depict Aeneas showing deep emotions for other characters only when they are dead. He mentions Creusa and Pallas along with Dido. Typically, Lyne assumes that this must be related to a pervasive ethical principle (Stoicism) and be intended to establish a consistent and important character trait and that the results of that character trait must comment on "the Stoical attitude to life and the imperial attitude to life" (183). My explanation of this phenomenon is, naturally, to create pathos. Before explaining how this was done, I will add to Lyne's examples. With three exceptions, which I will discuss, it is only in speeches to characters who are dead that Aeneas displays intense, heartfelt love or affection: Hector (2.279-86), Anchises (5.740-2; 6.697-702; cf. 3.710-15), Deiphobus (6.500-508) and Lausus (10.825-30). One of the three exceptions is Venus (1.405-9). Aeneas speaks to her as she is evaporating from his sight and expresses his agony at not being able to have human contact with her. The same extremely pathetic situation is the basis of his emotional interactions with the other members of his family, except Ascanius, who cannot die in the epic. Of Creusa he says, *maestus ... Creusam nequiquam ingeminans iterumque iterumque vocavi* (2.769-7); and after she speaks he desperately, but *frustra*, tries to grasp her as she evaporates (792-4). The same words are used for Aeneas' interaction with Anchises in 6.697-702, and he expresses his torment at this situation in 5.740-2; as he does at the very similar situation with Dido (6.465-6), the only other person with whom he has a familial relationship. He says to her *quem fugis?*. The same verb is used of Venus (1.406), Creusa (2.793) and Anchises (5.740,742; 6.701). Aeneas' relationship with Pallas and Lausus was not of a nature that would make him desperate to re-establish human contact with them. There the pathos is for the death of youths of promise, both of whom Aeneas addresses as *miserande puer* (10.825; 11.42), and for his helplessness to do for them what he thinks he should. Catullus 101 is very similar (*nequiquam*), as are Meleager's poem in *A.P.* 7.476 and *Iliad*

18.324ff., the beginning of which closely resembles the first part of Aeneas' speech to Pallas. Scholia bT comment on line 333, it is "περιπαθές ... to speak to the dead". Hector and Deiphobus died in the process of Troy's destruction. I have pointed out that Aeneas' love for Troy is the major way Vergil creates pathos for him. The other exceptions, besides Venus, to the rule that Aeneas' speeches which display intense love or affection are to the dead are also in a way ghosts from his Trojan past: Andromache and Helenus (3.313-19,492-505).

The considerations mentioned above indicate that Vergil's purpose in the Aeneas-Dido scene in Book 6 was not only to exculpate Aeneas. It was also to create pathos for him. While discussing Greek tragedies, I summarized Heath's observation (1987.82-8) that modern scholars, working on the assumption that characters must be portrayed consistently, do not see that the centre of 'sympathetic interest' is mobile, shifting from one character to another. I also quoted his illustration that towards the end of the *Antigone*, the 'focus of emotional engagement' moves from Antigone to Creon, who earlier had been portrayed unsympathetically as her persecutor and adversary. When analysing the pathos Vergil created for bereaved parents and for characters suffering from a guilty conscience, I pointed out that he did this with Mezentius. In Book 6, lines 455 to 476, he does this with Aeneas. He also uses this passage to devise as happy an ending for Dido as was possible, once her tragedy was over. Sychaeus *respondet curis aequatque ... amorem*, which Aeneas never did.

It is noteworthy that Catullus 64, whose influence on the Dido episode is obvious and profound, has a much more radical and unprepared shift of sympathetic focus, from Ariadne to Aegeus. Also, in 64.251-264 Catullus devised a happy ending for his pathetic heroine with a loving male partner. That section shows how unimportant not only consistency of character development and story line, but even mood, was for Catullus. As Jenkyns observes about Catullus 64 (1982.91),

> When it opens with a rich evocation of the voyage of the Argo, we do not suspect that ... [it] ... will be ... about the wedding of Peleus and Thetis; when we reach the wedding, we do not anticipate that it will be interrupted by a description of a tapestry occupying more than half the entire piece ... after the jubilation of the marriage ceremony we do not expect the wedding song to be given to the aged and sinister Parcae ...

These observations are part of Jenkyns' attack on critics who ignore the impact of the parts of Catullus 64 in their quest for systematic messages and meanings. Yet even he falls into that trap. He argues (139-40) that because Theseus is depicted sympathetically in lines 81ff and 101ff. the reader is not intended to believe Ariadne's accusations against him.

I. *The Gods in the Dido-Aeneas Episode and in Ancient Amatory Literature*

I have offered explanations for the way Vergil makes Dido and Aeneas behave in the Dido episode. An explanation must now be given for the behaviour of the other major protagonists: the gods and fate. The *Aeneid* begins by announcing that *fatum* drove Aeneas to Italy (Servius on 1.2) and that his purpose is *inferret ... deos Latio* (1.6). In Book 12 (192) Aeneas says his contribution to Italy will be *sacra deosque*. Furthermore, Vergil attributes every important occurrence in the epic to the gods (Heinze 1915.16; Perret 1965.130). If the *Aeneid*'s main purpose is to present a message, the gods must be part of it. That is the way they are always interpreted. Those critics who think Vergil intended to proclaim, define and explain the greatness of Rome interpret the role of the gods accordingly: "The gods in Vergil have a high sense of right and wrong. They are, as Ilioneus reminds Dido (1.543), *memores fandi atque nefandi* (Hahn 1931.17); *Virgile a voulu que son récit des aventures d'Enée symbolisât toute l'aventure romaine et son achèvement en Auguste,* but Aeneas and his men cannot be fully aware of the significance of their adventures so the gods inform the reader of it by their foreknowledge (Perret 1965.132); V. Pöschl, in pages 714 to 715 of his entry in *ANRW* 2.31.2 entitled *Virgil und Augustus* agrees and asserts that Vergil was the greatest and nearly the only Roman theologian.

The application of this outloook to Book 4 usually results in regarding one of its main functions as illustrating "a conflict between belief in a man-centred universe [represented by Dido] and belief in a divinely controlled world [represented by Aeneas]" (R. Williams 1972, on 4.379ff.), Dido's attitude being Epicurean (*ibid.*). For, her attribute of being "skeptical of the intervention of divine beings in human concerns" is one of those by which "Dido exhibits not a few characteristics of the typical

Epicurean, and as such stands in sharp contrast to the ... Stoicism of Aeneas" (Pease 1935.36-7,cf.43). But from her first appearance as *regina ad templum* (1.496), which she built and whose size and lavishness are described in 1.446-93, Dido is constantly depicted as making offerings to the gods, trusting in their benevolence and seeking their guidance.[3] (The only exception, 4.371-87, will be discussed later.) She does this despite losing the man whom she regards as her husband. Let us look, by contrast, at Aeneas' reaction when he loses his wife, which has incomparably less devastating results for him than Dido's loss for her. His own account shows his responsibility. Austin (1966) paraphrases 2.741 as, "I never gave her a thought, lost though she was" (cf. on 743). Yet Aeneas attributes his negligence to a *male numen amicum* (2.735) and says, *quem non incusavi ... deorum* (745; cf.2.402,428,396; 3.2; *pace* Serv. on 2.326). Donatus, who often used ridiculous arguments to exculpate Aeneas of insignificant possible accusations (e.g. on 1.453-6), commented on lines 738-40, *iterum neglegentiam suam fatis adscribit ... omnia autem culpae eius fuerunt*. Aeneas' unfair accusation of the gods for making him lose his wife follows shortly after the gods reminded him of his obligation to her (589-98), led him out of the battle to her (632) and made it possible for him to take her from Troy (673-704; cf.1.382). By contrast, the gods constantly treat Dido with brutal, heartless indifference. They even use her religious piety to hasten her death (4.450-5, where *infelix* as well as *exterrita* is caused by *fatis*).

Many critics have noticed the amorality and sometimes immorality of the gods in the Dido episode and elsewhere in the *Aeneid*. They, like those who think that the gods are thoroughly good, assume that this must be part of a consistent message running through the poem, whether that message is an indictment of the gods (e.g. Austin 1966.xix-xxi) or another 'voice' (e.g. Commager 1981; Lyne 1987.18-19,26-7,84-5,196-7; 35-44,50-3,61-99; cf. Perkell 1986 on the *Georgics*). Some relate the portrayal in the *Aeneid* to the general Roman attitude that the gods and fate were arbitrary, unpredictable and vindictive (e.g. Camps 1969.48-9; Matthaei 1971.13). The tendency of the ancient Greeks and Romans

---

[3] 1.632,731-4;4.56-64 (*principio*), 382 (where "*si* ... with the indicative ... does not imply any doubt ... but the reverse": Page 1894, on 3.433; cf. Nisbet and Hubbard 1975, on 32.1; Norden 1957, on 459),453,509-21 (see Austin 1955, on 521),607-21.

to think that way is obvious not only from their literature but also from their epitaphs (e.g. Lattimore 1942.157-8,183-4). Attacks on divine capriciousness and vindictiveness were also a standard part of orations for the dead (Norden 1957, on 868-71). Significantly, Norden is commenting here on this *di invidi* theme when spoken by Anchises. It is indicative of how much more highly Vergil valued pathos than logic that he had a dead spirit, who is showing the greatness that the gods and fate will grant to Rome, say that they cut short Marcellus' life because they did not want Rome to be too powerful. With similar incongruity the same dead spirit makes another common, pathetic statement: offerings to the dead are useless (885-6; cf. Catull. 101.3-4).

I think Vergil used the commonly accepted arbitrariness, heartlessness, amorality and immorality of the gods to arouse pathos and other emotional responses in the Dido episode and elsewhere, without intending any message. Before demonstrating how he did that, I will show that it was the normal literary practice.

The influence of Greek tragedy on the Dido episode was especially strong, as has been frequently observed (Suerbaum, *ANRW* 2.31.1.pp.134-5, 267-8; Muecke 1983; Heinze 1915.133-8; Pöschl 1978.76). Moreover, the scholia on the *Iliad* "follow closely the lead of Plato and Aristotle" in interpreting it in terms of tragedy (Richardson 1980.270). And those scholia had a profound influence on the composition of the *Aeneid* (Schlunk 1974). Indeed, Vergil explicitly compares Dido to two tormented characters in Greek tragedies (4.469-73). It is significant that the first and maybe the second are from plays by Euripides, perhaps mediated through Roman adaptations, and that both characters are described as being tormented by divinities. Euripides was very adept at using the gods' brutality to create compassion and terror. His lack of interest in portraying the gods systematically is evident from the lack of consensus among scholars who try to deduce his views on them from his plays: *la nature des sentiments religieux d'Euripide varie avec chacun de ses commentateurs* (de Romilly 1961. 126). Heath (1987.49-64) demonstrates that "Euripides' plays ... presuppose internally the world-view of traditional mythology and ... his *dominant* concern in them was ... to exploit the emotive potential of that mythology" (50, Heath's italics) and that it was very common in Greek literature from Homer on for characters to criticise divine cruelty (51). Similarly in many passages in Apollonius' *Argonautica* success depends on respecting and obeying the moral order of Zeus and the other Olympian gods (Lawall 1966. 143-6). But sometimes Zeus brutally punishes humanitarian deeds (*ibid.* 144) and success depends on criminal acts which defy the gods (147).

Let us now look at how the gods are treated in the love poetry of Vergil's contemporaries. First, it should be noted that none of them probably took the gods they mention very seriously as real beings who intervene in human affairs. Horace's renunciation of Epicureanism in *Ode* 1.34 is clearly not serious (Nisbet and Hubbard 1975.377); and, oddly to us, he equates *deus* with *Fortuna*: god's existence is manifested in violent, arbitrary unpredictability. Propertius in 2.6.35-6 mentions the total neglect of the gods and their temples. Significantly, he says the gods deserve this because of their indifference to infidelity. That is the most common view of the gods in Latin love poetry. They do not punish lovers' perjuries (Murgatroyd 1980, on 1.4.21-2) and are cruel (*ibid.* on 1.4.35-6). (In 1.4.35 Tibullus puts this standard complaint, *crudeles divi*, in the mouth of a god, with the same indifference to logic as Vergil showed in Anchises' statements about the gods in *Aeneid* 6.) Especially, "the gods of love were traditionally cruel ... and unconcerned, even amused, by mortals in love" (Murgatroyd 1980, on 1.10.57-8; cf. Leir 1914.17,29-33; Nisbet and Hubbard 1975, on 19.1 (*saeva*); Pease 1935, on 412; Coleman 1977, on 8.43-5 and 10.29-30; Preston 1916.47-8). I have already pointed out these ideas in my discussions of Catullus 76 (with 109), Propertius 1.1, Horace's *Ode* 1.5 and mythological love stories. They are also assumed in Lucretius' contrast between agonizing 'love as we know it', which is caused by a wound inflicted by Venus (4.1048-52), and painless affection, which has no divine causation (1278).

All these common themes were used by Vergil in Damon's song in *Eclogue* 8.17-60, which, despite its short space, contains many basic motifs found in Roman love poetry, including the Dido episode. It introduces the beloved as a *coniunx*, although that is objectively impossible (29-30), and the lover as *indigno ... deceptus amore ... extrema moriens ... hora*, calling on the gods, even though he has not benefited at all from them (18-20). Indeed, the only god who enters the poem's action, Hesperus, does so to help the beloved's marriage (30; see Coleman 1977, on 18 (*deceptus*) and 30).

Yet, she does not believe that any god cares for human affairs (35). The lover fell in love at first sight, which was a *malus error* (41). Approximately one-fifth is devoted to an outburst against *Amor* and Venus (42-50); where *Amor* is twice called *improbus*, as he is in *Aeneid* 4.412 and Propertius 1.1.4-6. It ends with the lover's suicide.

Why were the gods portrayed in this way? One obvious reason is that the Romans felt love to be cruel, painful and destructive, and the gods' behaviour explains this. Indeed, they often spoke of the gods and the forces they represented interchangeably. So Quintilian (*Inst.* 6.3.20) paraphrased *Camenae* in Horace's *Satires* 1.10.44 5 with *natura*. This was especially true of Venus and *Cupido/Amor*. Pichon in pages 61 to 73 of his concordance of the Latin love poets (1902) points out that in very many passages there is no agreement among editors as to whether to print 'Venus', *Cupido* and *Amor* with capital or small letters and tries to offer his own answer for most. He concedes that he cannot decide for some. He does not observe that ancient writers and readers would not have anticipated such a problem and that these gods and their effects were sometimes explicitly linked (e.g. Prop. 1.12, with Enk 1962.169-72). Indeed, from *Odyssey* 22.444-5 on, 'Aphrodite' or 'Venus' sometimes simply meant sexual intercourse or the ability to perform it (Murgatroyd 1980, on 1.5.39-40). Lucretius uses 'Venus' for Love, love and sexual intercourse (4.1048-59, 1073,1172,1200). Undoubtedly, that underlies his contrast between painful love, caused by Venus, and painless affection, without divine causation. He also describes the object of passion as 'Venus' (1071). It was common to speak of the beloved and *Amor/amor* and 'Venus' interchangeably (Pichon 1902.85-6; Plaut. *Bacch*.217; Prop. 1.1.1-4,9.11-14,10.19-20,19.5; 2.10.7-8; Ov. *Am.* 2.18.15-18). So Love, love and the loved one, expressed by the same word, dominated the lover (Nisbet and Hubbard 1975, on 27.14) and caused or were the fire that burned him (Preston 1916.48n73; Tib.3.8.5-6). Thus, the Romans' assumption that love is cruel, painful and destructive partially explains the way they depicted both those gods and those people who caused it. And it is noteworthy that just as Lucretius interchanges Love shooting its traditional arrows with the beloved shooting love (4.1052-4), so in the simile which summarizes Dido's tragedy (4.69-73) Aeneas has this attribute of Love, a fact which Donatus and Servius Danielis pointed out.

Another cause of the portrayal of the gods as being cruel to lovers is that it increased the impression that their suffering was undeserved. I have explained that one of the main reasons why Vergil and other ancient authors constantly portrayed characters as tormented by a guilty conscience although they did nothing wrong was the feeling that pity was aroused by people who suffered undeservedly (Schrijvers 1978.485-90; Isoc.16.48). So Servius and Donatus glossed *indigna morte* in *Aeneid* 6.163 (of Misenus, who was killed by a god for no moral fault) with *miserabilis*. So Vergil introduced the lover in Damon's song in *Eclogue* 8 (18-20) as *indigno ... deceptus amore dum queror et divos, quamquam nil testibus illis profeci ... adloquor* and the lover in *Eclogue* 10 (10) as *indigno ... amore peribat*. The assumption that a lover's undeserved suffering was caused by the gods was so natural that it was made even when there was no indication of divine intervention. An example is Ovid's *Heroides* 5, where the lover, Oenone, writes, *Quis deus opposuit nostris sua numina votis?/Ne tua permaneam, quod mihi crimen obest?/Leniter, ex merito quidquid patiare, ferendum est./ Quae venit indigno poena, dolenda venit* (5-8). But Vergil left no doubt as to the divine causation of Dido's misery, which to the Romans, as opposed to us, meant that she *merita nec morte peribat, sed misera ante diem* (4.696-7). (As was pointed out in my discussion of the theme of the premature death of young people in the *Aeneid*, the last two words were also extremely pathetic.)

However, there are passages in Latin love poetry where the gods, and Venus in particular, are assumed to punish those who mock and lie to lovers (e.g. Tib. 1.2.79-80,6.83-4,8.71-2,9.3-4,19-20; Prop. 2.16.47-56) and where the gods of love are assumed to watch over and protect lovers (e.g. Murgatroyd 1980, on 2.27-8; Tib. 1.5.57-8) or, at least, set them free from a painful love (e.g. Tib. 1.9.81-4). Why did this inconsistency exist? Of course, the ancient Greeks and Romans did not have our interest in religious orthodoxy and consistency. However, the contrast in question usually seems to follow a definite pattern. Ancient authors commonly had characters assert or assume that the gods are or should be moral (e.g. Eur. *Hipp.* 114-20,*Bacch.* 1348), but showed by what happens that they are not (cf. Winterbottom 1989). That is certainly true of the Dido episode (e.g. 1.543,603-5, which will be discussed later). Especially the love poets, in the desperation they depicted themselves as being, frequently expressed the assumption that the gods are concerned and just and invoked them to witness, guard or avenge *fides* (Pichon 1902.129). When discussing Catullus' Lesbia poems as being typical of this genre, I mentioned that in 109 he calls on the gods to bring it about that her promise of a *iucundus perpetuus amor* is sincere and will be fulfilled, and in 76 he says that the gods do not want him to be miserable and will help him because they pity the wretched and reward *pietas*. I also pointed out that the course of the affair, as he describes it, shows that these assumptions and hopes about the gods are not true. (Fordyce (1961) in his note on Catullus 76.17-26 observes its similarity to *Aeneid* 1.603-5.)

Sometimes the love poets realized that the desire for gods who help lovers was wishful thinking (e.g. Ov. *Am.* 3.8.65-6). And when they stepped back from their affairs and viewed them objectively, as in Propertius 1.1, they described the gods as being hostile or, at best, indifferent. They displayed the same knowledge when addressing other lovers. So Propertius in 3.20.1-6 tells a woman that she is *stulta* to trust the *durus* man who left her to make his fortune in Africa and to trust in the gods by whom he swore. And when they portrayed other people's love affairs, like Dido's, they brought out the contrast between the lovers' attitude to the gods and reality. There is a great deal of self-delusion in love. The Roman love poets dwelt on it; for instance, the lover thinking he is married or that the loved one promised marriage even when that is impossible, or resorting to magic in his desperation, or deluding himself about the beloved's appearance (Lucr. 4.1153-69, with Brown 1987 *ad loc.*; Quint. *Inst.* 6.2.6; Farron 1983,93-4n41; Nisbet and Hubbard 1975, on 18.14 (*caecus*) and 19.6 (*purius*)). Similarly, lovers deluded themselves about the gods.

Vergil and other poets used this misplaced trust of lovers in the gods to increase their pathos in several ways. I have observed that the common theme of the lover betraying her country and family and thus leaving herself nowhere to turn when her beloved betrays her fulfils Cicero's tenth *locus communis* for arousing pity and tears (*Inv.* 106-9): *inopia, infirmitas, solitudo demonstratur*. The constant emphasis on the gods' cruelty or indifference to the trusting lovers adds to this. I have also pointed out that the *benefacta* to the beloved in distress fulfils Cicero's fourth, sixth and thirteenth *loci communes*: doing and suffering things unworthy of one's former fortune, rank and good deeds; not only not receiving the reward one expects, but being thrown into great misery and being badly treated by those whom one expected to help. These happen to lovers in their relationship with gods as well as with their loved ones. Indeed, in Catullus 63, where the only participants are the devout human and heartless god, these are used very powerfully, along with Cicero's first means for producing pathos: contrast between past good things and present troubles, which Vergil also uses constantly in the *Aeneid*.

The fact that the trusting lover was *nescius/inscius* of the indifference or hostility of the gods was also used by Vergil's contemporaries for pathetic effects. For example, in Horace's *Ode* 1.5, which I have pointed out is the first love poem in the *Odes* and is typical, he says, *Heu quotiens fidem mutatosque deos flebit et aspera nigris aequora ventis emirabitur insolens, qui nunc te fruitur credulus ... nescius aurae fallacis*. Here the lover's pain will come from the realization that he has been too trusting in two typical objects: the beloved's *fides* and the gods. That the storm at sea will be caused by the gods is evident from the last two lines, *potenti ... maris deo* (or *deae*).

I have observed the similarities between Tarpeia in Propertius 4.4 and Dido: she *obstipuit* at first sight of the beloved (19-21), hopes to have children by him (55), assumes he will marry her (82,cf. 90), talks about her marriage bed (62) and dies because she helps him, her country's arch-enemy. Her death is caused by Jupiter (85-6), and Propertius several times says that she deserved it (17-18,87,89-94 (reading *iniuste*), cf. 1). However, typically, Propertius focuses on her suffering and arouses great sympathy for her. That suffering is caused by the intensity of her love (e.g. 23-8) and her guilty conscience at betraying Vesta (e.g. 36,43-4), for which she compares herself to Scylla and Ariadne (39-42). But Jupiter is indifferent to her suffering (29-30) and Vesta, whom she assumes to be totally good, increases her passion: *nescia vae furiis accubuisse novis, nam Vesta ... culpam alit et plures condit in ossa faces* (68-70).

Vergil emphasized Dido's ignorance of the supernatural forces controlling her affair with Aeneas and used that ignorance to increase greatly her misery. Like Tarpeia, *inscia Dido insidat quantus miserae deus* (1.718-19), where *inscia Dido* is at the end of its line, *miserae* and *deus* are juxtaposed and *deus* is emphasized by ending a sentence before a bucolic diaeresis. *Insido* has military connotations, and throughout the Dido episode she is constantly described in terms of a city being attacked, captured and burned (Newton

1957). That makes her like Troy in Book 2. Another similarity is that Venus describes Cupid's attack on her as a *dolus* (1.673,682, 684, cf. 688). I pointed out while discussing Nisus and Euryalus that the Greek victory in Book 2 is constantly attributed to *doli* and *insidiae* and that the Romans despised such means.

Much more significant for Dido's tragedy is her introduction, *fati nescia Dido* (1.299, also at the end of its line). Vergil tended to introduce characters with a short description, in a seemingly casual manner, which, however, mentions the attributes that will be basic for their significant actions and/or tragedies (Farron 1989). He wanted this introductory description enough to create a logical absurdity. Dido is called *fati nescia* when Jupiter sends Mercury to prevent her from barring the Trojans from her land. But, as Page (1894, *ad loc.*) observed, she would have been much more likely to drive them from Carthage if she knew fate than if she was ignorant of it. Page's solution is that the meaning of *fati nescia* be 'left vague and mysterious'. But there is nothing vague or mysterious about it. Commager (1981.101-110) pointed out that in the Dido episode *fata* very often means what Jupiter said, that Vergil shows Dido as its victim and as being terribly ignorant of it and that this introduction of Dido follows immediately after Jupiter's glowing prediction of Rome's future; so "we might almost understand it as 'Dido, who had not heard Jove's speech'" (105).

Commager interpreted these facts in terms of the 'two voices' approach. He did not consider the possibility that Vergil could have wanted Dido to be miserable for no other reason than to arouse pathos, and he did not point out most of the ways in which her ignorance of the workings of Aeneas' fate is a, if not the, main cause of her (and Aeneas') agony in Book 4. Dido never believes Aeneas that fate and Jupiter are forcing him to leave her; except parenthetically in 4.614 and 651, where her expressions may be as imprecise and meaningless as our 'God willing' (cf. Tib. 1.5.20). Since she is *fati nescia* she interprets the reason for his leaving her as purely personal (e.g. *mene fugis?* in 314). Moreover, she is forced to humble herself painfully (412-15,424) in the belief that he can at least delay his departure (429-35).

When discussing how Vergil used divine intervention to keep Dido's torment unrelieved while excusing Aeneas, I mentioned several other results of her being ignorant of divine compulsion on Aeneas. In lines 425-8 she expresses agonized perplexity as to *cur mea dicta negat duras demittere in auris.* But twelve lines later Vergil tells us, *fata obstant placidasque viri deus obstruit auris.* Placidas ('kindly') and *duras* are emphatic as the first words in their clauses, *viri* and *deus* are pointedly juxtaposed and *placidas* restates *tractabilis* in the previous line (cf. *dulcis* in 4.317-18 and 281). Moreover, it does not occur to her that Aeneas does not display compassion for her misery because of the gods, although Vergil makes that abundantly clear to the reader. So in lines 365-7 she says Aeneas is the product of "places in the mysterious North to express coldness and cruelty, as in *G* IV 517ff" (Austin 1955, on 366f.) because he did not *ingemuit, lumina flexit* or *lacrimas dedit* (369-70). However, in 331-2 Vergil informed us that that was because of Jupiter's instructions; and in 395 he *multa gemens* for her; but she has fainted, and he cannot stay to show her his feelings because *iussa tamen divum exsequitur* (396).

I have pointed out that the Romans were fascinated by the terrible pathos involved in the contrast between the lover, who cares about nothing but his all-consuming passion, sacrifices everything for it and often cannot live when it ends, and the beloved, who regards the affair as a pleasant interlude or means to an end and leaves it with indifference. Among the examples I used were Horace's *Ode* 1.5, Lesbia's *culpa* in Catullus 11.22-4 and Ariadne in Catullus 64. So Scylla in *Ciris* 415 bemoans Minos' lack of interest in her lament, and she ends it (454-8) with the passionately expressed wish that Minos pay attention to her suffering and that it was caused by fate, chance, or a deserved punishment, *omnia nam potius quam te fecisse putabo.* Vergil used Dido's condition of being *fati nescia* to make her believe this most painful of possibilities: that Aeneas alone is causing her misery and that he is emotionally indifferent to it. If a lover believed that her beloved left her because of the will of the gods, she could forgive him (e.g. Parth. 4).

Dido's belief that Aeneas is leaving her of his free will increases her agony in still another way. Self-esteem was extremely important to the ancient Romans and Greeks (e.g. Pöschl 1977. 110-11). That was especially true of Dido (*ibid.*; Highet 1972.135-7,cf. 182-3). The objective concomitant of self-esteem was *fama.* That was the ultimate obstacle to Dido indulging her love for Aeneas (4.91,170), and even after the affair began she tried to protect it (172). But Vergil emphasizes that she was unsuccessful (173-95), a fact which was extremely painful to her (321-3).

Because of the ancient obsession with self-esteem and reputation, lovers and others in Roman and Greek literature constantly thought they were being laughed at and disgraced, and this was regarded with horror and often produced terrible results (Farron 1989.110n7). Dido assumes that her former suitors are laughing at her (534-6) and, because she is *fati nescia*, she assumes that Aeneas shares the contempt he caused. In lines 591-2 she is furious and tormented that he will leave, but even more that he *inluserit* her; where the future perfect connotes 'get away with' (Austin 1955, *ad loc.*). To prevent that she utters the curses that will cause Aeneas' future misery and the Punic Wars (612-29).

From the discussion above, it is obvious that the Roman love poets, and especially Vergil, constantly used lovers' ignorance of the nature and operations of the gods to have them constantly make ironic statements and actions. They are ironic in that "the words of a character ... unconsciously betray ignorance of his true situation" and "depend on a gap in knowledge between the audience and the protagonist as to the meaning of a given situation". This definition is from page 137 of Muecke's article (1983), in which she demonstrates how pervasive this irony is in the Dido episode and how that was influenced by Greek tragedy. But she mentions none of the passages I have discussed, and she argues (145-6) that since Aeneas tells Dido several times in Books 2 and 3 that he is fated to go to Italy, she is not *fati nescia* in Book 4 and it is because of the 'nature of her passion' that she does not apply her knowledge of fate to her situation. But the cause of her ignorance is much more terribly ironic. It is her trust in the gods' benevolence which prevents her from believing that they could destroy her by forcing Aeneas to leave her, as I have shown and will demonstrate further.

I have already referred to the tremendous influence Greek tragedies had on the Dido episode and the tendency for the *Iliad* to be interpreted as a tragedy by Plato, Aristotle and the scholia on it. Since antiquity it has been frequently observed that much of the impact of Greek tragedies derives from this type of irony. "Some measure of ignorance followed by realization is present in nearly all [Greek] plays" (Lucas 1978.291,cf. 292-8). Indeed, "The tragedy of error, of ... blindness ... represents an experience and a vision of life ... [that] is an intrinsic part of their [the Greeks'] myth and history stated in terms of myth" (*ibid*. 307). It was basic to

Aristotle's evaluations in the *Poetics* (*ibid.* 291-2,299-307; Muecke 1983.142). It was especially prominent in Sophocles' *Oedipus Tyrannus* (Reinhardt 1979.97-111,116-29,134; Lyne 1987.194n62), as Aristotle and the ancient scholia appreciated (Stanford 1939.165-73). Vergil used it throughout the *Aeneid* (Quinn 1979.330-9).

Aristotle says that pity is especially aroused when suffering is caused by dear ones and relatives (*Poet.* 1453b14-1454a13). This corresponds with several of Cicero's *loci communes* for producing pity and tears (*Inv. Rhet.* 1.106-9). Some of the incongruous juxtapositions listed in note 2, on page 119, emphasize that Pygmalion caused great suffering to Dido although he was her brother. Aristotle also says that this suffering caused by dear ones and relatives can be done with knowledge or in ignorance (*ibid.*). He gives as an example of the latter the *Oedipus Tyrannus*, where this is true not only of Oedipus but also Jocasta and the Corinthian messenger, whose attempts to help Oedipus ironically cause misery for him and them. Anna and Barce clearly resemble Jocasta in this. Both have obvious antecedents in Greek tragedies among nurses and other confidantes who hurt those whom they want to help. Barce does only one thing: *gradum studio celerabat anilem* (641), where the incongruous juxtaposition stresses that in her eagerness to help Dido she ran although her age made that difficult. But Dido's purpose in sending her on this mission is *quam primum abrumpere lucem* (631). Vergil undoubtedly meant us to feel that when Barce discovers Dido's intention, her reaction will be similar to the one Anna expresses with an incongruous juxtaposition in line 675. Apuleius saw the terrible irony in line 641. He imitated it in *Metamorphoses* 6.14.1, where Psyche *studiose gradum celerans*, ostensibly to perform an errand she was instructed to do, but really *inventura vitae pessimae finem*.

Vergil used the ironic discrepancy between Dido's trust in the gods and their true nature to increase her misery in still another way. That is in the one passage (4.371-380) where she questions divine benevolence. This violation of her deeply rooted outlook was extremely painful for her. It also involved terribly ironic statements. Vergil used incongruous juxtapositions to emphasize them and the agony this lapse from her normal views caused. That passage is in answer to the last of only three speeches made by Trojans to Dido in Books 1 and 4. The first two also contain horribly ironic assertions about divine justice and benevolence. In the first Ilioneus tells her that she will not regret helping the Trojans because, *sperate deos memores fandi atque nefandi* (1.543). He is asking there for very little (551-2). Dido replies by offering incomparably more than was requested (569-74). Aeneas reacts to her generosity by promising, *Di tibi, si qua pios respectant numina, si quid usquam iustitiae est ... praemia digna ferant* (603-5). (*Si* with the indicative "does not imply any doubt ... but the reverse": Page 1894, on 3.433; cf. Nisbet and Hubbard 1975, on 32.1; Norden 1957, on 459.). The only other speech by a Trojan to Dido in Books 1 and 4 is Aeneas' in 4.333-61. There, after she has told him that his departure will cause her death, he tells her that the gods are forcing him to leave her.

In her answer to that claim (371-87), Dido recalls Aeneas' reasons why the gods will reward her (compare 4.373-5 with 1.598-600) and, for the only time, wavers in her faith in divine benevolence. It is her statements there that the proponents of her Epicureanism assert reveal this basic character trait. Lines 371-2 (*iam iam nec maxima Iuno nec Saturnius haec oculis pater aspicit aequis*) is usually interpreted as meaning even Juno and Jupiter are no longer just. But there are three reasons for construing *nec* with *aspicit* rather than with *aequis*; meaning that although Jupiter is a *pater*, he and Juno do not see these things with their *aequi* eyes. First, the normal interpretation ignores *pater*. The Romans derived Jupiter's name from *iuvans pater* (Pease 1958.712; cf. 718 for the derivation of Juno from *iuvando*). I have discussed Vergil's and other Romans' assumption of the naturalness of parental affection and his tendency to juxtapose with a word or clause an attribute (or attributes) of its subject or object which make it incongruous in some way, so 'although' is suggested (note 2). Vergil especially often applied *pater* to a character to indicate that in that passage he is acting in a manner incongruous with the love, compassion, assistance in distress and/or fairness that is expected from a father.[4] So in 4.372 *pater* is connected closely with *aequis*, which

---

[4] E.g. Fairness: 1.237;4.234 (with Williams 1972, *ad loc.*). Compassion and assistance in distress: 2.652-3,674-77 (with Donatus on 674). Love: 6.820-21;7.327. *Parens* and *genitor* are used similarly in 2.664-67 and 7.359-60. Failure to see this pattern has caused 2.617-18 (*Ipse pater Danais animos virisque secundas sufficit, ipse deos in Dardana suscitat arma*) to be misconstrued. *Ipse* is usually interpreted as suggesting Jupiter's majesty (e.g. Austin 1966 and Conington 1884 *ad loc.*). But *ipse* emphasizes that "Even the father himself [who should be loving and protecting] ..." An apt parallel is 7.327 (*odit et ipse*

means 'impartial', 'pitying' and 'favoring' (Hellegouarc'h 1963. 150-1; cf. *Aen.* 6.129-30), and this is an example of Vergil's incongruous juxtapositions. Second, if *nec* is construed with *aspicit,* lines 371-2 are similar in meaning to 379-80. Third, that produces a very effective pathetic irony of a type common in Dido's relations with the gods. She is saying that Juno and Jupiter do not see *haec,* which refers to the general situation of Aeneas deserting what she regards as a marriage and in specific to his not showing compassion for her (369-70). But the reader knows that Juno instigated this fatal affair and made their union in the cave seem like a marriage and that Jupiter is forcing Aeneas to leave and not show compassion for her (331-2). However, Dido so trusts the gods that she cannot imagine that they could be cruel to her. She still regards Jupiter as a compassionate *pater* who views human affairs with *oculi aequi.* But in this one instance (*iam iam*) he and Juno incongruously do not see what is happening. (Notice that her pain would be as great if the normal interpretation of lines 371-2 is correct.)

Dido proceeds in 4.373-5 to recall Aeneas' reasons in 1.598-605 why the gods will reward her, *si quid <u>usquam</u> iustitiae est.* So she naturally introduces that recollection with the assertion *nusquam tuta fides* and follows it by paraphrasing ironically his claim of divine compulsion now (*nunc... nunc... nunc*) (376-8). Her recollection of her generosity to Aeneas and his reaction to it in Book 1, in contrast with his current claim, lead her to state that the gods do not care about human affairs as a general principle, no longer as a temporary lapse from their normal conduct (379-80). But she still makes this statement only as an ironic echo of the belief she is casting doubt on, and her natural religiosity causes her to regard this assertion as a result of temporary insanity: *heu, furiis incensa feror* (376). Nowhere else does Dido describe herself so strongly as mentally deranged, not even in 4.595, where she realizes that she has just been giving orders to men who are not there. There is again a terrible irony here. I have pointed out that *furor* and its related nouns, adjectives and verbs are applied to Dido more than twice as often as to any other character in the *Aeneid* (Farron 1985.

---

pater Pluton (of Allecto)). The fact that even Jupiter the *pater* is hostile is Venus' ultimate evidence that the Trojan cause is hopeless. Therefore (619), *eripe, nate, fugam.* As often, Donatus and Servius (on 2.617; cf. Servius on 2.326) provide the correct explanation.

621). It "is frequently applied to people ... driven mad by the gods, in whose plight pity ... is our dominant feeling" (R. Williams 1960a, on 6). Indeed, *pour les Anciens, tout égarement de la raison était d'origine divine* (Allain 1946.196). Greek tragedies often portrayed characters made delirious by the gods because *le délire est à la fois le plus intense des émois* and so is effective at providing pathos (De Romilly 1961.91,cf.90-107). Vergil explicitly compares Dido to such characters in 4.469-73. The second of these, Orestes, "came to be a type of madmen in general" for the Romans and was a very popular character (Pease 1935.383). Here Dido says that it is because of *furor* that she is saying that the gods do not care about mortal concerns. But the reader knows that she is *furiosa* throughout Book 4 because of what the gods do to her.

Most modern scholars do not see that all of lines 371 to 380 are devoted to Dido's agony at divine indifference to her suffering. For example, Austin (1955, *ad loc.*) paraphrases *nusquam ... fides* (373) as "nowhere can I safely put my trust" and comments on lines 373-5, "Dido's egoism is clear here". And twentieth-century editors and commentators, except Sabbadini and Pease, interpret *heu, furiis ... feror* (376) as being parenthetical or commenting on the preceding lines. But, although Dido's speeches in book 4 tend to jump emotionally from thought to thought without explicit connections, they have a coherent development and overall pattern (Heinze 1915.425; R. Williams 1972, on 4.522f. and 584f.).

The ancient commentators understood these lines correctly, for the most part. Donatus explained that Dido mentions Juno in line 371 because *regina deorum vindicare debuit iniusta* (cf. Serv. Dan. *ad loc.*), quoted as a very apt parallel for *nusquam ... fides* Terence's *pro Iuppiter, ubinam est fides?* and filled in Dido's unexpressed thoughts when she mentions Aeneas' claim of divine compulsion (376-8) as *si ista vera sunt, cur non extiterunt ante beneficia mea?* Servius explained *furiis ... feror* as *quia multa erat in deos locutura*. (Servius Danielis said that Aeneas calls himself *amens* when he accuses the gods in 2.745 *quia in furore incusavit deos*.) The author of the letter from Dido to Aeneas in *Anthologia Latina* 83R also understood this speech. In lines 100 to 117 Dido repeats four times the refrain *cui digna rependes,/si mihi dura paras?* Lines 112 to 114 recapitulate *Aeneid* 4.373-5. Then Dido says (120-3), *si nil pia facta merentur,/ esse deos natura docet, non esse timendos/ rerum facta probant. Quid enim non credere possum?/ Tutus fraude manes et nos pietate perimus!* Her *pia facta* and *pietas* must refer to Aeneas' assertion in 1.597 to 605 that the gods will reward her if they *pios respectant*. She says that if they do not, then the Epicurean conception of them is correct. After that she expresses amazement that she would think such a thing. This passage has been misconstrued in the same way as its model in the *Aeneid* has. Riese punctuated it with a full stop after *merentur*, and Purser (*apud* Palmer 1898.xxn1) stated that in the line following that, "the author proclaims his Epicurean views".

To return to Dido's speech in the *Aeneid*, because she thinks of herself as raving when she says that the gods are not concerned with mortal affairs, she does not regard that as a refutation of Aeneas' claims. Immediately afterwards she stops talking to herself and says to him *neque ... dicta refello* (380). Then, as soon as she stops thinking about her generosity to Aeneas and his claim of divine compulsion, her normal religiosity returns: *si quid pia numina possunt* (382). On the basis of that assumption she makes the threats in lines 384-7. Her anguish and confusion are so extreme here that she does not have a clear idea of what she is saying. If she had simply said *sequar absens* in line 384 and *umbra adero* in 386, they would have been by far the most radical instances of incongruous juxtaposition in *Aeneid* 4, so much so that they could be explained only with great ingenuity. But Vergil emphasized *absens* by placing it at the end of its line and added to it the concrete, explicit *atris ignibus*. He also added the concrete, explicit *omnibus locis* to *umbra adero*, and in the next line stated that her *umbra* will be where it should be, *Manis ... sub imos*. These additions make even farfetched, metaphorical explanations impossible. Immediately after these threats, Vergil says that Dido *his medium dictis sermonem abrumpit* and fainted (388-92).

The unintelligibility of lines 384 to 387 is attested by desperate attempts to explain them. Servius and Donatus mention several ancient interpretations. Austin (1955, on 387) refers to several 'drastic' modern attempts to make sense of Dido's 'illogicality' and dismisses them as 'frigid'. In his note on 384ff. he says, "Editors have laboured much to explain ... Dido's threat ... but is not mystery a prerogative of prophecy, and is not Virgil a poet?" However, the meaning of no other threat or prophecy in the *Aeneid*, whether by Dido or anyone else, is so unclear; and Austin does not point out here, as he does on line 30, that the fact that Vergil was a poet is sometimes manifested by his having characters give indications that what they say cannot be believed. It is significant that in 659 Dido says resignedly *moriemur inultae*, showing that she does not remember or does not take seriously her confused, incomprehensible predictions in 384 to 387. (Lines 612 to 629 are prayers for what others will do.)

However, Vergil had no interest in making a systematic statement about the gods in the Dido episode. Just as Aeneas could display compassion for her after her tragedy had run its course, so could the gods (4.693-705). Also, they fulfil the prayer she makes in lines 607-29 (Kepple 1976.357-60; Austin 1955, on 615,618,619). So for the period after her death she is not only not *fati nescia*, she causes what is fated. Similarly, in Catullus 64 Ariadne's curses are fulfilled, to bring misery to the next focus of sympathetic interest.

J. *Similarities Between the Gods in Book 2 of the* Aeneid *and in the Dido-Aeneas Episode*

My interpretation of Vergil's use of the gods in the Dido episode can be tested by their role in Book 2, where it might seem that he is making an even more explicitly negative statement about them. Palmer (1938.373-5) points out that the gods' hostility to Troy and the Trojans "is hammered home ... by a striking device. Throughout the second book there runs a *Leitmotiv* that is repeated and emphasized". That is "the sacrilege committed with impunity by Greeks at altars and in holy places". His examples are: "Pallas, whose temple the Greeks had violated (165) and who signified her displeasure *nec dubiis ... monstris* (171), gives refuge to the very serpents who have removed the only obstacle to success ... 226"; "Neptune allows his priest to be slain while sacrificing at his own altars ... 202"; "the Trojans place the horse in the hallowed citadel ... 245"; "they decorate the shrines of the gods ... 248"; "later ... the bodies of the slain lie even in the temples and holy places ... 364-6"; when the Trojans attain some success, yet, *heu nihil invitis fas quemquam fidere divis! ... trahebatur ... Priameia ... a templo ... adytisque Minervae, ad caelum tendens ... lumina* frustra (402-5); "Coroebus falls at the altar ... 425ff."; "nor did his piety nor even the fillet of Apollo avail Panthus ... 429-30"; then *Vidi Hecubam centumque nurus, Piamumque* per aras *sanguine foedantem* quos ipse sacraverat ignis (501-2) and *ingens* ara *fuit, iuxtaque ... laurus incumbens arae, ...*

complexa penates. *Hic Hecuba et natae* nequiquam altaria circum ... *condensae et* divom amplexae simulacra ... (512-17); "Hecuba restrains Priam ... with the words: *haec* ara *tuebitur omnis* (523) ... Priam calls upon the gods *si qua est caelo pietas* to avenge ... his son. Yet Pyrrhus drags him *altaria ad ipsa* (550)" and kills him there.

Many additions can be made to Palmer's observations. In lines 141-4 Sinon ends his lies about himself by appealing for pity *per superos et conscia numina veri, per si qua est ... mortalibus usquam intemerata fides*. And the Trojans do pity him, which causes their destruction. In 201 Laocoon is described as a priest of Neptune, which he was not anywhere else. This change emphasized divine perfidy, because the snakes that killed him came from Neptune's element, the sea, and Vergil twice calls Troy *Neptunia* when talking of its destruction (2.625; 3.3; cf.2.610-12). Moreover, he emphasizes that Laocoon was performing the sacrifice properly (Austin 1966, on 202), for which he was rewarded by being *perfusus sanie vittas atroque veneno* (221). The Trojans bring the horse into Troy in the form of a religious rite (Austin 1966, on 239) because they are *caeci ... furore* (244). And they are constantly described as being motivated by insanity and frenzy (Allain 1946.195-7), which, as was pointed out, was thought to be of divine origin. Indeed, in lines 336 to 337 Aeneas describes himself as being driven into battle by *numen divum* and Erinys (i.e. *furor* personified: Farron 1985).

Sinon is *fatis ... deum defensus iniquis* (257). Later he is *victor ... insultans* (329-30), as is Pyrrhus (469-70). Jupiter is called *ferus* by Panthus (326), on which Servius observed, *summae necessitatis est, cum etiam sacerdos in convicia ruit deorum*. In 396 the Trojans attack *haud numine nostro*. In 410-11 they are overwhelmed by spears thrown by their own men from the roof of a temple. In 426-8 *cadit et Rhipeus, iustissimus unus ... et servantissimus aequi (dis aliter visum)*. Lines 501-2 were mentioned in my summary of Palmer's article. Servius in his note on 502 points out their similarity to 365 and draws the obvious conclusion: *per quod ostenditur ... nihil prodesse religionem*. Donatus draws the same conclusion in his notes on 424-6 and 426-8. Austin (1966, on 608ff.) calls the revelation of the gods destroying Troy an "apocalypse of terror ... all the *numina magna deum* engaged in active destruction of Troy in ruthless alliance with the Greeks" and comments on line 615, "Pallas, the protectress of citadels, is herself present at the destruction of this citadel where but lately the Trojans had set the Horse to do her honour". In the first two lines of Book 3 the destruction of Troy is summarized as *res Asiae Priamique evertere gentem immeritam visum superis*, where *immeritam* is the first word in its line (cf. 1.479). Furthermore, I pointed out while discussing Nisus and Euryalus that Vergil emphasizes that Troy was captured by *doli* and *insidiae*. It was these means that the gods supported, the gods whom Dido expects to enforce *fides*.

As with other questions, three basic approaches have been followed by modern scholars in explaining what Vergil intended by having the gods operate the way they do in Book 2. Those who regard the *Aeneid* as completely pro-Roman must find some means of justifying the gods, since they are the guarantors of Rome's future. So Conway (1906.32) asserts, "the cause of the fall of Troy was the Trojans' own cowardice which led them first to leave Laocoon to perish unaided, and then to see in his death the sign, not of their own wrong-doing, but of his". Those who regard the *Aeneid*'s purpose as contrasting a public with a private voice argue that the gods are brutal to individual characters but benevolent to Rome. An example is Camps (1969.46-9), who mentions many other episodes, besides Books 2 and 4, in which the gods "exploit the reverence ... for them as a means of deceiving men to their own harm" (46-7) and points out that "repeatedly ... a victim of the gods is *insons* or *immeritus*, or his fate *iniquus*" (47). His examples of this being stated explicitly, in addition to Troy (3.2) and Dido (4.696), are Turnus (10.630) and Palinurus (5.841). (He does not mention that *insonti* is the first word in 5.841 and is followed, two words later, by *deus*.) Other critics regard Book 2 as an attack on the gods, which must mean on Aeneas' mission. For example, Austin in the introduction to his edition of Book 2 (1966.xx-xxi) observes that in the revelation of the gods destroying Troy, "no mortal misdeed has caused the ruin of Troy, but *divum inclementia, divum* ... (602f.). The repetition of *divum* comes with stabbing shock" and that "the passage ends abruptly: *apparent dirae facies inimicaque Troiae numina* ... It is a fantastic apocalypse, gods in devilry, gloating over their horrid work like demons ... The intensity of the lines is remarkable; every word is urgent". His conclusion is that this scene is the result of a "deeply disturbing intensity of poetic vision", that Vergil "had suddenly, blindingly, seen that human *pietas* - the linch-pin of the whole structure of the

Aeneid—has no protection against the arbitrary ruthlessness of the gods, no necessary recognition from them" and that "perhaps here ... lies the ultimate reason for his wish that the *Aeneid* should be destroyed".

However, Austin also observes that 'a few moments' after this scene "Aeneas reaches his home safely *ducente deo*", that Anchises' prayer to Jupiter is answered "so that in simple faith he cries to the gods of Troy *Vestrum hoc augurium, vestroque in numine Troia est*" and that "the departure from Troy is invested with the full ritual sanction of divine augury". Since Austin assumes that at every point in time Vergil must have intended a consistent statement about the gods, he asserts, "the conclusion is irresistible that the whole Venus-scene" was written later and that the horrible vision of the gods which inspired it must have come to Vergil "near the end of his life".

There are, however, three reasons why this conclusion is untenable. First, as Austin himself points out (xix-xx), the gods are consistently portrayed as brutal and amoral throughout Book 2 up to the Venus-scene. He himself calls it 'the climax' to a 'mounting indictment'. Second, the gods are frequently depicted this way throughout the *Aeneid*. For example, Panthus (2.429-30) is not the only character whose *pietas* gains no protection or recognition from the gods. As was pointed out, Dido's does not, although Aeneas assures her it will (1.603-5); nor does Aeneas', at least from Juno, as Vergil emphasizes in 1.9-11. Third, as was also pointed out, this type of portrayal of the gods was very common in ancient Greek and Roman literature. For example, Austin (1966, on 506-83) observes that Priam killed at an altar or other holy place was a popular subject in literature and art. And the obvious inference from this was often explicitly drawn; for example, *nihil Hercei profuit ara Iovis* (Ov. Ib. 284).

In fact, the parallelism with the Dido episode is very close. After the tragedy of Troy had run its course, the gods could be concerned, helpful and compassionate (cf.4.693-705). Panthus' *plurima pietas* did not help him; but Anchises' prayer, *si pietate meremur* (2.690), is answered. And, just as the gods fulfil Dido's prayer for revenge after she is dead, so they fulfil Priam's prayer that *si qua est caelo pietas quae talia curet*, they *persolvant grates dignas et praemia reddant debita* to Pyrrhus (2.535-8). As Page points out (1894) in his note on 3.332 (*patriasque obtruncat ad aras*), "Pyrrhus had slain Priam and his son Polites at the altar and Virgil clearly intends us to recall his own description of Pyrrhus in 2.663: *Natum ante ora patris, patrem qui obtruncat ad aras.*" I have quoted the examples Palmer gave of "sacrilege committed with impunity by Greeks at altars", which he described accurately as a "*Leitmotiv* that is repeated and emphasized" throughout Book 2. But when Vergil no longer wanted this motif, such sacrilege could be punished.

Why did Vergil want this motif and similar depictions of divine brutality and amorality in most of Book 2? What purpose did they serve? The same as other occurrences of gods hurting and destroying trusting and devout humans undeservedly. They provided what the ancient Romans wanted most from literature: pathos; and they provided it in the manner in which they expected it: emphasizing the characters' helplessness and weakness and having the characters receive misery from those for whom they performed *benefacta* and expected good treatment in return. Moreover, it was by no means only ancient readers who were affected powerfully by these and the other means Vergil used to create pathos. Book 2 has always been, and still is, immensely popular and admired, perhaps more than any other book in the *Aeneid* except Four. The reason is not, and has never been, the views it expresses on the gods, patriotism, moral codes, the meaning of life, etc. Indeed, there is no agreement on what these views are.

Here again there are close parallels in the Homeric epics and Greek tragedies. Gould (1991) demonstrates that they were based on πάθος in the Greek sense; that is (ix) "catastrophic suffering, undergone by some great figure ... far in excess of the sufferer's deserts". The similarity to *Aeneid* 2 and 4 is obvious, as is the fact, which Gould also shows, that this undeserved suffering was usually caused by a god or gods and that, although πάθος is what makes tragedies tragic, "we must not insist that the ... final excitement of a play be an exhibition of *pathos*. 'Philosophy' may triumph in the final scene or the final pages" (207). By "philosophy" he means events or series of events which are morally or intellectually intelligible. Gould's observations on the way critics distort ancient literature also resemble mine (257):

> the greatest poets have all found ways to mix "poetry" and "philosophy". Literary criticism, therefore, that dwells on the subtleties

of a drama's "philosophy" is ... wrong ... if this element ... is singled out as the essence of the power and profundity of the work.

Philosophers (ancient and modern) also resemble critics of the *Aeneid* in that they "unlike poets, usually hunger for a single, internally consistent explanation ... The thrill of *pathos* is treated by them as something that must be eliminated, neutralized, or shown to be of minor importance" (207).

Donatus and Servius warned against thinking that the *Aeneid* provides a philosophical, internally consistent explanation of the gods and religion. The former (in his introduction to Book 1: page 5, line 26 to page 6, line 12 of Georgii's edition) first mentions obvious contradictions: that the gods exist and that they do not exist; that they do not care about what people do, that they do care; that fate exists, that it does not exist; that people die on a set day, that they die before their predetermined time; that the dead feel and perceive something, that there is nothing after death. Then he explains that Vergil was not guided by the function of one making claims (*officium adserentis*), but he used and dispensed with these ideas in accordance with the person, passage or situation involved. And he points out that Vergil never professes to be the propounder of any profound knowledge or philosophy. Servius in his comments on 10.467 (*stat sua cuique dies*) puts the same observations into a broader perspective. He notes that this statement conflicts with *ante diem* in 4.697 and explains that we find contradictory views in the same poem because poets always (*semper*) use the ideas of various philosophical sects in accordance with the nature of the situation at hand (*pro qualitate negotiorum*) and never allign themselves with one sect. The only exception he allows is those poets whose subject is philosophy, of whom he gives Lucretius as an example.

POSTSCRIPT

The test of any hypothesis is whether it explains the facts better than other hypotheses. The most striking fact about the *Aeneid* is that nearly all readers of it from Vergil's time to ours have reacted in the way Pococurante does in Chapter 25 of *Candide*, by the very un-romantic champion of monarchy Voltaire:

> le second, le quatrième et le sixième livre ... sont excellents; mais, pour son pieux Énée, et le fort Cloanthe, et l'ami Achates, et le petit Ascanius, et l'imbécile roi Latinus, et la bourgeoise Amata, et l'insipide Lavinia, je ne crois pas qu'il y ait rien de si froid et de plus désagréable

In other words, the characters and passages which are part of the *Aeneid*'s plot and pertain to its 'message' are dull, unexciting and uninteresting. Its greatness is in its depiction of grief and love. For, even in the revelation of Rome's future heroes in Book Six, Vergil's interest and certainly that of his readers has been in the pathetic, like Marcellus, not the triumphant. Of course, Pococurante's purpose, as his name suggests, is to throw cold water on Candide's ardor for great works of literature. So he overgeneralizes Aeneas' lack of interest for the reader, ignoring those parts where he is the focus of attention and sympathy, like Book Two, and he dwells on the *Aeneid*'s weaknesses. When Voltaire discussed the *Aeneid* in his own person, in pages 36 to 41 of his *Essay Upon the Epic Poetry of the European Nations*, written in English, his judgement was overwhelmingly positive, except for one 'defect': "the latter Part of the Poem is less animated than the first". The reason is that the "Match between *Aeneas* and *Lavinia* ... and a War ... could not indeed command our Concern as well as the burning of *Troy*, and the Love of *Dido*". But Vergil should not be blamed because "Tis a great Mistake to believe an Author can soar, when the subject sinks". In other words, Vergil had to devote too much of the last books to the plot, *arma virumque*.

It is instructive to compare Camps' discussion of what he regards as the *Aeneid*'s 'two imperfections' (1969.135-6):

> The first ... is that the emphasis ... required by its [the story's] basic conception on the ... grievous weight of the trials endured by Aeneas and his party on their voyage ... to Italy is simply not sustained by the narrative of these trials, and this inadequacy is

thrown into relief by the contrasted intensity of the suffering of Dido.

Camps here is more honest than many modern scholars who argue that the emphasis of the first half of the *Aeneid* does fall on Aeneas' trials. But the intensity of the suffering of Dido and other episodes unrelated to the plot bothered nearly no reader until about a century before Camps wrote this. They, including even Pococurante, regarded these passages as the glory of the *Aeneid*.

Camps' second imperfection is the same as the one Voltaire pointed out in his *Essay*:

> Our concern for the hero and our interest in the 'Roman' significance of the *Aeneid* are both satisfied by the end of the eighth book, and the concluding books are from this point of view an anticlimax, though they engage our interest on behalf of the ... resisters. It seems unlikely that Virgil intended the interest to shift so markedly from his hero in these last three books; for they would be to the mind of his age the most 'epic' part ... the tale of *arma* promised in the *Aeneid*'s opening line. ... [However] he had been successful in diversifying the war ... by ... distinctive characters ... Nisus and Euryalus, Pallas, Lausus, Mezentius, Camilla ... the more exigent requirements of plot in this part of the *Aeneid* leave no scope for magnificent episodes, such as the fall of Troy, the fate of Dido and the descent into the world of the dead

At the end Camps explains the relative lack of interest of the last books in the way Voltaire and I do. But his presuppositions cause bizarre convolutions in the rest of his discussion. He begins by assuming that the focus of interest in the first eight books was on Aeneas and Rome, which contradicts his ending and his first 'imperfection', and he assumes that the successful parts of the last books could not have been what Vergil and his contemporaries wanted to be successful, the plot and meaning.

It is only since the late nineteenth century that the assumption that the parts of a work of literature must serve its plot and meaning has caused the literary weakness of plot and message of the *Aeneid* to become a crisis which requires elaborate explanations: we must not be misled by the romantic-sentimental outlook of our culture into concentrating on the emotionally intense parts of the poem and so miss its Roman/Stoic subject; or, they are the most memorable parts of the *Aeneid* because Vergil got carried away by them and so destroyed the epic's balance; or, he wanted his readers to focus on the emotionally intense books, like two, four and six to show how Aeneas develops/suffers, etc. to perform his mission; or, the purpose of bringing suffering so strongly to the readers' attention was to demonstrate that Aeneas' mission is destructive or to hear it against the background of another voice; etc.

My hypothesis, that we are meant to concentrate on grief and love for their own sake, not only explains the nearly universally recognized strengths and weaknesses of the *Aeneid* better than other modern hypotheses, it also explains another very prominent fact: that the *Aeneid* has always been regarded as great literature because of its portrayal of grief and love.

If my hypothesis is correct, the *Aeneid* is three-dimensional. Other modern critics try to flatten it into either one dimension, as Grandsen (1984.3) in the assertion quoted at the beginning of chapter 3, or two dimensions; for instance, "the purpose of the *Aeneid* is ... to show the conflict of great principles" (Pease 1935.32).

The modern approach is to treat the *Aeneid* as if it is like Silius' *Punica*. That epic begins by announcing a plot similar to the *Aeneid*'s: *Ordior arma, quibus caelo se gloria tollit Aeneadum.* But this plot does control the *Punica*. That is the reason why even if Silius possessed Vergil's linguistic and metrical brilliance, his poem would still be incomparably thinner and poorer than Vergil's. Yet, modern critics try to reduce the *Aeneid* to the level of the *Punica* and to deny or explain away what readers, including Silius, have regarded as the cause of its greatness.

I will now illustrate this point with a brief look at a few works of European literature which have been regarded as great by nearly all readers. As I have pointed out, from the ancient Greeks on, the Homeric epics have been admired for their episodes, not their plots. There has also been general consensus that the *Iliad* is greater than the *Odyssey*. Perhaps one reason is that its plot is much less dominant than is the plot of the *Odyssey*, as defined by Aristotle (*Poet.* 1455b16-23). This difference is evident in the way the Analysts treated the two epics. As the modern Analyst Von der Mühll asserted, the *Iliad* grew out of the Anger-poem, but "the *Odyssey* was always an *Odyssey*". Indeed, the last half of the *Odyssey* suffers from the same defect as the last third of the *Aeneid*: dominance of plot. Another reason for the generally recognized superiority of the *Iliad* over the *Odyssey* and *Aeneid* and the greater interest of its hero may be that the plot itself, the poem's subject, what it is 'about', is negative. Achilles is most appealing and memorable when he questions the value of heroism in Book 9, denounces and curses his anger (against Agamemnon) in Book 18 and ends his anger (against Hector) in Book 24. But Odysseus cannot question, curse or reject establishing himself at home or killing the suitors, and Aeneas cannot do that with regard to his mission. Aeneas is appealing when he ignores his mission, as in Book 2, or regards it as a encumbrance, as in Book 3.

The nearly universally recognized literary superiority of Dante's *Inferno* over his *Purgatory* and *Paradise* was caused in part by the *Divine Comedy*'s theological subject being less prominent there, thus giving Dante more scope to present a three dimensional portrayal of people and emotions.

As for Shakespeare's *Hamlet*, few readers agree with T.S. Eliot's judgement in "Hamlet and his Problems" (*The Sacred Wood*, pages 95-103) that it is 'an artistic failure' (98), but most share Eliot's impression that it "is possibly the ... [play] on which Shakespeare spent most pains" (98) and is more 'interesting' than his other plays (99). Eliot insists that to interpret *Hamlet* it is necessary to regard it as 'a stratification'; it is "superposed upon much cruder material which persists even in the final form" (96-7), and its immediate source was Thomas Kyd's *Hamlet*. Eliot argues that in that play "the motive was a revenge-motive simply ... the action or delay is caused ... solely by the difficulty of assassinating a monarch surrounded by guards" (97). In Shakespeare's *Hamlet*, on the other hand, "there is a motive which is more important than ... revenge, and which explicitly 'blunts' the latter; the delay in revenge is unexplained" (97). *Hamlet* is 'an artistic failure' largely because Shakespeare could not 'impose' his version "successfully upon the intractable material of the old play" (98) and because there is no 'objective correlative' for Hamlet's emotions (100-101), although "the intense feeling, ecstatic or terrible, without an object or exceeding its object, is something which every person of sensibility has known" (102).

Eliot's source for Shakespeare's *Hamlet* is a play that is no longer extant, but we have prose versions of the Hamlet story by Saxo and Belleforest, and the latter "is clearly revealed as, directly or indirectly, a main source [of Shakespeare's play]" (Jenkins 1982.96). Eliot asserts that it was the version "upon which Kyd's *Hamlet* must have been based" (97). Among the changes which Shakespeare introduced is that "Belleforest, following Saxo, likens

Amleth to Hercules: the comparison persists in Shakespeare, but those who were like are now unlike (I.II.152-3). The mind of Hamlet, confronting the enigma of man's life, is not in Belleforest at all" (Jenkins 1982.95).

Eliot's approach is strikingly similar to the Analytic approach to the *Iliad*: reconstructing a simple, uni-dimensional *Ur*-story on which the finished poem is based, insisting that its stratification is basic for its interpretation and pointing out the defects caused by inconsistencies. However, Eliot did not do what the Analysts of the *Iliad* did: state that they are glad that the more complex and sophisticated layers were added because they are what make the finished poem great. I think nearly every reader of Eliot's essay has reacted in that way: if Eliot's assertions about Shakespeare's relation to Kyd are correct, then the additions and changes are what make *Hamlet* great because the marvellous parts of *Hamlet*, like those of the *Iliad*, are those which are irrelevant to its plot or those in which the hero regards the plot, his basic activity, as a terrible problem. (The same is obviously true of *Macbeth*.)

For Goethe's *Faust* we have the author's own comments in his conversations with Eckermann of May 6, 1827 (cf. July 5,1827; Jan. 3,1830; Feb. 13, 1831):

> They come and ask me what idea I sought to embody in my *Faust*. As if I knew ... that myself! ... Indeed, that would have been a fine thing, if I wanted to string such a rich, variegated ... life ... upon the meagre thread of a single ... idea! It was completely not my manner as a poet to strive for the embodiment of something abstract.

In his conversation with Eckermann of April 18, 1927 Goethe discussed some of the inconsistencies in Shakespeare's plays, many of which involve fundamental aspects of their plots (e.g. Hamlet's description of death as "the undiscovered country from whose bourn no traveller returns"). He stated, "the poet always lets his characters say what in some particular place is fitting, effective, and good, without worrying a great deal ... whether these words contradict another passage".

Another instructive illustration of my hypothesis is provided by Tolstoy's *War and Peace*. It was profoundly influenced by the Homeric epics (Steiner 1959.47 and *passim*), is commonly regarded as Russia's national epic and by general, if not universal, consensus as the great epic of modern Western literature. For, as

Aristotle and Horace knew, the presence or absence of meter is irrelevant for the classification of a work of literature in a genre. The war which begins its title was incomparably more real, important and emotionally stirring to Tolstoy's contemporaries than the *arma* of the *Aeneid* was to Vergil's contemporaries. Miller (1927.42) asserted, "Vergil took the story of Aeneas, which no one before him seemed to have found particularly thrilling or inspiring, and felt the thrill, the inspiration". (Cf. "It was the *Aeneid* itself ... who [*sic*] transformed Aeneas into a national hero": Horsfall 1986.11.) Miller contrasts that with Ovid's recreation in the *Metamorphoses*, where "Ovid is sick and tired of Aeneas". But nearly all readers since Ovid have felt as he did. If Vergil felt any thrill in Aeneas' story he was totally incapable of communicating it. By contrast, few readers of *War and Peace* do not feel that Tolstoy's "brain was boiling over with patriotic zeal when he wrote, 'The walls of Moscow witnessed the shame and defeat of the invincible armies of Napoleon'" (Troyat 1967.52). Yet no one (except perhaps a few eccentrics) has regarded the narration of the course of the war itself or the historical meaning which Tolstoy extracted from it as being the elements which make *War and Peace* great. Its greatness lies in its representation of "life in all its fullness and diversity" (*ibid.* 386), which surrounds the plot and which the plot activates. As Tolstoy noted telegraphically in his diary in March 1865, the 'poetry of the novelist' often springs from "the picture of manners based on a historical event — *Odyssey, Iliad, Year 1805*" (Steiner 1959.47).

I will conclude by comparing my approach to the three most widely held modern views of the *Aeneid* and adding one more criticism of them. One view is that the *Aeneid* concentrates on personal loss and suffering in order to attack Aeneas, his mission and Rome. I agree that the *Aeneid* concentrates on grief, but I think that it does so as an end in itself. Moreover, although very few readers have felt a thrill in the narration of the military-political exploits of Aeneas and his followers in the pursuance of their mission, I and many others sense that genuine feeling is involved in some of the predictions of the achievements of Rome (e.g. by Jupiter in Book 1) and of Augustus (e.g. by Anchises in Book 6). In this I agree with the view that the *Aeneid*'s purpose was to announce and explain the future greatness of Rome and Augustus. But I think that this interpretation totally ignores or distorts the vast majority of the poem's episodes. The view with which I am in closest agreement is that there are two voices, one of public success, the other of personal loss. However, this interpretation, like the others, applies to the *Aeneid* the modern critical obsession with unity and meaning, which is completely alien to ancient literature. It therefore assumes incorrectly that the voices must contribute to an overall message by commenting on each other.

The criticism I will now add is of the usual assumption of the proponents of the propagandistic and 'two voices' views that the pronouncements of public success must be motivated by public devotion and duty. The 'two voices' approach contrasts with that the voice of private loss and suffering, which emanates from Vergil's personal feelings and resonates in the emotions of his readers (cf. the Stoic interpretations of Bowra and Fowler, discussed in chapter 3). But why should patriotic enthusiasm be assumed to emanate from a non-emotional source? It is not only Robert Ardrey who has maintained that national self-identification and assertiveness are fundamental, animal constituents of human emotions. The Marxist Régis Debray argued that also (*New Left Review* 105, September, 1977, 25-41). This nationalistic urge is certainly one of the primal drives which Sigmund Freud thought must be controlled or sublimated in order for civilization to exist. The ancient Greeks and Romans were fully aware of this necessity, and that was a major reason why Freud found them so congenial. That most definitely included Vergil. The line which Freud chose for the title page of *The Interpretation of Dreams*, which he and most of his admirers regard as his masterpiece, is *Aeneid* 7.312 (*flectere si nequeo superos, Acheronta movebo*). There the world below (below the conscious mind — the subconscious — as well as below the physical world) is represented by Allecto, who arouses the forces of nationalism and militarism which are latent in the human mind.

Great literature is one of the highest and most fragile manifestations of civilization. Among the emotions that must be curbed to produce it are patriotism, enthusiasm for strong leaders and militarism. If Nazism had succeeded politically and militarily, it still could not have produced literature in the sense that the *Iliad* is literature, with its sympathy for the home-loving enemy Hector and its hero's lachrymose empathy with Hector's father. Plato knew that Homer and Greek tragedy had to be banned from his ideal state. That ideal state largely reflects an atavistic longing for the small hunting groups in which humans and proto-humans lived for nearly their entire existence and by which their emotions were formed. That is true of its isolation, its hierarchical and disciplined organization, its unquestioningly obedient citizens and its contempt for trade and private property. As Adam Smith pointed out, trade and private property do not exist among animals. Plato's ideal state is also extremely militaristic in its goals and values. When Plato has Socrates summarize it in *Timaeus* 17c-19c, he ends with its ultimate activity: waging war. Such a society would be destroyed by the powerful emotions engendered by Homer and tragedy (*Resp.* 607A). So the only "literature" which can be allowed are "hymns to gods and encomia of good people" (*ibid.*); that is, people who "with body and soul have accomplished noble and difficult works and obeyed the laws" (*Leg.* 801E). The suffering which was the basis of Greek literature must be shown to make moral and intellectual sense by helping those who endure it (*Resp.* 380A-B). Very many interpretations of the *Aeneid* argue that its purpose is to fulfil these criteria.

As I have said, I think that the *Aeneid* does contain genuinely enthusiastic praises of Rome's and Augustus' triumphs, but they are as literarily barren as are the dull, uninspired and uninspiring accounts of Aeneas' military-political actions in the pursuance of his mission (as opposed to his military actions in Book 2, which are in opposition to his mission). Even in the last third of the epic Vergil contrived to devote most of the narrative to the characters who do not advance Aeneas' mission: Mezentius, Camilla, Turnus, etc. However, there is no need to doubt the sincerity of Vergil's patriotism and admiration for Augustus. On the contrary, those are powerful emotions which must be held in check to be a poet, or indeed a civilized person. On the other hand, Vergil's depictions and evocations of love and grief, which have always been regarded as what made him a great poet, were largely 'public'. Fascination with them and the manner and form of their narration derived largely from his literary culture. Indeed, in general, compassion is much less natural and much more the product of socialization and acculturation than patriotism, militarism and hero-worship. The same is true of love. As Stendhal said of Madame Rênal, she would have known earlier that she was in love if she would have read more novels; and the form love takes is very influenced by one's culture (Griffin 1976a.88-9).

Here again, *War and Peace* is instructive. It begins with Anna Pavlovna talking about "the infamies and atrocities of the Antichrist" (Napoleon). Most of her guests agree with her assessment, as with her assertion that "Russia alone is the saviour of Europe. Our benefactor knows his lofty destiny ... our good and sublime emperor". But one of the book's two heroes, Andrey, tries to be fair to Napoleon, and its other hero, Pierre, horrifies his fellow guests by calling him a great man. However, when Tolstoy presents Napoleon as a character, his presentation is completely negative. As a result, critics from Dostoevsky on have observed that Napoleon is the one inauthentic, uni-dimensional character in the novel. Do Andrey and Pierre represent Tolstoy's 'private voice' slipping through his public obligations? Are public obligations the cause of his failure with Napoleon? On the contrary, in the opening scene Tolstoy was fulfilling his public obligation as an author to see and describe characters and events from all sides, an obligation which Greek and Roman authors from Homer on fulfilled brilliantly. This involved making the plot, the war against Napoleon, problematic for those engaged in it; as Homer did with Achilles' anger and Shakespeare with Hamlet's revenge. But when depicting Napoleon, Tolstoy was overcome by private, patriotic emotion to neglect his public duty to respect and display the complexity of people and their social interactions.

However, because Tolstoy usually did perform this public duty, *War and Peace* is the great Russian national epic and, indeed, the great epic of the modern Western world. It succeeded despite its author's patriotism, the historical message he tried to extract from its plot, and (because of?) its lack of unity.

The same is true of the *Aeneid*.

APPENDIX

RECENT INTERPRETATIONS OF THE
NISUS-EURYALUS EPISODE

Examples of the First Approach

Some scholars who think that 9.446-9 is irrelevant to most of the episode attribute it to a quirk caused be Vergil's culture. For example, Heinze (1915.219) says, *sie haben gefehlt, indem sie beide sich fortreissen liessen, ihre nächste Pflicht anderen Wünschen hintanzusetzen.* But in a footnote he adds, *es ist mir freilich zweifelhaft ob Virgil und seine Hörer die Verfehlung des Nisus ... als Pflichtverletzung so empfunden haben* because of their 'southern', impulsive nature. He discusses 9.446-9 on page 372, but does not mention it on 219. However, his qualifying footnote was almost certainly caused by it.

Other critics think the irrelevance was caused by a personal quirk of Vergil's. An example is Griffin (1986.94):

> So profoundly is Virgil moved by the death of the two lovers that he breaks out 'lucky pair ...' We seem to see him trying to put that essentially homosexual sensibility at the service of the patriotic purposes of his poem; and preferring to forget that Nisus should have gone on alone to warn Aeneas and avert general ruin.

G. Williams, Lyne and Duckworth are examples of critics who, like Heinze and Griffin, think that 9.446-9 praises Nisus and Euryalus for their loyalty to each other and that it is irrelevant to most of the episode, but who argue that the irrelevance is deliberate. Williams (1983.205-6, 226-7, 230-1) says that the apostrophe expresses 'personal admiration' and "they are lucky [*Fortunati*] because, loving one another, they died together". But the episode is about the conflict between 'patriotism', which here involves 'getting a message to Aeneas', and the 'twelfth-century heroic ethic' of slaughtering the enemy and obtaining plunder. So the episode is 'morally ambiguous', and Vergil "transcends the delivery of a verdict by his apostrophe". Lyne (1987.229-30,235-7), like Williams, describes 9.446-9 as 'personal' and, like Griffin, as "a romantic response to the preceding text". He argues that the romantic end of the episode and apostrophe are part of a 'voice' which undermines the 'epic voice' to which most of the episode belongs. The epic voice is 'patriotic' and 'imperial' (p.2). Lyne also asserts that the apostrophe to Lausus (10.791-3) is similar. Duckworth (1967.148) regards the main purpose of 9.446-9 as prefiguring 10.791-3.

All the scholars whose views are discussed above interpret 9.446-9 as referring to Nisus' and Euryalus' loyalty to each other. There are, however, a few scholars who recognize the seriousness of their faults and who take 9.446-9 into consideration and regard it as praise, but who think it is patriotic. They, like the above scholars, regard it as irrelevant to most of the episode. They resemble Williams in viewing the episode as morally ambiguous and resemble Lyne in interpreting the apostrophe as undermining it in a disturbing manner. For that reason they describe it as 'ironic'. Examples are Di Cesare (1974.161-6) and Johnson (1976.61-6).

The former points out Nisus' and Euryalus' "rashness and impetuosity ... the mission itself ... they completely lost sight of ... The damage they wrought, the plunder ... were directly damaging to the mission". He also observes, "Their fame and their *fortuna* [cf. *Fortunati* in 9.446] ... is that they acquitted themselves well within their limits. They were so devoted to each other that Nisus joined Euryalus in death when he might have escaped". All this agrees with my analysis except the qualification 'within their limits'. But because Di Cesare, like the other critics, does not think their loving devotion is sufficiently important to dominate the episode, he says of 9.446-9, "The patriotic force is undeniable." And he resembles Williams somewhat in arguing that "the whole episode belongs in a larger perspective ... of the past ... of the kind of heroism and ... individualism that might have been appropriate before but now carry their own irony".

Johnson also appreciates the effect of the episode's end and does not see that the same feeling pervades the entire episode:

> the death of Euryalus is possessed of an extraordinary loveliness ... yet the beauty of these verses calls attention to itself in a way that impedes the progress of the narrative ... the verses exhibit something that smacks of the grotesque, of *Liebestod*. Though Vergil is careful to understate the eroticism of the entire passage, he gives it vivid emphasis at the climax ... the physical beauty of Euryalus ... give[s] emotional significance to the final act of the dying Nisus ... [which] attains ... nobility both by ... his gesture of love ... and by ... Vergil's patriotic apostrophe to the reckless, vainglorious lovers.

He realizes that this interpretation raises two obvious questions: "The glamorous broken doll and his lover are eternal patriots of Rome? What have their deaths, their romance, their mindless, murderous rampage to do with the destiny of Rome?" His answer is that in relation to the episode's end "the patriotic apostrophe ... [is a] foil with ironic indecorum".

I mention when outlining the four approaches to this episode that the first has two defects. The first, not seeing that Nisus' and Euryalus' love and loyalty pervades the episode, is obvious from many of the quotations above and statments like Lyne's (1987.229) that the 'erotic image' of the simile of the cut flower "adds an additional and unexpected nuance". The second defect, minimizing the glowing praise of 9.446-9, is also obvious from many of the statements quoted above and in those like Heinze's (1915.219) that if Nisus *aus geschütztem Hinterhalt den Freund sterben sähe und, zu vernünftig um den aussichtslosen Kampf gegen die Überzahl aufzunehmen, pflichtgemäss fürbass zöge*, he would have *für kalt und lieblos gegolten*. Alternatively, Williams (1983.205) asserts that *fortunati* "does not mean 'lucky because you will be celebrated in my poem'. They are no luckier in that respect than all the others mentioned in the *Aeneid*". But 9.446-9 manifestly does promise them special fame, and, as I show, later Romans acknowledged that. Lyne (1987.236) says that "a reader inclined to hearken to the epic voice [of most of the episode] need not be irritatingly diverted" by the 'further voices' of the episode's end and apostrophe because they are 'discreet'.

Examples of the Second Approach

When Otis (1963) mentions the Nisus-Euryalus episode without regard to 9.446-9, he says that its 'purpose' is to show the damage caused by lust for battle and plunder, for which they 'pay the penalty' (363-4,393; cf.315, 317,345,381). But when he takes the apostrophe into consideration, he must contradict that, since he assumes it refers to their military actions. On pages 349-50 he says that Nisus and Euryalus

> possess *virtus* ... but are overcome ... by the excessive, irrational violence of the one and the desperate *eros* of the other ... His is a *Liebestod* ... marked by utter forgetfulness of his ... manifest duty ... Yet Vergil [writes] ... 'Fortunati ambo ...' He here shows that he admires their heroism in spite of all the reservations he has ... expressed.

However, if *fortunati ambo* refers to their heroism, why does Vergil single out for such glowing praise an instance of heroism that is so flawed and ultimately futile? Otis' longest analysis of the episode is the most interesting (388-9):

> the episode is essentially paradigmatic, a ... *exemplum virtutis* ... What, however, gives Virgil's *exemplum* its emotional power is precisely the empathy by which Virgil makes us ... share the feelings of Nisus (esp. from 1.386 on) ... His use of the remarkable Catullan simile [433-7] ... is here a key ... The simile is ... preceded by [431-2] ... and followed by [438-9] ... So Vergil's pause here, to mark by the simile the ... meaning of the event ... beauty ruthlessly cut off ... takes us ... into his own ... feeling that is also ... that of the protective lover, Nisus ... We thus can proceed with little sense of discontinuity from the ... conclusion [444-5] ... to the overt editorializing of 'Fortunati ambo ...' In the end the episode is assimilated to ... the ideology of Roman patriotism.

Here Otis' analysis of the text itself leads to the correct explanation of why they are praised. But his assumption that the episode must be about patriotism and the proper conduct necessary for bringing about the Roman people causes him to subordinate that explanation to the hypothesis that Nisus and Euryalus are an *exemplum virtutis*, a hypothesis which his own analyses elsewhere show to be indefensible.

Pavlock (1985), like Otis, describes Nisus' and Euryalus' behaviour as completely negative when she does not consider 9.446-9. Indeed, she says that her principal difference with Fitzgerald, whose views will be discussed below, is on the issue of 'ironic distance' (207n4). She points out Nisus' and Euryalus' hideous brutality to the Rutulians (213-16). Indeed, she mentions examples of it which I have not used. She also says that Vergil "shows the ... side of *amor* that can be destructive" since because of it Nisus "abandons his public mission" (219). And she quotes

9.498-9 to demonstrate that as a result they "impeded the public cause" (222). Pavlock asserts that their conduct in Book 5 forshadows that in Book 9 by showing that "both ... are very concerned with material rewards ... at the expense of ethical conduct" (212-13). Moreover, although she recognizes that Nisus' friendship with Euryalus is a form of *pietas*, she says that that "leads him first to behaviour in Book 5 that cannot be deemed pious and second to total abandonment of the civic *pietas* ... in the night-raid" (222).

However, in her last paragraph (224) she quotes 9.446-9. Then, like Otis, she feels obliged to mention their positive qualities. These are "their vitality, their potential as warriors, and their great bond of friendship". But throughout the rest of her article she had argued that these qualities cause totally immoral and destructive actions. So why should they be granted this extraordinary apostrophe?

Pavlock's analysis suffers from the same defect as the others. She fails to realize how important and admirable love was for Vergil and his contemporaries. She could not see that the fact that Nisus is *insignis ... amore pio* for the beautiful boy Euryalus makes all other considerations insignificant. This deficiency is clear in her discussion of *pietas*. She realizes that it is multi-vocal in the *Aeneid* (221-2 and *passim*), and she had only to look at the passages cited under *pietas* and *inpii* in Pichon (1902) to know that among Vergil's contemporaries *pietas* frequently meant loyalty in erotic relationships. But she asserts that in 5.296 "*pius* ... signals ... that Nisus and Euryalus are not physically involved" (218) and that Nisus "put his friendship with Euryalus on a higher [*sic*] level ... of a familial relationship" (222).

It should be noted that many critics only narrowly avoid the type of self-contradictions committed by Otis and Pavlock. An example is Heinze, discussed above.

Examples of the Third Approach

Examples of critics who ignore 9.446-9 are Nethercut (1971.138-9), who interprets Nisus' and Euryalus' conduct as typical of the Trojans' destructiveness and immorality; Hornsby (1970.10-11,32-3, 66,69-70,120), Dutra (1987.82-3,85) and Saylor (1990), who regard Nisus' and Euryalus' 'savage destruction', 'terrible irresponsibility', 'madness and fury' and anarchic, un-Vergilian heroism as similar to Turnus'; and Jenkyns (1985.75), who describes Euryalus as "a pitiable fool, who brings about the needless destruction of his lover and himself" and uses that to illustrate that Vergil was a 'melancholy optimist' since Euryalus and Nisus are among "the sad side-effects of the progress of the Roman destiny".

An example of a critic who argues that 9.446-9 should not be taken seriously is Huxley (1974). He dwells on Nisus' and Euryalus' immorality, brutality and negligence in Books 9 and 5. Until his last sentence he asserts that that makes their episodes in both books literary failures, which "strike a false note and call for drastic revision" (76). In his last sentence he suggests a possible purpose for their deficiencies: to "contrast the[ir] irrational pietas ... with the rational pietas of their absent leader". He attributes the high regard their episode in Book 9 enjoys to

9.446-9, but asserts that the apostrophe was caused by a strong tendency on Vergil's part to side with the winning against the losing side (75). It is not worth the space to attempt a systematic refutation of this assertion. Whatever readers of the *Aeneid* have viewed its purpose as being, most have been struck by "Vergil's habit of siding with the 'under-dog'", to quote from Hahn's excellent study of this subject (1925.185). With regard to Huxley's argument that Vergil does not end Dido's or Camilla's story with a eulogy because they are on the losing side (75), I should point out that Vergil follows the ultimate victory of the ultimate victor, Aeneas, with lines that are very far from eulogy (12.951-2).

Quinn (1969), Boyle (1972) and Fitzgerald (1972) are examples of critics who argue that 9.446-9 is ironic in that it means the opposite of what it seems to mean and so reinforces the negative portrayal of Nisus and Euryalus. Quinn (12-16) first discusses them among cases of the futile 'heroic impulse' to kill and be killed, which he says pervades the *Aeneid*. To that he attributes Nisus' suicidal behavior at the end of the episode. So his and Euryalus' deaths are "the price they pay for" the "indiscriminate slaughter of the sleeping Rutuli". He then discusses them as part of his analysis of the entire *Aeneid* (200-7). There also Nisus' death is "a useless gesture of self-immolation and destruction" (206), and he and Euryalus "who deal out death with so little thought for their victims are perhaps not so greatly to be pitied ... when death overtakes them" (205). As for the apostrophe, it "strikes an almost openly ironical note" since after it "the spotlight falls on the gleaming helmet of Messapus and the *phalerae* of Rhamnes" (206-7).

Boyle and Fitzgerald view Nisus' and Euryalus' conduct as illustrations of the values of Aeneas' mission, which they regard as negative. Boyle says (79),

> the hollowness of the ... *fama* and *laudes* which the Trojan pair had sought and the moral repugnance of the imperial process for which they sacrificed their lives [*sic*] are brought sharply to the reader's attention by the forceful irony of ... 446-49 (the irony consists in the blatant appeal to the very values responsible for the destruction ... Nisus and Euryalus perpetrated and to which inevitably they ... were subject). (Cf. Boyle 1986.121,89-92.)

Fitzgerald argues that they make manifest 'the possible consequences' of the attitudes which underlie Aeneas' mission (120). These are 'strong desire, direct enthusiasm' (118) and 'unexamined and simplistic zeal' (126). So, *'Fortunati ambo!* (446). This is ... the ideology of patriotism ... But I doubt that Vergil's judgment is *'fortunati'*" (116-17,cf.136). For (126),

> How can men ... grant adulation ... to such devastation, to such blatant failure ... Can such values as we see ... in this episode ... go uncriticised by the world of the poet, Rome in the twenties B.C.? Can this be how men live and aspire to live? Can Virgil seriously approve the judgement, *fortunati ambo*?

Fitzgerald's rhetorical questions betray the weakness of all the modern critics who analyze this episode. They do not see that 'the world of the poet' was fascinated by passionate, agonizing, self-destructive love.

A modified form of the third approach is Winnington-Ingram's

(1971-2). He points out some of the military and patriotic defects which Nisus and Euryalus manifest (68-9) and expresses sympathy with Boyle's interpretation, but says, "to me ... this seems to swing too far away from the old simple notion of Virgil as a propagandist". He finds the key in Parry's 'two voices' approach (68,70). So the apostrophe expresses 'the tensions and contradictions' in the epic (70).

Examples of the Fourth Approach

Klingner (1967) points out the uniqueness and tremendous force of the praise expressed in 9.446-9 (561,563). He also emphasizes its 'lyrical' quality, a term he seems to use to mean what Otis calls 'sympathy' and 'empathy'. Klingner observes this quality also in the descriptions of Pasiphae's, Orpheus' and Dido's sufferings (109,353,451,cf.434,521,548). Like many other scholars, his analysis is sensitive and accurate when he concentrates on the events leading to the apostrophe. For instance, he observes that in 9.432ff. *der Erzähler sieht Euryalus mit den Augen des Liebenden* (564), and that something of the 'lyrical' quality, *lebt ... nicht nur in ... fortunati ambo usw., sondern schon in der Erzählung von Nisus und Euryalus überhaupt, besonders in den ... Versen, die den Tod der beiden enthalten ... Liebesgefühl durchatmet auch diese Verse* (564) and

> Nisus ... wirft sich ... über den toten Euryalus ... [as in *Ecl.* 5.22 and *Aen.* 11.150, which] sind rückhaltlose Gebärden der Liebe ... Das Unvergleichliche der Verse [444-5] ... liegt darin, dass jene Gebärde zugleich die beiden im Tode vereint und ... das Mitfühlen ... ist wichtiger ... als die Darstellung der Begebenheit an sich (565).

However, Klingner also resembles the other critics in that he does not consider the possibility that the episode's primary interest could be 'merely' overwhelming love. He, like the others, assumed that its purpose must be to comment on the subject of the *Aeneid*, and the subject of the *Aeneid* is Roman patriotism, whether Vergil was praising or attacking it. So he qualifies the assertions he makes on page 564 by saying that the love which pervades the end of the episode is not of the type in Catullus 64, *sondern, die Liebe zwischen den beiden jungen Helden, Liebe, die zu Taten befeuert.* And he follows the last passage quoted above with the following paragraph, which concludes his discussion:

> In der Erzählung von Nisus and Euryalus ist ein lyrischer Zug, ja etwas von einem Liebesgedicht mit erhalten. Dass sie dabei ... ein Preis elder, zu höchstem Sinn und Tun befeuernder Freundschaft, dass sie ein gültiges Glied ... des Rom-Gedichts geworden ist, das erst macht sie unbergleichlich.

And on page 561 he says,

> Sein [Vergil's] Herz ist ihrer Freundesliebe, ist der Blüte ihrer Jugend zugewandt. Dies Gefühl allein würde aber schwerlich genügt haben, sie so überschwenglich zu preisen. Virgil erlaubt sich ... nichts Abgesondertes ... Dieser Bezug zeigt sich hier ... in den Worten des Aletes [247-50] ...

Klingner goes on here, as elsewhere, to assert that Aletes' words provide the key to lines 446-9. But Aletes says that the existence of such youths shows that Rome will endure because of their intention to get through to Aeneas. Their love for each other, which occasions the praise in 446-9, causes them to forget that intention, just as in Book 5 it causes them to cheat. Klingner tries to get around the fact that their mission is unsuccessful the first time he mentions Aletes' words (560). He points out that the situation of the Trojans makes their mission desperately important and they fail, *jedoch ihr Tun offenbart in der Not Kräfte des Innern, die den Eingeschlossenen Mut und Hoffnung zu geben vermögen. Als ... Aletes* (246ff.) ... Klingner says that this is based on *Iliad* 10, where the Greeks' fortunes are also at their most desperate, *und ein Handstreich ... unterbricht das bänglich gespannte Wesen und gewinnt der Nacht Erstaunliches ab*. But that is just the point. Odysseus and Diomedes succeed brilliantly and as a result their episode ends with the Greeks rejoicing (10.541,565). Nisus and Euryalus totally fail to accomplish the goal which encouraged Aletes and the others. So the ultimate result of their actions for the Trojans is *torpent infractae ad proelia vires* (499).

Lennox (1977) in the first paragraph of his study of this episode states (331),

> In a ... admirable study Klingner ... illustrated the great importance of ... vv.446-9 [which Vergil wrote] ... because his heart was drawn towards the loving comradeship of these two ... because ... here was proof that all was not lost for the Aeneadae (see Aletes' words vv.247-250).

On page 341 he paraphrases with approval Klingner's observations that Vergil "envelops the final destruction of the pair in a poignant lyricism with elements borrowed from *Liebesgedicht*" and that "the flower-simile [shows] ... what motivated Nisus to abandon his mission".

Lennox adds three elements to Klingner's analysis. First (334n19), he points out that the introductions of Nisus and Euryalus in Books 5 and 9 "provide information ... which is ... closely relevant to the episode". Second (341-2), he says that Vergil

> models the promises which Iulus makes to Nisus upon those which Agamemnon makes ... in Iliad IX ... showing that ... the absence of Aeneas is as serious ... as was that of Achilles ... [Thus] the carrying of a message to Aeneas assumes its true importance.

Third, Lennox tries to refute the accusations that the attack on the Rutulians is sneaky, brutal and unnecessary and that Nisus should not have gone back for Euryalus. These are considerations which Klingner ignores.

Lennox acknowledges that Euryalus is 'rash, unthinking' (341) and that he causes his destruction by needlessly taking plunder and indulging in blood-lust (336-7). But he argues (336-9) that slaughter and plunder were not part of Nisus' original plan. Nisus slaughters the Rutulians because "with the spirit of a hungry lion [he] cannot pass by [this] ... chance". However, if Lennox is correct, then Nisus' blood-lust, graphically illustrated by the vicious lion, does not interrupt his main purpose; it interrupts his only purpose, which is worse. And Lennox demonstrates how important that purpose was. Lennox also asserts (337) that the Rutulians' drunkenness stresses not the needlessness of the slaughter but "the *mollitia* of these 'barbarians' (they are likened to *molle pecus* at 341)". But *molle pecus* is part of the effect created in 340-1 of the brutality of the attack (R. Williams 1973, on 9.340). And what of the Trojans' drunkenness in 2.265? Lennox does not consider other objections to the attack on the Rutulians. He proceeds to "Nisus' second alleged error of judgement ... Without hesitation he returns in search of his friend" (339). He points out (340) that "Nisus is ... faced with a ... choice between ... two duties: that to his people ... and that to his bosom-friend ... Virgil gives no hint of condemnation". The last observation is an extreme understatement. Lennox concludes (342): "Here they are now, the youth upon which the Aeneadae will depend for their future ... Here is an example of what might be hoped for from Augustus' ... youth policy." And he ends by quoting Aletes' words in conjunction with lines 446-9.

However, even assuming that Lennox had successfully refuted all objections to Nisus' part in the attack on the Rutulians, could Vergil still have singled out Nisus and Euryalus for extraordinary praise for the reasons quoted above? Lennox acknowledges Euryalus' self-destructive faults and Nisus' choice to ignore a vitally important mission. Could the Trojans' future depend on such people? Lennox also acknowledges Nisus' 'unsporting' conduct in Book 5 (333n19). Could this have been an example for Augustus' youth policy? Moreover, they are homosexual lovers, which makes them poor guarantors of the Trojans' future continuation and poor examples for Augustus' social programs, which tried strenuously to promote family life and procreation.

Thornton (1976) does not mention Klingner, and her book was published the year before Lennox's article, but she shares their view that 9.446-9 is praise, that it is very important and that the episode must be evaluated with reference to it. In the first two paragraphs of her discussion of the episode (164), she says about the apostrophe,

> if noticed, [it] is then taken to be ironical. This is inevitable if the episode is interpreted as an instance of evil *furor* and ... [its] consequences ... [But 9.446-9 is] so weighty and serious that irony is out of the question ... whatever Nisus and Euryalus did must, in Virgil's eyes, be honourable and great so as to deserve his praise.

Like Lennox, she tries to defend the attack on the Rutulians. She argues that it is necessary because Nisus says it is (167-8). But I have amply demonstrated that Vergil leaves no doubt that it is not necessary. Nisus may have been misled by his blood-lust or may be giving an excuse. She proceeds to assert (168) that "slaughtering the enemy means fame ... in a just cause ... Virgil represents the war of the Trojans against the Latins and Rutulians as just". But in the beginning of the next book (10.8-14) Vergil has Jupiter explicitly contrast this war with a just war. Furthermore, many of the passages cited in my discussion of the episode, especially Livy 42.47, show that the methods used by Nisus and Euryalus were regarded as contemptible even in a just war. My analysis also refutes another of Thornton's arguments: "when Nisus is compared to a hungry lion ... that is a description of ... warriordom which ... is ... glorious" (168). Again like Lennox, she defends Nisus for going back for Euryalus. She points out (169-70) that "when Virgil calls the love of Nisus for Euryalus *pius* (5.296) he means it: Nisus is loyal to the bitter end"; and that (171) "there is ... no hint of a condemnation of Nisus for neglecting his duty. The only derogatory statement ... is ... *imprudens* 9.386, that is, without taking care that Euryalus was following him" and she compares Book 5.

However, like the other critics who make perceptive observations about the last part of the episode, she is unable to follow them to their logical conclusion because she could not believe that the extraordinary praise in lines 446-9 could be granted for love alone. Love must subserve something 'higher': "they were ... true warriors - and they had this love for battle in common" (172).

The clash between a sensitive analysis of the Nisus-Euryalus episode and the preconception that the glory promised in the apostrophe could not be for 'merely' love is perhaps most stark in Kraggerud (1968.191-8). He emphasizes Vergil's admiration for Nisus' personal devotion to Euryalus in Books 5 and 9 and that "Vergil hat die beiden Nisus-Euryalus-Episoden ... aufeinander bezogen und dadurch eine sinnvolle Einheit geschaffen" (193). And he points out the importance of 9.466-9 (194). But he asserts about it:

> Die Verse drücken Dankbarkeit und Verpflichtung ... gegenüber jungen Männern solcher Art und Gesinnung aus. Die Beständigkeit des römischen Imperiums hängt von solchen Leistungen ab. Nisus und Euryalus sind ... hervorragende Vertreter jener Qualitäten und Fähigkeiten, die Rom gross gemacht haben. (198)

Makowski (1989) expresses his admiration for the analyses of Thornton, Lennox, Kraggerud and Klingner, but he does recognize that Vergil attributes central importance to Nisus' and Euryalus' love in Books 5 and 9 and asserts that it is "of paramount importance to read the *aristeia* performed by Nisus and Euryalus *qua erastes* and *qua eromenos*" (11-12). But even he assumes that these characters cannot be the subject of a long narrative and glowing praise 'merely' because they love each other. For him also their importance is their *aristeia*. Their love is important because it motivates totally admirable conduct in both their episodes.

As I explain in chapter 1 when I outline the four approaches above, all the evaluations of the episode in this Appendix are from 1963 or later, except Heinze's. I will now discuss briefly eight from before 1963. These are mentioned by Duckworth in the beginning of his article (1967.129-30) and seem to be similar to my interpretation. The first two, from Pease (1935.6) and Cartault (1926.667), are also quoted by Thornton (1976.164). Pease is quoting from De Witt (1930, discussed below) with whom he expresses disagreement (6n29). Cartault's full statement is *l'épisode ... n'est pas seulement la glorification de l'héroïsme, mais aussi de l'amitié*. Those by Mendell (1938-9.16-17 and 1951.216-17) are *obiter dicta* made in passing as parts of discussions of the frequency of Catullan reminisces in the *Aeneid* and whether the episode was originally an independent poem. Büchner's (1960.109) is a single sentence in which he says this episode is 'perhaps' (*vielleicht*) an exception to the rule that everything in the *Aeneid* serves the epic's goal. The three others are parts of analyses of the meaning of the episode whose conclusions are at variance with Duckworth's description of them. De Witt (1930.34-5) says that Nisus was 'overindulgent' to Euryalus, that he died a 'hero's death' and that the episode in Book 9 teaches "a sad philosophy of life ... that virtues in excess may bring ruin". Richardson (1938) maintains that in the episode "there is a pointed contrast uniformly maintained *passim* between the two types of warriors: Nisus ... and Euryalus" (140-1) and that "the love of N. and E. ... is .. nowhere (in Book IX) stated by Virgil" (141n2). Colmant's article (1951) is entitled "L'Épisode de Nisus ... ou le poème de l'amitié". But his interpretation follows the fourth approach discussed above. He says that by this episode *Virgile voulut inspirer ... à la fois une conception haute et pure de l'amitié ainsi que l'ambition de servir la patrie jusqu'au péril même de la vie* (91) and Nisus' *grand souci est de développer dans son frère d'armes le goût de la fidélité au service du Prince* (97). In his concluding paragraph on the episode (98) he states, *En résumé, Virgile nous montre ... la* virtus romana *dans la jeunesse ... rend apte à servir l'État*.

There is one more analysis I will mention, which comes closest to mine. Bellincioni (1985.424-6) points out the importance of Nisus' *pius amor* and Euryalus' beauty in Books 5 and 9 and that the apostrophe is for Nisus' love. But she cannot resist seeing a moral in the episode: *Niso ... paga con la vita la debolezza di aver accettato come compagno in una difficile impresa l'immaturo E.; e il fanciullo che nella sua infantile vanità ... scambia la guerra per un gioco*.

BIBLIOGRAPHY

R. Allain 1946: "Une 'Nuit spirituelle' d'Énée", *REL* 24, 189-198.
W. Anderson 1956: *Ethos and Education in Greek Music* (Cambridge, Mass.).
W. Arrowsmith 1959: "The Criticism of Greek Tregedy", *The Tulane Drama Review* 3, 31-57.
R. Austin 1955: *P. Vergili Maronis Aeneidos Liber Quartus* (Oxford).
———, 1966: *P. Vergili Maronis Aeneidos Liber Secundus*, corrected edition (Oxford).
———, 1971: *P. Vergili Maronis Aeneidos Liber Primus* (Oxford).
———, 1977: *P. Vergili Maronis Aeneidos Liber Sextus* (Oxford).
D. Shackleton Bailey 1956: *Propertiana* (Cambridge).
W. Barrett 1966: *Euripides, Hippolytus*, corrected edition (Oxford).
W. Bates 1930: *Euripides: A Student of Human Nature* (New York).
M. Bellincioni 1985: "Eurialo", *Enciclopedia Virgiliana*, Vol. 2 (Rome) 424-426.
C. Bowra 1933: "Aeneas the Stoic Ideal", *G & R* 3, 8-21.
A. Boyle 1972: "The Meaning of the *Aeneid*: A Critical Inquiry: Part I", *Ramus* 1, 63-90.
———, 1986: *The Chaonian Dove* (Leiden).
A. Bradley 1969: "Augustan Culture and a Radical Alternative: Vergil's *Georgics*", *Arion* 8, 347-358.
C. Brink 1963: *Horace on Poetry, I: Prolegomena to the Literary Epistles* (Cambridge).
———, 1971: *Horace on Poetry*: The Ars Poetica (Cambridge).
R. Brown 1987: *Lucretius on Love and Sex* (Leiden).
S. Bruwer 1974: "The Theme of Exile in Virgil's Aeneid", unpublished doctoral dissertation at the University of Stellenbosch, South Africa.
K. Buchner 1960: "Vergil's *Aeneis*", *Studi in onore di Luigi Castiglioni* (Florence) 105-126.
F. Buffière 1956: *Les Mythes d'Homère et la pensée grecque* (Paris).
A. Bulloch 1985 "Hellenistic Poetry", *The Cambridge History of Classical Literature*, Vol. 1, 541-621.
F. Cairns 1974: "Some Observations on Propertius 1.1", *CQ* 24, 94-110.
———, 1989: *Virgil's Augustan Epic* (Cambridge).
W. Camps 1961: *Propertius, Elegies, Book I* (Cambridge).
———, 1967: *Propertius, Elegies, Book II* (Cambridge).
———, 1969: *An Introduction to Virgil's Aeneid* (Oxford).
———, 1980: *An Introduction to Homer* (Oxford).
A. Cartault 1926: *L'Art de Virgile dans l'Énéide* (Paris).
H. Clarke 1967: *The Art of the Odyssey* (Engelwood Cliffs, New Jersey).
R. Coleman 1977: *Vergil, Eclogues* (Cambridge).
P. Colmant 1951: "L'Épisode de Nisus et Euryale ou le poème de l'amitié", *LEC* 19, 89-100.
S. Commager (editor) 1966: *Virgil: A Collection of Critical Essays* (Englewood Cliffs, New Jersey).
———, 1974: *A Prolegomenon to Propertius* (Cincinnati).
———, 1981: "Fateful Words: Some Conversations in *Aeneid* 4", *Arethusa* 14, 1, 101-114.
J. Conington 1884: *The Works of Virgil*, Vol. 2, 4th ed., rev. by H. Nettleship (London).
L. Constans 1938: *L'Énéide de Virgile* (Paris).

R. Conway 1906: "An Unnoticed Aspect of Vergil's Personality", *Proc of the Classical Assoc.* 28-37.
———, 1921: *New Studies in a Great Inheritance* (London).
E. Curtius 1963: *Kritische Essays zur europäischen Literatur*, 3rd ed. (Berne).
H. Dahlmann 1953: "Varros schrift De Poemetis und die hellenistisch-römische Poetik", *Abhandlungen der Akademie ... Mainz* 3, 89-152.
R. Dawe 1963: "Inconsistency of Plot and Character in Aeschylus", *PCPhS* 89, 21-62.
J. de Romilly 1961: *L'Évolution du pathétique d'Eschyle à Euripide* (Paris).
N. De Witt 1907: *The Dido Episode in the Aeneid of Vergil* (Chicago).
———, 1930: "Vergil and the Tragic Drama", *CJ* 26,19-27.
M. di Cesare 1974: *The Altar and the City: A Reading of Vergil's Aeneid* (N.Y.).
K. Dover 1974: *Greek Popular Morality in the Time of Plato and Aristotle* (Oxford).
G. Duckworth 1964: "Variety and Repetition in Vergil's Hexameters", *TAPhA* 95, 9-65.
———, 1965-6: "Hexameter Patterns in Vergil", *PVS* 5, 39-49.
———, 1966: "Vergil's Subjective Style and its Relation to Meter", *Vergilius* 12, 1-10.
———, 1967: "The Significance of Nisus and Euryalus for *Aeneid* IX-XII", *AJPh* 88, 129-150.
D. Dudley 1961: "A Plea for Aeneas", *G&R* s.s. 8, 52-60.
J. Dutra 1987: "The Fortunes of War: The Birth of a Legacy", *AugAge* 6, 80-91.
J. Ellsworth 1986: "Ovid's '*Aeneid*' Reconsidered (*Met.* 13.623-14.608)", *Vergilius* 32, 27-32.
G. Else 1963: *Aristotle's Poetics: The Argument*, corrected edition (Cambridge, Mass.).
P. Enk 1962: *Sex. Propertii Elegiarum Liber Secundus* (Leiden).
E. Fantham 1975: "Vergil's Dido and Seneca's Tragic Heroines", *G&R* s.s. 22, 1-10.
S. Farron 1979: "The Portrayal of Women in the Iliad", *AClass* 22, 15-31.
———, 1979-80, "The *Odyssey* as an anti-Aristocratic Statement", *Studies in Antiquity* 1, 59-101.
———, 1979-80a: "The Roman Invention of Evil", *Studies in Antiquity* 1, 12-46.
———, 1980: "The Aeneas-Dido episode as an Attack on Aeneas' Mission and Rome", *G&R* s.s. 27, 34-47.
———, 1980a: "*Aeneid* VI, 826-835 (The Vision of Julius Caesar and Pompey) as an Attack on Augustan Propaganda", *AClass* 23, 53-68.
———, 1981: "The Death of Turnus Viewed in the Perspective of its Historical Background", *AClass* 24, 97-106.
———, 1982: "The Abruptness of the End of the *Aeneid*", *AClass* 25, 136-141.
———, 1983: "The Sentimentalism, Romanticism and Emtionalism of the Ancient Greeks and Romans, with Specific Reference to *Aeneid* 4", *AClass* 26, 83-94.
———, 1985: "Furie/Furore", *Enciclopedia Virgiliana*, Vol. 2 (Rome) 620-622.
———, 1986: "Aeneas' Revenge for Pallas as a Criticism of Aeneas", *AClass* 29, 69-83.
———, 1988: "Sentimentalismo", *Enciclopedia Virginilana*, Vol. 4 (Rome) 776-778.
———, 1989: "The Introduction of Characters in the *Aeneid*", *AClass* 32, 107-110.
———, 1992: "*Pius Aeneas* in *Aeneid* 4.393-6", *Studies in Latin Literature and Roman History, Collection Latomus*, Vol. 6 (Bruxelles) 260-276.
L. Feder 1954: "Vergil's Tragic Queen", *CJ* 49, 197-209.
D. Feeney 1983: "The Taciturnity of Aeneas", *CQ* 33, 204-19.

J. Ferguson 1970: "Fire and Wound: The Imagery of *Aeneid* IV. 1ff", *PVS* 10, 57-63.
N. Fisher 1979: *"Hybris* and Dishonour: II", *G&R* s.s. 26, 32-47.
G. Fitzgerald 1972: "Nisus and Euryalus: A Paradigm of Futile Behaviour and the Tragedy of Youth", *Cicero and Virgil: Studies in Honour of Harold Hunt*, ed. J. Martyn (Amsterdam) 114-137.
C. Fordyce 1961: *Catullus: A Commentary* (Oxford).
——, 1977: *P. Vergili Maronis Aeneidos Libri VII-VIII* (Oxford).
W. Fowler 1919: *The Death of Turnus* (Oxford).
H. Fränkel 1975: *Early Greek Poetry and Philosophy*. Translated by M. Hadas and J. Willis (Oxford).
E. Fraenkel 1957: *Horace* (Oxford).
——, 1962: *Aeschylus, Agamemnon*, corrected edition (Oxford).
R. Frank 1968: "Catullus 51: *Otium* versus *Virtus*", *TAPhA* 99, 233-239.
E. Fredricksmeyer 1965: "On the Unity of Catullus 51", *TAPhA* 96, 153-163.
M. Geymonat 1973: *P. Vergili Maronis Opera* (Turin).
M. Gigante 1950: "La cultura letteraria a Pompei", *Pompeiana* (Naples) 111-143.
——, 1979: *Civiltà delle forme letterarie nell'antica Pompei* (Naples).
F. Goodyear 1981: *The Annals of Tacitus, Books 1-6*, Vol. 2 (Cambridge).
H. Gotoff 1984: "The Transformation of Mezentius", *TAPhA* 114, 191-218.
T. Gould 1991: *The Ancient Quarrel Between Poetry and Philosophy* (Princeton).
A. Gow 1952: *Theocritus*, Vol. 2, 2nd ed. (Cambridge).
K. Grandsen 1984: *Virgil's Iliad: An Essay on Epic Narrative* (Cambridge).
W. Grant 1952: "Elegiac Themes in Horace's *Odes", Studies in Honour of Gilbert Norwood*, ed. M. White (Toronto) 194-202.
J. Griffin 1976: "Homeric Pathos and Objectivity", *CQ* n.s. 26, 161-187.
——, 1976a: "Augustan Poetry and the Life of Luxury", *JRS* 66, 87-104.
——, 1977: "The Epic Cycle and the Uniqueness of Homer", *JHS* 97, 39-53.
——, 1980: *Homer on Life and Death* (Oxford).
——, 1985: *Latin Poets and Roman Life* (Oxford).
——, 1986: *Virgil* (Oxford).
R. Griffith 1985: "Literary Allusion in Virgil, *Aeneid* 9.435ff.", *Vergilius* 31, 40-44.
G. Grube 1965: *The Greek and Roman Critics* (London).
E. Hahn 1925: "Vergil and 'the Underdog'"", *TAPhA* 56, 185-212.
——, 1931: "Pietas versus Violentia in the *Aeneid*", *CW* 25, 9-21.
S. Halliwell 1986: *Aristotle's Poetics* (London).
E. Havelock 1963: *Preface to Plato* (Cambridge, Mass.).
M. Heath 1986: "The Origins of Modern Pindaric Criticism", *JHS* 106, 85-98.
——, 1987: *The Poetics of Greek Tragedy* (London).
——, 1987a: "'Iure Principem Tenet': Euripides' *Hecuba*", *BICS* 34, 40-68.
——, 1989: *Unity in Greek Poetics* (Oxford).
R. Heinze 1915: *Virgils Epische Technik*, 3rd ed. (Leipzig).
J. Hellegouarc'h 1963: *Le Vocabulaire latin des relations et des partis politiques sous la République* (Paris).
J. Henderson 1975: *The Maculate Muse* (New Haven).
J. Henry 1878: *Aeneidea*, Vol. 2 (Dublin).
A. Heubeck, S. West, J. Hainsworth 1988: *A Commentary on Homer's Odyssey*, Vol. 1 (Oxford).
G. Highet, 1972: *Speeches in the Aeneid* (Princeton).
R. Hornsby 1970: *Patterns of Action in the Aeneid* (Iowa City).
N. Horsfall 1986: "The Aeneas-Legend and the *Aeneid*", *Vergilius* 32, 8-17.

M. Humbert 1972: *Le Remariage à Rome* (Milan).
R. Hunter 1989: *Apollonius of Rhodes, Argonautica, Book III* (Cambridge).
H. Huxley 1974: "Fortunati Ambo: Raid and Reputation", *Proceedings of the North-West Conference of Foreign Languages* 25, 73-77.
R. Jebb 1876: *The Attic, Orators from Antiphon to Isaeos*, Vol. 1 (London).
H. Jenkins 1982: *Hamlet* (London).
R. Jenkyns 1982: *Three Classical Poets: Sappho, Catullus and Juvenal* (London).
——, 1985: "Pathos, Tragedy and Hope in the *Aeneid*", *JRS* 75, 60-77.
W. Johnson 1976: *Darkness Visible* (Berkeley).
D. Joly 1978: "Présence des *Bucoliques* à Pompéi", *Présence de Virgile*, ed. R. Chevallier (Paris).
J. Jones 1987: "*Aeneid* 4.238-278 and the Persistence of an Allegorical Interpretation", *Vergilius* 33, 29-37.
W. Kaufmann 1968: *Tragedy and Philosophy* (Garden City, N.Y.).
E. Kenney 1971: *Lucretius, De Rerum Natura, Book III* (Cambridge).
L. Kepple 1976: "Arruns and the Death of Aeneas", *AJPh* 97, 344-360.
W. Ker 1926 (editor): *Essays of John Dryden*, Vol. 2 (Oxford).
H. Kitto 1956: *From and Meaning in Drama* (London).
F. Klingner 1967: *Virgil, Bucolica, Georgica, Aeneis* (Zürich).
C. Knapp 1917: "Molle atque Facetum", *AJPh* 38, 194-199.
B. Knox 1950: "The Serpent and the Flame: The Imagery of the Second Book of the *Aeneid*", *AJPh* 71, 379-400.
D. Konstan 1977: *Catallus' Indictment of Rome: The Meaning of Catullus 64* (Amsterdam).
E. Kraggerud 1968: *Aeneisstudien* (Oslo).
E. Langmuir 1976: "Arma Virumque ... Nicolò Dell'Abate's *Aeneid*", *Journal of the Warburg and Courtauld Institutes* 39, 151-170.
R. Lattimore 1942: *Themes in Greek and Latin Epitaphs* (Urbana, Illinois).
G. Lawall 1966: "Apollonius' *Argonautica*: Jason as Anti-Hero", *YClS* 19, 121-169.
P. Lennox 1977: "Vergil's Night-Episode Re-examined (*Aeneid* IX, 176-449)", *Hermes* 105, 331-342.
A. Lesky 1978: *Greek Tragedy*. Translated by H. Frankfort. 3rd ed. (N.Y.).
B. Lier 1914: *Ad Topica Carminum Amatoriorum Symbolae* (Stettin).
D. Lucas 1978: *Aristotle, Poetics*, corrected edition (Oxford).
T. Luce 1977: *Livy: The Composition of his History* (Princeton).
G. Luck 1959: *The Latin Love Elegy* (London).
R. Lyne 1978: *Ciris: A Poem Attributed to Vergil* (Cambridge).
——, 1978a: "The Neoteric Poets", *CQ* n.s. 28, 167-187.
——, 1980: *The Latin Love Poets* (Oxford).
——, 1987: *Further Voices in Vergil's Aeneid* (Oxford).
J. Mackail 1930: *The Aeneid* (Oxford).
C. Macleod 1982: *Homer, Iliad, Book XXIV* (Cambridge).
J. Makowski 1989: "Nisus and Euryalus: A Platonic Relationship", *CJ* 85, 1-15.
H. Marrou 1956: *A History of Education in Antiquity*. Translated by G. Lamb (N.Y.).
C. Martindale 1984: *Virgil and his Influence* (Bristol).
L. Matthaei 1917: "The Fates, the Gods, and the Freedom of Man's Will in the *Aeneid*", *CQ* 11, 11-26.
P. Mazon 1959: *Introduction à l'Iliade* (Paris).
A. McKay 1987: "Book Illustrations of Vergil's *Aeneid*, A.D. 400-1980", *AugAge* 6, 227-237.

K. Mcleish 1972: "Dido, Aeneas and the Concept of *Pietas*", *G&R* s.s. 19, 127-135.
T. Means 1929: "A Comparison of the Treatment by Vergil and Ovid of the Aeneas Dido Myth", *CW* 23, 41-44.
C. Mendell 1938-9: "Vergil's Workshop", *CJ* 34, 9-22.
——, 1951: "The Influence of the Epyllion on the *Aeneid*", *YCLS* 12, 205-226.
F. Miller 1927: "Ovid's *Aeneid* and Vergil's: A Contrast in Motivation", *CJ* 23, 33-43.
R. Monti 1981: *The Dido Episode and the Aeneid* (Leiden).
W. Moskalew 1982: *Formular Language and Poetic Design in the Aeneid* (Leiden).
F. Muecke 1983: "Foreshadowing and Dramatic Irony in the Story of Dido", *AJPh* 104, 134-155.
P. Murgatroyd 1980: *Tibullus I* (Pietermaritzburg, South Africa). (Most of his references can also be found in K. Smith, *The Elegies of Albius Tibullus*, 1913.)
C. Murgia, 1967: "Critical Notes on the Text of Servius' Commentary on *Aeneid* III-V", *HSPh* 72, 311-350.
G. Murray 1934: *The Rise of the Greek Epic*, 4th ed. (Oxford).
W. Nethercut 1971: "The Imagery of the *Aeneid*", *CJ* 67, 123-143.
H. Nettleship 1885: *Lectures and Essays on Subjects Connected with Latin Literature and Scholarship* (Oxford).
S. Newmyer 1990: "Some Lesser Lights at Dido's Pyre: Forgotten Musical Portraits of Vergil's Queen", *Vergilius* 36, 35-41.
F. Newton 1957: "Recurrent Imagery in *Aeneid* IV", *TAPhA* 88, 31-43.
R. Nisbet and M. Hubbard 1975: *A Commentary on Horace: Odes, Book 1*, corrected edition (Oxford).
R. Nisbet and M. Hubbard 1978: *A Commentary on Horace: Odes, Book 2* (Oxford).
E. Nitchie 1966: *Vergil and the English Poets* (N.Y.).
E. Norden 1957: *P. Vergilius Maro, Aeneis, Buch VI*, 4th edition (Stuttgart).
R. Ogilvie 1965: *A Commentary on Livy, Books 1-5* (Oxford).
B. Otis 1963: *Virgil: A Study in Civilized Poetry* (Oxford).
——, 1970: *Ovid as an Epic Poet* (Oxford).
S. Owen 1924: *P. Ovidi Nasonis Tristium Liber Secundus* (Oxford).
T. Page 1894: *The Aeneid of Virgil, Books I-VI* (London).
A. Palmer 1898: *P. Ovidi Nasonis Heroides* (Oxford).
L. Palmer 1938: "Ara Invisa Sedebat", *Mnemosyne* 6, 368-379.
T. Papanghelis 1987: *Propertius: A Hellenistic Poet on Love and Death* (Cambridge).
A. Parry 1963: "The Two Voices of Virgil's *Aeneid*", in Commager 1966, 107-123.
B. Pavlock 1985: "Epic and Tragedy in Vergil's Nisus and Euryalus Episode", *TAPhA* 115, 207-224.
T. Pearce 1968: "Virgil, *Aeneid* IV, 440", *CR* n.s. 18, 13-14.
——, 1968a: "A Pattern of Word Order in Latin Poetry", *CR* n.s. 18, 334-354.
A. Pease 1920: *M. Tulli Ciceronis De Divinatione, Liber Primus* (Urbana, Illinois).
——, 1935: *Publi Vergili Maronis Aeneidos Liber Quartus*, (Cambridge, Mass.).
——, 1958: *M. Tulli Ciceronis De Natura Deorum Libri Secundus et Tertius* (Cambridge, Mass.).
C. Perkell 1978: "A Reading of Virgil's Fourth *Georgic*", *Phoenix* 22, 211-221.
——, 1986: "Vergil's Theodicy Reconsidered", *Vergil at 2000*, ed. J. Bernard, 67-83 (N.Y.).
J. Perret 1965: *Virgile*, 2nd ed. (Paris).

———, 1967: "Optimisme et tragédie dans l'Énéide", *REL* 45, 342-362.
E. Phinney Jr. 1964-5: "Dido and Sychaeus", *CJ* 60, 335-359.
R. Pichon 1902: *De Sermone amatorio apud Latinos Elegiarum Scriptores* (Paris).
V. Pöschl 1977: *Die Dichtkunst Virgils*, 3rd ed. (Berlin).
———, 1988: "Virgile et la tragédie", *Présence de Virgile*, ed. R. Chevallier (Paris) 73-79.
H. Prescott 1927: *The Development of Virgil's Art* (Chicago).
K. Preston 1916: *Studies in the Diction of the Sermo Amatorius in Roman Comedy* (Chicago).
W. Pritchett 1974: *The Greek States at War: Part II* (Berkeley).
M. Putnam 1961: "The Art of Catullus 65", *HSPh* 65, 165-205.
———, 1970: *Virgil's Pastoral Art: Studies in the Eclogues* (Princeton).
K. Quinn 1963: "Horace as a Love Poet", *Arion* 2, 59-77.
———, 1969: *Virgil's Aeneid: A Critical Description*, corrected edition (London).
———, 1984: *Horace, the Odes*, corrected edition (London).
E. Rand 1931: *The Magical Art of Virgil* (Cambridge, Mass.)
K. Reinhardt 1979: *Sophocles*. Translated by H. and D. Harvey (Oxford).
L. Richardson 1938: "In Defence of Nisus", *Hermathena* 51, 140-145.
N. Richardson 1980: "Literary Criticism in the Exegetical Scholia to the *Iliad*: A Sketch", *CQ* n.s. 30, 265-287.
E. Rhode 1914: *Der griechische Roman und seine Vorläufer*, 3rd ed. (Leipzig).
D. Ross Jr. 1987: *Virgil's Elements: Physics and Poetry in the Georgics* (Princeton).
A. Rostagni 1956: "L'influenza greca sull' origine dell'elegia erotica latina", *Entretiens sur l'Antiquité Classique* 2 (Geneva) 59-82.
C. Saylor 1986: "Some Stock Characteristics of the Roman Lover in Vergil, *Aeneid* IV", *Vergilius* 32, 73-77.
———, 1990: "Group vs. Individual in Vergil *Aeneid* IX", *Latomus* 49, 88-94.
W. Schadewalt 1955: "Furcht und Mitleid? Zur Deutung des Aristotelischen Tragödiensatzes", *Hermes* 83, 129-171.
K. Schefold 1957: *Die Wände Pompejis* (Berlin).
A. Schlegel 1809-11: *Course of Lectures on Dramatic Art and Literature*. Translated by J. Black, revised by A. Morrison (1846) (London).
R. Schlunk 1974: *The Homeric Scholia and the Aeneid* (Ann Arbor.).
M. Schrijvers 1978: "La Valeur de la pitié chez Virgile (dans 'l'Enéide) et chez quelques-uns de ses interprètes", *Présence de Virgile*, ed. R. Chevallier (Paris) 483-495.
R. Seaton 1912: *Apollonius Rhodius, The Argonautica* (Cambridge, Mass.).
C. Segal 1966: "Orpheus and the Fourth *Georgic:* Vergil on Nature and Civilization", *AJPh* 87, 307-325.
W. Sellar 1908: *The Roman Poets of the Augustan Age*, 3rd ed. (Oxford).
M. Skinner 1983: "The Last Encounter of Dido and Aeneas: *Aen.* 6.450-476", *Vergilius* 29,12-18.
S. Smith 1942: W. Leonard and S. Smith, *T. Lucreti Cari De Rerum Natura Libri Sex* (Madison, Wisconsin).
W. Stanford 1939: *Ambiguity in Greek Literature* (Oxford).
———, 1983: *Greek Tragedy and the Emotions: An Introductory Study* (London).
K. Stanley 1965: "Irony and Foreshadowing in *Aeneid* I, 462", *AJPh* 86, 267-277.
G. Steiner 1959: *Tolstoy or Dostoevsky* (N.Y.).
J. Sullivan 1976: *Propertius: A Critical Introduction* (Cambridge).
O. Taplin 1978: *Greek Tragedy in Action* (London).
A. Thornton 1976: *The Living Universe: Gods and Men in Virgil's Aeneid* (Leiden).
O. Touchefeu-Meynier 1968: *Thèmes odysséens dans l'art antique* (Paris).

A. Traina 1970: *Vortit barbare: Le traduzioni poetische da Livio Andronico a Cicerone* (Rome). (Unfortunately, the revised edition of 1974 was inaccessible to me.)
H. Troyat 1967: *Tolstoy* Translated by N. Amphoux (N.Y.)
D. Vessey 1969: "Nescio quid Maius", *PVS* 9, 53-76.
B. Vickers 1979: *Towards Greek Tragedy: Drama, Myth, Society* (London).
J. Voisin 1979: "Le Suicide d'Amata", *REL* 57, 254-266.
H. Waddell 1934: *The Wandering Scholars*, 7th ed. (London).
F. Walbank 1960: "History and Tragedy", *Historia* 9, 216-234.
A. Waldock 1951: *Sophocles the Dramatist* (Cambridge).
T. Webster 1966: "The Myth of Ariadne from Homer to Catullus", *G&R* s.s. 13, 22-31.
A. Wheeler 1910: "Propertius as *Praeceptor Amoris*", *CPh* 5, 28-40.
T. von Wilamowitz-Moellendorff 1917: *Die dramatische Technik des Sophokles* (Berlin).
G. Williams 1958: "Some Aspects of Roman Marriage Ceremonies and Ideals", *JRS* 48, 16-29.
——, 1968: *Tradition and Originality in Roman Poetry* (Oxford).
——, 1983: *Technique and Ideas in the Aeneid* (New Haven).
R. Williams 1960: "The Pictures on Dido's Temple (*Aeneid* 1.450-93)", *CQ* n.s. 10, 145-151.
——, 1960a: *P. Vergili Maronis Aeneidos Liber Quintus* (Oxford).
——, 1967: *Virgil* (Oxford).
——, 1969: "Changing Attitudes to Virgil: A Study in the History of Taste from Dryden to Tennyson", *Virgil*, edited by D. Dudley (London) 119-138.
——, 1972: *The Aeneid of Virgil, Books 1-6* (London).
——, 1973: *The Aeneid of Virgil, Books 7-12* (London).
R. Williams (and T. Pattie) 1982: *Virgil: His Poetry Through the Ages* (London).
S. Wiltshire 1989: *Public and Private Voice in Vergil's Aeneid* (Amherst).
M. Winterbottom 1989: "Speaking of the Gods", *G + R* s.s. 36, 33-41.
T. Wiseman 1985: *Catullus and his World: A Reappraisal* (Cambridge).
H. Yeames 1913: "The Tragedy of Dido: Part I", *CJ* 8, 139-150.

INDEX

(Characters in works of ancient Greek and Latin literature, except the *Aeneid*, are not listed. The only exception is when they are referred to by later authors.)

Achilles (regarded as a passionate lover): 16-18. (compassionate treatment of Priam used as a model): 55-56.
Acro (Pseudo-): 21n6, 49.
Aeneas: xii, 31-33, 56-58, 62-65, 68-69, 70-81, 85, 90-91, 96-97, 99, 102, 107-114, 116-25, 128, 132-41, 146, 159.
Aeneid: passim; Book 2: 31, 63-65, 111-12, 132, 137n4, 140-44, 146, 149; Book 5: 62-3; Book 6: 22-24, 31, 120-23, 146.
Aeschylus (see also "Tragedy"): 35, 43.
afid≈w (see also *Pudor*): 105-107.
Amata: xii, 102-103, 105, 146.
Amor (the god): (in Vergil): 127-28, 131-32; (elsewhere): 86, 94, 127-29.
Anchises: 63, 69, 122, 126-27.
Andromache: (in the *Aeneid*): 123; (in reactions to the *Iliad*): 40.
Anna: 72, 76-77, 87-88, 92, 100, 107, 116, 135.
Anthologia Latina: 29-30, 72-73, 138-39.
Apollonius Rhodius' *Argonautica*: 16, 56-58, 61-62, 89, 92, 96-99, 104-105, 107, 127.
Aristophanes: 48, 50.
Aristotle: 34-35, 37-39, 43-46, 49, 52-53, 126, 134-35.
Ascanius: see "Iulus".
Augustine (Saint): 73, 77-78, 110.
Augustus: 22, 33, 49, 51, 71, 101, 151, 153, 162.
Ausonius: 27, 77.

Benefacta: 84, 86, 93-94, 97-100, 104, 107, 117, 138, 144.
Brutus (in the *Aeneid*): 68.

Callimachus: 18.
Camilla: 69, 147, 153.

Catharsis: 44-45.
Catullus: (Poem 64): 3, 15, 58-59, 89, 92, 94-95, 98-99, 106, 115-18, 120, 123-24, 140; (Lesbia Poems): 14, 15, 82-86, 89, 93-94, 98, 114-15, 127, 130; (other poems): 81, 93, 116, 122, 131.
Cicero: 2, 3, 19n5, 41, 60, 64, 67, 70, 87, 98, 130, 135.
Ciris: 16, 92, 95-96, 104-106, 116, 133.
Comedy (see also "Aristophanes"): (Roman): 15-16, 105.
Creusa: 63, 122.
Cupid: see *Amor*.

Daedaulus (in the *Aeneid*): 68.
Dido: x-xii, 1, 18, 22, 27, 31-33, 43, 57-58, 61-62, 68-140, 142-47, 160.
Dolus: 2-8, 132, 142.
Donatus (Aelius): 33, 40, 83.
Donatus (Tiberius Claudius): 2, 7-9, 12, 14, 18, 23, 29, 52, 64-65, 69, 74-76, 100, 116-18, 125, 128-29, 137n4, 138-39, 141, 145.
Dying for love: (in the *Aeneid*): (of Nisus and Euryalus): 1, 11-14, 18-19, 28-30; (other characters): xii, 18-19, 22-23, 84-85; (in the *Eclogues*): 20, 23-24, 127; (in the *Georgics*): 20-21; (elsewhere): 17-19, 28-29, 71, 84, 92-97, 108, 131.

Eclogues: 7, 15, 20, 23-24, 49, 59-60, 63, 81, 87, 89, 93, 127-29, 160.
Ennius: 60, 64, 99, 118n2.
Epic Cycle: 18, 64.
Euripides (see also "Tragedy"): 34-37, 43-44, 47-48, 50, 64, 97, 99, 106, 126.
Euryalus: see "Nisus and Euryalus".
Euryalus' mother: 66-67.
Evander: xii, 65.

Fraus: 2, 4-7.

INDEX

Furor (includes references to insanity, madness, etc.): 9, 86-88, 92, 94-95, 102, 112, 137-38, 141.
Furtum: 4-5, 7.

Georgics: 3, 15, 20-21, 49, 70, 88, 114, 160.
Gods (except *Amor*, Juno, Jupiter, Mercury and Venus, who are listed individually): (in the *Aeneid*): 75-76, 80-81, 84, 86, 116-19, 124-27, 129-45; (in the *Eclogues*): 127-29; (elsewhere): 84, 86, 91, 95-96, 118, 125-31, 134, 145.
Graffiti (at Pompeii): 19n5, 27, 86.
Greek Tragedy: see "Tragedy".
Guilty Conscience: (in the *Aeneid*): 100-103, 107-108, 129; (elsewhere): 88, 103-108, 129, 131.

Hamartia: 44.
Hector: (in the *Aeneid*): 55, 64, 122-23; (in reactions to the *Iliad*): 28, 40.
Hecuba: 40, 66, 140-41.
Homer (see also *Iliad* and *Odyssey*): 17, 92, 144, 150, 153.
Horace: (hexameters): 3; (*Ars Poetica*): 41, 48-51, 53; (*Odes*): 15, 51, 91, 93, 127, 131; (*Satires*): 15, 21n6, 49, 128.
Hubris: 45.

Iarbas: 71-72, 78.
Iliad (see also "Homer"): 3, 13, 16-18, 21, 40, 51-56, 61-62, 103, 123, 126, 148-49, 151-52.
Insidiae: 4-8, 142.
Iulus: 66, 146.

Juno: xii, 65, 136-37, 143.
Jupiter: (in the *Aeneid*): 66, 117, 132-33, 136-37, 141, 143, 151; (elsewhere): 131, 143.

Latinus: xii, 65-66, 102, 146.
Lausus, 19n5, 25, 122, 147, 155.
Livy: 6-7, 9, 64.
Lucan: 40.
Lucretius: 3, 87-88, 103, 127-28, 130, 145.

Macrobius: 62, 67, 78.
Marcellus: 33, 47, 69.

Marriage (see also "Remarriage") (assumed or claimed by and for lovers): (of Dido): 74, 95, 116-17; (in the *Eclogues*): 127; (elsewhere): 83, 94-95, 116, 130-31.
Mercury: 75, 80-81, 117.
Metre: 3-4, 11-12, 21, 51.
Mezentius: 67-68, 102, 147, 153.
Mobile Focus: 46-47, 67, 123-24, 140, 143-44; cf. 35.

Nisus and Euryalus: xii, 1-4, 8-14, 18-19, 24-30, 33, 43, 66, 81-82, 88, 108-109, 147, 155-64. (Nisus alone: 69, 71).

Odyssey (see also "Homer"): 16, 18, 40, 51-56, 61-62, 97, 128, 148-49, 151.
Ovid: (*Amores*): 14, 19n5, 87, 89; (*Ars Amatoria*): 24, 71; (*Fasti*): 5n2, 16, 71-72, 74-77; (*Heroides*): 17, 19n5, 22, 70-71, 75, 92, 97, 99, 104, 129; (*Metamorphoses*): 16, 19n5, 24, 51, 59, 71, 83, 85, 95-97, 104, 151; (*Remedia Amoris*): 19n5, 71, 95; (*Tristia*): 22, 27-28.

Painting: (Ancient Greek): 17, 64; (at Pompeii): 17-18, 59, 97; (on manuscripts): 73-74, 78.
Pallas: 122-23, 147.
Parthenius: 16, 19n5, 82, 93-95, 105, 118, 121, 133.
Pathos: 65, 85, and *passim*.
Pietas: 2, 18, 19n5, 25, 27-29, 37, 71, 73, 76, 84, 106, 130, 136, 138-39, 142-43, 158, 163.
Plato: 17, 38-39, 48, 126, 152-53.
Plautus: 15, 107.
Plutarch: 5, 42, 118.
Polybius: 5-6, 63-64.
Pompeii: see "Grafitti" and "Painting".
Priam: (in the *Aeneid*): 8, 56, 64, 140-41, 143-44; (in reactions to the *Iliad*): 40-41, 55, 66; (elsewhere): 143.
Propertius: 14-16, 19n5, 24, 51, 59, 85-87, 89-93, 95, 97-98, 104, 127-28, 130-31.
Pseudo-Acro: see "Acro".
Pudor (and *Pudicitia*) (see also αἰδώς): 75, 100-102, 106-107.

Quintilian: 42, 128.

Remarriage (see also "Marriage"): 100-102.

Sappho: 42, 88-89, 121.
Scholia: (on Homer): 40, 46, 52, 103, 123, 126; (on tragedy); 46; (on Sophocles): 135; (on Euripides): 106; (on Theocritus): 118; (on Juvenal): 74.
Seneca: 19n5, 27, 49, 99, 103-104, 107.
Servius (including Servius Danielis): 4, 7-8, 11-15, 17, 22-23, 33, 40, 49-50, 52, 61-62, 64-65, 67, 69, 74, 83, 98, 100, 116-18, 124-25, 128-29, 137n4, 138-39, 141, 145.
Silius Italicus: 72, 75-77, 120-21, 148.
Sophocles (see also "Tragedy"): 35-36, 43, 46-47, 67, 135.
Statius: 2, 28-29.
Stoicism: 76, 80, 109-111, 113, 120-22, 125, 152.

Terence: 15, 60, 105.
Theocritus: 15, 19n5, 62.
Thucydides: 41, 64.
Tibullus: 14, 19n5, 81, 85, 89-90, 93, 98, 103-104, 127, 129.
Tragedy: (Classical Greek): 18, 36-37, 39-40, 44-48, 51-52, 64, 92, 126, 134-35, 138, 144-45, 153; (post-Euripidean): 15, 19n5; (Roman): 15, 39, 64.
Turnus: xii, 8, 10, 69, 102, 110-11, 117, 142, 153, 158.

Venus: (in the *Aeneid*): xii, 63, 66, 117, 122, 132, 143; (elsewhere): 86-88, 94, 127-29.

SUPPLEMENTS TO MNEMOSYNE

EDITED BY A.D. LEEMAN, C.J. RUIJGH AND H.W. PLEKET

4. LEEMAN, A.D. *A Systematical Bibliography of Sallust (1879-1964)*. Revised and augmented edition. 1965. ISBN 90 04 01467 5
5. LENZ, F.W. (ed.). *The Aristeides 'Prolegomena'*. 1959. ISBN 90 04 01468 3
7. McKAY, K.J. *Erysichthon. A Callimachean Comedy*. 1962. ISBN 90 04 01470 5
11. RUTILIUS LUPUS. *De Figuris Sententiarum et Elocutionis*. Edited with Prolegomena and Commentary by E. BROOKS. 1970. ISBN 90 04 01474 8
12. SMYTH, W.R. (ed.). *Thesaurus criticus ad Sexti Propertii textum*. 1970. ISBN 90 04 01475 6
13. LEVIN, D.N. *Apollonius' 'Argonautica' re-examined*. 1. The Neglected First and Second Books. 1971. ISBN 90 04 02575 8
14. REINMUTH, O.W. *The Ephebic Inscriptions of the Fourth Century B.C.* 1971. ISBN 90 04 01476 4
16. ROSE, K.F.C. *The Date and Author of the 'Satyricon'*. With an introduction by J.P. SULLIVAN. 1971. ISBN 90 04 02578 2
18. WILLIS, J. *De Martiano Capella emendando*. 1971. ISBN 90 04 02580 4
19. HERINGTON, C.J. (ed.). *The Older Scholia on the Prometheus Bound*. 1972. ISBN 90 04 03455 2
20. THIEL, H. VAN. *Petron. Überlieferung und Rekonstruktion*. 1971. ISBN 90 04 02581 2
21. LOSADA, L.A. *The Fifth Column in the Peloponnesian War*. 1972. ISBN 90 04 03421 8
23. BROWN, V. *The Textual Transmission of Caesar's 'Civil War'*. 1972. ISBN 90 04 03457 9
24. LOOMIS, J.W. *Studies in Catullan Verse*. An Analysis of Word Types and Patterns in the Polymetra. 1972. ISBN 90 04 03429 3
27. GEORGE, E.V. *Aeneid VIII and the Aitia of Callimachus*. 1974. ISBN 90 04 03859 0
29. BERS, V. *Enallage and Greek Style*. 1974. ISBN 90 04 03786 1
37. SMITH, O.L. *Studies in the Scholia on Aeschylus*. 1. The Recensions of Demetrius Triclinius. 1975. ISBN 90 04 04220 2
39. SCHMELING, G.L. & J.H. STUCKEY. *A Bibliography of Petronius*. 1977. ISBN 90 04 04753 0
44. THOMPSON, W.E. *De Hagniae Hereditate. An Athenian Inheritance Case*. 1976. ISBN 90 04 04757 3
45. McGUSHIN, P. *Sallustius Crispus, 'Bellum Catilinae'. A Commentary*. 1977. ISBN 90 04 04835 9
46. THORNTON, A. *The Living Universe. Gods and Men in Virgil's Aeneid*. 1976. ISBN 90 04 04579 1
48. BRENK, F.E. *In Mist apparelled. Religious Themes in Plutarch's 'Moralia' and 'Lives'*. 1977. ISBN 90 04 05241 0
51. SUSSMAN, L.A. *The Elder Seneca*. 1978. ISBN 90 04 05759 5
57. BOER, W. DEN. *Private Morality in Greece and Rome. Some Historical Aspects*. 1979. ISBN 90 04 05976 8
61. *Hieronymus' Liber de optimo genere interpretandi (Epistula 57)*. Ein Kommentar von G.J.M. BARTELINK. 1980. ISBN 90 04 06085 5
63. HOHENDAHL-ZOETELIEF, I.M. *Manners in the Homeric Epic*. 1980. ISBN 90 04 06223 8
64. HARVEY, R.A. *A Commentary on Persius*. 1981. ISBN 90 04 06313 7

65. MAXWELL-STUART, P.G. *Studies in Greek Colour Terminology. 1.* γλαυκός. 1981. ISBN 90 04 06406 0
68. ACHARD, G. *Pratique rhétorique et idéologie politique dans les discours 'Optimates' de Cicéron.* 1981. ISBN 90 04 06374 9
69. MANNING, C.E. *On Seneca's 'Ad Marciam'.* 1981. ISBN 90 04 06430 3
70. BERTHIAUME, G. *Les rôles du Mágeiros.* Etude sur la boucherie, la cuisine et le sacrifice dans la Grèce ancienne. 1982. ISBN 90 04 06554 7
71. CAMPBELL, M. *A commentary on Quintus Smyrnaeus Posthomerica XII.* 1981. ISBN 90 04 06502 4
72. CAMPBELL, M. *Echoes and Imitations of Early Epic in Apollonius Rhodius.* 1981. ISBN 90 04 06503 2
73. MOSKALEW, W. *Formular Language and Poetic Design in the Aeneid.* 1982. ISBN 90 04 06580 6
74. RACE, W.H. *The Classical Priamel from Homer to Boethius.* 1982. ISBN 90 04 06515 6
75. MOORHOUSE, A.C. *The Syntax of Sophocles.* 1982. ISBN 90 04 06599 7
77. WITKE, C. *Horace's Roman Odes.* A Critical Examination. 1983. ISBN 90 04 07006 0
78. ORANJE, J. *Euripides' 'Bacchae'.* The Play and its Audience. 1984. ISBN 90 04 07011 7
79. STATIUS. *Thebaidos Libri XII.* Recensuit et cum apparatu critico et exegetico instruxit D.E. HILL. 1983. ISBN 90 04 06917 8
82. DAM, H.-J. VAN. *P. Papinius Statius, Silvae Book II.* A Commentary. 1984. ISBN 90 04 07110 5
84. OBER, J. *Fortress Attica. Defense of the Athenian Land Frontier, 404-322 B.C.* 1985. ISBN 90 04 07243 8
85. HUBBARD, T.K. *The Pindaric Mind.* A Study of Logical Structure in Early Greek Poetry. 1985. ISBN 90 04 07303 5
86. VERDENIUS, W.J. *A Commentary on Hesiod: Works and Days,* vv. 1-382. 1985. ISBN 90 04 07465 1
87. HARDER, A. *Euripides' 'Kresphonthes' and 'Archelaos'.* Introduction, Text and Commentary. 1985. ISBN 90 04 07511 9
88. WILLIAMS, H.J. *The 'Eclogues' and 'Cynegetica' of Nemesianus.* Edited with an Introduction and Commentary. 1986. ISBN 90 04 07486 4
89. McGING, B.C. *The Foreign Policy of Mithridates VI Eupator, King of Pontus.* 1986. ISBN 90 04 07591 7
91. SIDEBOTHAM, S.E. *Roman Economic Policy in the Erythra Thalassa 30 B.C.-A.D. 217.* 1986. ISBN 90 04 07644 1
92. VOGEL, C.J. DE. *Rethinking Plato and Platonism.* 2nd impr. of the first (1986) ed. 1988. ISBN 90 04 08755 9
93. MILLER, A.M. *From Delos to Delphi.* A Literary Study of the Homeric Hymn to Apollo. 1986. ISBN 90 04 07674 3
94. BOYLE, A.J. *The Chaonian Dove.* Studies in the Eclogues, Georgics, and Aeneid of Virgil. 1986. ISBN 90 04 07672 7
95. KYLE, D.G. *Athletics in Ancient Athens.* 2nd impr. of the first (1987) ed. 1993. ISBN 90 04 09759 7
97. VERDENIUS, W.J. *Commentaries on Pindar. Vol. I. Olympian Odes 3, 7, 12, 14.* 1987. ISBN 90 04 08126 7
98. PROIETTI, G. *Xenophon's Sparta.* An introduction. 1987. ISBN 90 04 08338 3
99. BREMER, J.M., A.M. VAN ERP TAALMAN KIP & S.R. SLINGS. *Some Recently Found Greek Poems.* Text and Commentary. 1987. ISBN 90 04 08319 7
100. OPHUIJSEN, J.M. VAN. *Hephaestion on Metre.* Translation and Commentary. 1987. ISBN 90 04 08452 5

101. VERDENIUS, W.J. *Commentaries on Pindar. Vol. II.* Olympian Odes 1, 10, 11, Nemean 11, Isthmian 2. 1988. ISBN 90 04 08535 1
102. LUSCHNIG, C.A.E. *Time holds the Mirror. A Study of Knowledge in Euripides' 'Hippolytus'*. 1988. ISBN 90 04 08601 3
103. MARCOVICH, M. *Alcestis Barcinonensis.* Text and Commentary. 1988. ISBN 90 04 08600 5
104. HOLT, F.L. *Alexander the Great and Bactria.* The Formation of a Greek Frontier in Central Asia. Repr. 1989. ISBN 90 04 08612 9
105. BILLERBECK, M. *Senecas Tragödien: sprachliche und stilistische Untersuchungen.* Mit Anhängen zur Sprache des Hercules Oetaeus und der Octavia. 1988. ISBN 90 04 08631 5
106. ARENDS, J.F.M. *Die Einheit der Polis. Eine Studie über Platons Staat.* 1988. ISBN 90 04 08785 0
107. BOTER, G.J. *The Textual Tradition of Plato's Republic.* 1988. ISBN 90 04 08787 7
108. WHEELER, E.L. *Stratagem and the Vocabulary of Military Trickery.* 1988. ISBN 90 04 08831 8
109. BUCKLER, J. *Philip II and the Sacred War.* 1989. ISBN 90 04 09095 9
110. FULLERTON, M.D. *The Archaistic Style in Roman Statuary.* 1990. ISBN 90 04 09146 7
111. ROTHWELL, K.S. *Politics and Persuasion in Aristophanes' 'Ecclesiazusae'.* 1990. ISBN 90 04 09185 8
112. CALDER, W.M. & A. DEMANDT. *Eduard Meyer.* Leben und Leistung eines Universalhistorikers. 1990. ISBN 90 04 09131 9
113. CHAMBERS, M.H. *Georg Busolt. His Career in His Letters.* 1990. ISBN 90 04 09225 0
114. CASWELL, C.P. *A Study of 'Thumos' in Early Greek Epic.* 1990. ISBN 90 04 09260 9
115. EINGARTNER, J. *Isis und ihre Dienerinnen in der Kunst der römischen Kaiserzeit.* 1991. ISBN 90 04 09312 5
116. JONG, I. DE. *Narrative in Drama.* The Art of the Euripidean Messenger-Speech. 1991. ISBN 90 04 09406 7
117. BOYCE, B.T. *The Language of the Freedmen in Petronius' Cena Trimalchionis.* 1991. ISBN 90 04 09431 8
118. RÜTTEN, Th. *Demokrit — lachender Philosoph und sanguinischer Melancholiker.* 1992. ISBN 90 04 09523 3
119. KARAVITES, P. (with the collaboration of Th. Wren). *Promise-Giving and Treaty-Making.* Homer and the Near East. 1992. ISBN 90 04 09567 5
120. SANTORO L'HOIR, F. *The Rhetoric of Gender Terms.* 'Man', 'woman' and the portrayal of character in Latin prose. 1992. ISBN 90 04 09512 8
121. WALLINGA, H.T. *Ships and Sea-Power before the Great Persian War.* The Ancestry of the Ancient Trireme. 1993. ISBN 90 04 09650 7
122. FARRON, S. *Vergil's Aeneid: A Poem of Grief and Love.* 1993. ISBN 90 04 09661 2
123. LÉTOUBLON, F. *Les lieux communs du roman.* Stéréotypes grecs d'aventure et d'amour. 1993. ISBN 90 04 09724 4
124. KUNTZ, M. *Narrative Setting and Dramatic Poetry.* 1993. ISBN 90 04 09784 8
125. THEOPHRASTUS. *Metaphysics.* Introduction, Translation and Commentary by Marlein van Raalte. 1993. ISBN 90 04 09786 4
126. THIERMANN, P. *Die 'Orationes Homeri' des Leonardo Bruni Aretino.* Kritische Edition der lateinischen und kastellanischen Übersetzung mit Prolegomena und Kommentar. 1993. ISBN 90 04 09719 8
127. LEVENE, D.S. *Religion in Livy.* 1993. ISBN 90 04 09617 5
128. PORTER, J.R. *Studies in Euripides' Orestes.* 1993. ISBN 90 04 09662 0
129. SICKING, C.M.J. & J.M. VAN OPHUIJSEN. *Two Studies in Attic Particle Usage.* Lysias and Plato. 1993. ISBN 90 04 09867 4